Christmas On Stage

An Anthology of Royalty-Free Christmas Plays for All Ages

Edited by Theodore O. Zapel

MERIWETHER PUBLISHING LTD.
Colorado Springs, Colorado

Meriwether Publishing Ltd., Publisher
P.O. Box 7710
Colorado Springs, CO 80933

Cover design: Tom Myers
Editor: Theodore O. Zapel
Typography: Sharon E. Garlock

Library of Congress Cataloging-in-Publication Data

Christmas on stage : an anthology of royalty-free Christmas plays for
    all ages / edited by Theodore O. Zapel. -- 1st ed.
        p.   cm.
    ISBN 0-916260-68-2
    1. Christmas plays, American. 2. Children's plays, American.
3. Young adult drama, American.   I. Zapel, Theodore O., 1955-
PS627.C57C45   1990
812.008'033--dc20   90-53278
                                        CIP

4   5   6   7   8   00   01   02   03   04

DEDICATION

This anthology
is dedicated
to the many playwrights
who contributed their work
to make this book possible.
It is also dedicated
to the patrons of
Contemporary Drama Service
who have produced
these plays successfully
through the years.

PREFACE

The twenty-seven one-act plays and readings in this book are selected to provide a wide variety of material for Christmas programs. All of the plays are royalty free and are suitable for classroom, chancel, or drama club presentations. These plays have been production tested in hundreds of schools and churches nationwide.

Included are contemporary comedies, fantasies, classics, reenactments of the Christmas story, children's pageants, carol programs, mime and dance programs, even a "rap" play. All plays have been selected for easy staging. This book also offers several Readers Theatre plays, requiring no memorization and minimal rehearsal. For storytellers, several classic readings are available.

We have tried to provide something to fit almost any size cast, age group and staging situation. Production suggestions are at the beginning of each play to simplify rehearsal and performance. Many of the plays can be staged without scenery or special costumes. They may be used as part of a reading curriculum, tape recorded, broadcast over a public address system, or used for amateur videotape productions.

The main objective of this book is to help make Christmas more meaningful (and fun) for performer and audience alike. We feel that each of the plays contained here accomplishes this by portraying the true message and spirit of Christmas.

NOTE: The numerals running vertically down the left margin of each page of dialog are for the convenience of the director. With these he/she may easily direct attention to a specific passage.

TABLE OF CONTENTS

IV. Readers Theatre for Christmas

V. Adaptations from Classics and Legends

VI. Christmas Readings

ELEMENTARY GRADES

O Holy Night
by ARTHUR L. ZAPEL JR.

CAST

NARRATOR 1 (Girl)
She must be a good reader.
It would also help if she has some ability as an actress.

NARRATOR 2 (Boy)
He can be younger than Narrator 1.
Acting ability is required.

NARRATOR 3 (Girl)
She should be about the same age as Narrator 2.
Reading ability is required.

NARRATOR 4 (Boy)

A strong voice and reading ability is essential. He, together with Narrator 1, has the most lines and the most difficult interpretations.

NOTE: It is not necessary that there be two boy narrators and two girl narrators. It is possible that all four could be boys, or three boys and one girl. Four girl narrators is not recommended since the acting parts are all men characters. Under special circumstances, however, girls could portray men with, perhaps, slight adjustments in the script.

STAGING DIAGRAM

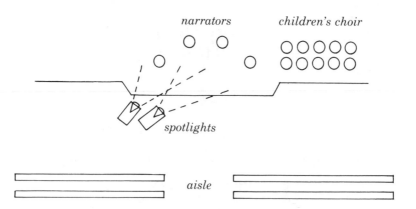

(A) Narrators 1 and 3 (Girls) should stand side by side. Narrators 2 and 4 (Boys) should also stand together to more easily move into dialog attitudes when required.

(B) Seat your children's choir as close to the players as the design of your church chancel will permit. Keep them as visible as possible. Everyone loves to watch children sing.

(C) We recommend positioning both spotlights to one side of the players. This "single source" for light will help heighten the drama of the scene and avoid double shadows on the faces of the actors. If possible, run the spotlights through a dimmer. Fading scenes in and out adds considerably to the dramatic effect.

PRODUCTION NOTES

It's always fun to sing out and sing along, especially at Christmas when we all find that words alone fall a little short.

It was this that motivated our development of this presentation. Christmas without carols is like spring without flowers. Over the years, perhaps, carol singing has been delegated to only a few while it should be a means of joyful and devout worship for everyone.

As I researched this project I was pleased to learn that the most beautiful of all carols were seldom created by great masters of music, but by common, devoted worshippers of Christ. They are songs from the heart and not the book.

Our most famous Christmas music is classic in its simplicity.

Let us then use this as the key to staging this presentation. Let's be direct — unprofessional if that's the way it goes — and above all, sincere to the mood of the music.

The best performers aren't necessary to make this program effective, but clearly spoken words will help. Choose readers that will speak up and out for all to hear. The younger the narrators the better, though vocabulary could be a snag here.

I endeavored to write language for elementary readers but unfortunately the subject matter does not permit too great a simplification. If you find that some of the words are too difficult for your children to read, change them. Rewrite as required. Your author isn't touchy at all if it will help the program.

In keeping with our suggestion of simplicity, I don't believe costumes are needed. A prop here and there might help, but I fear costumes could create problems. The changes would need to be too rapid.

This is essentially a musical presentation. Accordingly, I would suggest that you use your children's choir as much as possible. You may choose to have them sing the first chorus of every carol with the congregation singing the remaining. Or you may have them sing several of those indicated by themselves.

I hope you have as much fun putting it on as I had putting it down.

Arthur L. Zapel

1	NARRATOR 1:	The night before Jesus was born was quiet . . .
2		so very quiet.
3	NARRATOR 2:	The world was soon to be changed.
4	NARRATOR 3:	Something good was about to happen.
5	NARRATOR 4:	A little child would change everything . . .
6		everybody.
7	NARRATOR 1:	A little child would come into the world and
8		find his way into the hearts of everybody and speak what
9		they could not say.
10	NARRATOR 3:	It was a very quiet night.
11	NARRATOR 2:	So quiet that when shepherds talked to each
12		other they whispered.
13	NARRATOR 4:	In the dark, to the east, a star kept getting
14		brighter and brighter.
15	NARRATOR 1:	And if you listened softly — very softly — you
16		could hear faraway voices.
17	NARRATOR 4:	You could tell that they were waiting voices
18		. . . watching voices . . . praying voices.
19	NARRATOR 1:	Then . . . all of a sudden!
20	CHORUS:	*(With a sharp attack. Original music or this strain from*
21		*Handel's "Messiah.")*
22		Glory to God
23		Glory to God
24		Glory to God in the highest
25		And peace on earth.
26	NARRATOR 2:	This was music for the holy birth . . .
27	NARRATOR 3:	Music for the people to *sing* what they could
28		not say.
29	NARRATOR 1:	No one knows who first praised the Christ
30		Child in music, but some think it was the shepherds in
31		the fields.
32	NARRATOR 4:	It is said that they sang with the angels of the
33		Heavenly Host.
34	NARRATOR 3:	But no one knows for sure because that was
35		too long ago.

1	NARRATOR 2:	Some say the first carol was "The First Noel."
2	NARRATOR 3:	But no one can prove it. All they know for sure
3		is that it means the "First Chirstmas."
4	NARRATOR 2:	I wonder how it sounded that first holy night?
5		*(Congregation sings "The First Noel." Congregation sings the*
6		*verses and the children's choir, representing the angels, sings*
7		*the chorus.)*
8	NARRATOR 1:	Hardly any of the carols we sing were written
9		by one person.
10	NARRATOR 3:	Most of them were created by people who
11		never expected to write words for music or music for
12		words.
13	NARRATOR 1:	In 1867, on a night shortly before Christmas, a
14		young Episcopalian rector in Philadelphia was watching
15		feathery snowflakes fall gently to the ground outside his
16		study window.
17	NARRATOR 3:	He was planning a sermon for he was already
18		renowned as a preacher and a powerful orator.
19	NARRATOR 1:	But the words that came to Phillips Brooks
20		on this snowy night did not fit his style of flowery oratory.
21		The words were simple quiet words. Poetry. He was
22		remembering . . .
23	NARRATOR 2:	*(Looking at a piece of paper, he speaks as though he*
24		*is Phillips Brooks.)* Yes, this says it! This is Bethlehem at
25		Christmas.
26	NARRATOR 3:	Phillips Brooks had been to Bethlehem three
27		years before. He had attended the Christmas Eve service
28		in the Church of the Nativity close to the spot where
29		Jesus was born. Now the feelings of that evening came
30		together within him as an inspired poem.
31	NARRATOR 2:	*(Still acting as Phillips Brooks now talking to Lewis*
32		*Redner)* Lewis, I would like you to do something for me.
33	NARRATOR 4:	*(Acting as Lewis Redner)* Of course, Phillips.
34	NARRATOR 2:	*(As Brooks)* Look at this.
35	NARRATOR 4:	*(As Lewis)* It's a poem.

1   NARRATOR 2:   *(As Brooks)* It's about Bethlehem on Christmas
2   Eve. Would you set it to music?
3   NARRATOR 4:   *(As Lewis)* But you know that I'm not a composer.
4   I'm barely an organist.
5   NARRATOR 2:   *(As Brooks)* I believe you can do it. It would
6   be for our Sunday school program next Sunday.
7   NARRATOR 4:   *(As Lewis)* All right. I will try.
8   NARRATOR 1:   Lewis Redner did try. Every morning and
9   evening that week he tried and failed. At bedtime on
10   Saturday he gave up. He was convinced that it was not
11   in him to do this. Then as he slept something happened . . .
12   NARRATOR 4:   *(As Lewis talking to Brooks)* It came to me as if in
13   a dream. It was almost complete. I'm convinced that this
14   music is not from me. It is an "angel strain." You wrote
15   the words Phillips, but I'm sure angels wrote the music.
16   I would like to call it "St. Phillips."
17   NARRATOR 2:   *(As Brooks)* And I would like to call it "St.
18   Lewis." *(They both laugh.)*
19   NARRATOR 3:   But it was called neither of these titles. After
20   it was sung that next Sunday by six teachers and thirty-
21   six Sunday school children, it was published in a church
22   magazine. They titled it: "O Little Town of Bethlehem."
23   *(Congregation sings "O Little Town of Bethlehem.")*
24   NARRATOR 1:   In Douai *(Pronounced "Do-AY")*, France in 1740
25   an Englishman named John Francis Wade made his
26   living copying music for organizations of the Roman
27   Catholic church. Compositions and arrangements of
28   other musicians were brought to him to be neatly
29   transcribed on musical manuscript for individual voices
30   and instruments.
31   NARRATOR 3:   John Francis Wade found joy in his work
32   because it brought him into close contact with many of
33   the world's most talented composers.
34   NARRATOR 1:   Sometimes when he would finish the work of
35   the intricate masses, oratorios, and pastorales, he would

1   take some time for himself. He would express himself in
2   composing simple hymns and cradle songs.
3   NARRATOR 3:   Most of them he destroyed as idle doodlings.
4   He saw nothing in them that approached the beauty of
5   the music he prepared for others.
6   NARRATOR 1:   But occasionally he would be taken by what
7   he had created and he would timidly show his work to
8   the composers he most respected. They would say:
9   NARRATOR 2:   *(Acting as composer 1)* "Interesting, John. You
10   must keep trying."
11   NARRATOR 1:   Or they would say something like . . .
12   NARRATOR 4:   *(Acting as composer 2)* "Good! Good John! Now
13   about my work. I would like you to . . . " *(Fade)*
14   NARRATOR 3:   Soon John Francis Wade did not both to
15   show any of his melodies to anyone.
16   NARRATOR 1:   But several years later a Portugese priest was
17   sorting through some of Wade's manuscripts and he came
18   upon some musical scribblings with a Latin title that was
19   unfamiliar to him.
20   NARRATOR 4:   *(Acting as the Portugese priest)* "John, what is
21   this?" . . . asked the priest.
22   NARRATOR 3:   John looked and saw it was the Christmas
23   hymn that he had written two years before.
24   NARRATOR 4:   *(Still as the Portugese priest)* This is a beautiful
25   melody. It would make a fine processional for our
26   Christmas service. May we use it?
27   NARRATOR 1:   John was pleased to give permission. And
28   that was the first use of the Latin hymn that has been
29   sung by more people than any other Christmas song. It
30   has since been translated into more than 120 different
31   languages. In English we call it, "O Come, All Ye Faithful."
32   *(Congregation sings "O Come, All Ye Faithful.")*
33   NARRATOR 1:   It was a cold winter in Wayland, Massachusetts
34   a little over a hundred years ago. This night, two weeks
35   before Christmas, the village was sleeping beneath a heavy

1	snowfall. Only one light reached out into the midnight
2	darkness. Its warm reflections came from the second floor
3	window of the manse of the Unitarian Church.
4	NARRATOR 2: Reverend Edmund Sears sat in the flickering
5	light of a kerosene lamp writing a letter to the Massachusetts
6	State Senator.
7	NARRATOR 1: When he finished it he read it over carefully.
8	After a moment's reflection he tore it in two and let it
9	fall to the floor.
10	NARRATOR 4: He thought, "What a foolish man I am to think
11	that my words could turn the nation away from the vast
12	madness of these times. I barely have the courage to
13	deliver my weekly sermon, now I am telling a senator
14	what to do. I am indeed a silly, proud man."
15	NARRATOR 1: Reverend Sears was deeply disturbed by the
16	provisions of the new Fugitive Slave Law and the onrush
17	of what he believed to be inevitable war between the
18	states.
19	NARRATOR 2: More than anything else this shy, retiring
20	pastor wanted to find a way to speak of peace that others
21	would hear.
22	NARRATOR 3: In his despair that evening he began writing
23	some lines that only few people have ever heard.
24	NARRATOR 4: "Beneath the angel-strain have rolled
25	Two thousand years of wrong;
26	And man at war with man, hears not
27	The love song which they bring:
28	Oh, hush the noise, ye men of strife,
29	And hear the angels sing."
30	NARRATOR 3: These lines inspired more and long into the
31	evening Reverend Sears wrote until he had completed
32	one of the most heartfelt poems ever written.
33	NARRATOR 1: The next day he sent the stanzas to his close
34	friend, Dr. Morrison in Boston. He immediately arranged
35	that they be published in *The Christian Register*. Later

1	they reached the eyes of an outstanding young composer,
2	Richard Storr Willis, who set them to music. Before many
3	years this Christmas hymn was being sung in churches
4	of all denominations across America. Though the first
5	stanza he wrote about war is no longer included in this
6	carol, everyone knows the others. Reverend Edmund
7	Sears' carol is: "It Came Upon a Midnight Clear."
8	*(Congregation sings "It Came Upon a Midnight Clear.")*
9	NARRATOR 1: St. Francis of Assisi in 1223 was probably the
10	first man of the church who brought the events of the
11	manger to children to dramatize. He believed that at
12	Christmas children most understand Christ Jesus. A new
13	baby is born. By him the world is made new. The offices
14	and pronouncements of men are set aside as children
15	and grown-ups together worship a babe — an innocent,
16	unknowing infant.
17	NARRATOR 2: The humble German farmers of Pennsylvania,
18	too, often found more meaning in a simple birth in a
19	stable than in wordy sermons from a pulpit.
20	NARRATOR 3: It is now believed that someone — or some
21	group — among the Pennsylvania Lutherans were the
22	first to sing the cradle song generally credited to Martin
23	Luther.
24	NARRATOR 2: No one yet knows who that person or group
25	was.
26	NARRATOR 1: But unfortunately it was after the time of
27	Luther for he would have cherished it more than anyone.
28	He loved to sing. From his first young days as a choirboy
29	he loved most of all to sing of the infant Lord on his first
30	birthday.
31	NARRATOR 4: The mystery of the creation of this hymn is an
32	unimportant mystery, for the song is all that matters.
33	The quiet gentleness of this most beautiful cradle hymn.
34	NARRATOR 3: Let us together worship the baby Jesus. Let
35	us sing "Away in a Manger." *(Children's choir or congregation*

1   *sings "Away in a Manger.")*

2   NARRATOR 4: *(Acting as Charles Wesley)* **I never thought of**
3   **myself as a writer of anything except, perhaps, letters of**
4   **state or letters of business. But an event on shipboard**
5   **changed me. It inspired me to do more with words than**
6   **I thought I was able. While returning to England from**
7   **America in 1736, I listened to group of Moravians sing**
8   **hymns every night after dark. Their music came from**
9   **their soul and it reached into the deepest part of me. So**
10   **moved was I that I prayed that the gift of music be given**
11   **to me that I, too, could worship in this way.**

12   NARRATOR 1: **So spoke Charles Wesley telling of the event**
13   **which opened that part of him which later made him the**
14   **most famous of all writers of hymns.**

15   NARRATOR 2: **Charles, with his brother John, had spent a**
16   **year in America as secretary to General Oglethorpe,**
17   **founder of the colony of Georgia. Ill health and a great**
18   **longing for home put him on the ship that changed his**
19   **destiny.**

20   NARRATOR 3: **Counting from that event he wrote more than**
21   **6,500 hymns. His tireless inspiration brought music to**
22   **the world and helped considerably in the founding of the**
23   **Methodist faith.**

24   NARRATOR 1: **Among his favorite hymns was one put to the**
25   **music of Mendelssohn. Though the words and music were**
26   **created separately no greater marriage of mood has ever**
27   **been achieved than in the carol "Hark! The Herald Angels**
28   **Sing."** *(Congregation sings "Hark! The Herald Angels Sing.")*

29   NARRATOR 1: *(Continued)* **It is told that on December 23, 1818,**
30   **a young priest, Joseph Mohr, was called to the house of a**
31   **woodchopper far from his Austrian village of Oberndorf. A**
32   **young wife had just given birth to her first child.**

33   NARRATOR 3: *(Acting as the young mother)* **He is so small and**
34   **helpless. He is not even beautiful. But I will love him and**
35   **he will become strong.**

1	NARRATOR 1:	The radiant joy of this young mother brought
2		to Father Mohr's mind the joy of Mary when baby Jesus
3		was delivered of her. He could think of nothing else as
4		he rode back through the snowy forest to his church. The
5		stars, the quiet, the vision of the young mother with a
6		child cradled in her arms made him think of Bethlehem.
7		As soon as he returned to his room he wrote on a scrap
8		of paper the words that had come to him again and again
9		in the forest: "Silent Night, Holy Night." Looking at them
10		he knew that he must write more. As dawn came he had
11		completed the words for a Christmas hymn. He rushed
12		them to his schoolmaster friend at the neighboring
13		village of Arnsdorf.
14	NARRATOR 2:	*(Acting as Joseph Mohr)* **Franz, you must set**
15		**these words to music for me!**
16	NARRATOR 4:	*(Acting as Franz Gruber)* **Ja, ja,** *(German*
17		*pronunciation: Yah, yah)* **Joseph. But please now, you must**
18		**not be so excited.**
19	NARRATOR 2:	*(As Mohr)* **It is so soon that Christmas Eve will**
20		**be with us! We must sing them tonight in church.**
21	NARRATOR 4:	*(As Gruber)* **Tonight!**
22	NARRATOR 2:	*(As Mohr)* **Tonight, Franz! Our organ is broken**
23		**and we must have music for the midnight mass. Please**
24		**will you do this for me?**
25	NARRATOR 4:	*(As Gruber)* **Well, I will try, though you don't**
26		**give me much time.**
27	NARRATOR 1:	Very little time was needed. Franz Gruber
28		said the words sang themselves. The music was ready
29		that evening arranged for two voices and guitar. With
30		the elevation of the host at midnight, Gruber and Mohr
31		together sang the simple carol. Those who heard it said
32		it was the most beautiful music they had ever heard at
33		Christmas.
34	NARRATOR 3:	Except for a circumstance this simple song
35		may never have left St. Nicholas Church in Oberndorf.

1	Some months later when an organ master came to repair
2	the church organ he asked Gruber to play something.
3	Gruber played "Silent Night." The organ master thought
4	it a lovely song and memorized it.
5	NARRATOR 1: In turn he taught it to four children named
6	Strasser in his village. They sang it many times, one of
7	them during a visit to Leipzig where it was heard by the
8	music director of the Kingdom of Saxony. The year
9	following, the Strasser children were persuaded to sing
10	it for several members of royalty. It was repeated by many
11	singers for over thirty years with the title, "The Tyrolese
12	Song." Then in the 1850s the full choir of the Imperial
13	Church in Berlin sang it for King Frederick William IV.
14	He was so moved by it that he ordered a search for its
15	composers.
16	NARRATOR 3: When their identities were discovered, only
17	Franz Gruber was still alive. It was the only song either
18	of them had ever written. Many feel it is the most
19	beautiful of all Christmas songs. *(Congregation sings "Silent*
20	*Night, Holy Night.)*
21	NARRATOR 4: The world has been made richer by these
22	carols. The Holy Spirit visited each of the many people
23	who created them and it is with us today *(Tonight)* as we
24	sing.
25	NARRATOR 1: There are many other great carols and many
26	more will still be written.
27	NARRATOR 4: It is only important that we sing them with
28	meaning so that the world may continue to be changed
29	for the infant Jesus and all infants forever. *(Choir sings*
30	*"O Holy Night" or a musical benediction.)*
31	*CLOSING BENEDICTION*
32	
33	
34	
35	

The Little Match Girl
by HANS CHRISTIAN ANDERSEN
adapted by
JANET MEILI

CAST

LITTLE MATCH GIRL

NARRATOR

MOTHER

FATHER

TWO CHILDREN

GRANDMOTHER

AUTHOR'S NOTE: The actors in Scene I can double as the characters in the other scenes, but the audience should not feel they are seeing the same family in different circumstances. The children may be boys or girls. Change the script to suit.

STAGING DIRECTIONS

This production, as written, can be performed in any church chancel or in any meeting room without benefit of stage or curtains.

The only requirement for making this an effective dramatic program is the availability of two floodlights, two spotlights and a fader (rheostat). These can be improvised with photolights purchased from a photo shop or bright floodlights inserted into tomato can reflectors. Faders can be made by anyone with some electrical know-how.

This equipment may also be rented from any theatrical supply house or sometimes an electrical supply company.

The use of lights permits any staging area to be used as a stage without a curtain. Darkness alone becomes the curtain when audience attention is directed to different areas by spotlights.

When the main "scenes" of this playlet are darkened the props may be changed as necessary for the next episode.

The fading up and down of the lights becomes another device by which the director can control the dramatic pace of the production.

Every staging situation is different, of course, and the director will be challenged to make the best use of whatever resources are available. Try several ways to use both lights and space to advantage. It's surprising how adaptable the chancel area of a church really is — or what you can do in almost any meeting room if you can control the lighting.

The script has suggested cues for the lights. Try these first, then do what works best for your situation.

Properly staged, this story can be one of the most memorable you will ever present.

1   *SETTING:*   A hovel in a large city in the mid-nineteenth century.
2   A bare table, with the drunken FATHER sitting on a bench
3   holding an empty mug. The ill MOTHER is lying on a pallet
4   on the floor covered only by a shawl. The little MATCH GIRL
5   is sitting Upstage of her mother. Two CHILDREN, dirty and
6   in rags, sit on the floor alongside the pallet playing with a rag
7   ball or doll.
8
9   *PRELUDE:*   Optional use.
10 **PASTOR:**   **We are here today** *(Tonight)* **to celebrate the joy of**
11   **Christmas. And what a joyous event it is! But not for**
12   **everyone. The forgotten ones — the poor and lonely —**
13   **those without hope . . . their Christmas is very different**
14   **from ours. Though we all try to bring joy and hope to**
15   **everyone at Christmas time, some are still overlooked.**
16   **It was so in the time of Hans Christian Andersen and it**
17   **is still true today. For those forgotten ones, the great**
18   **Danish storyteller wrote one of the most moving stories**
19   **of all Christmas literature — "The Little Match Girl." It**
20   **may, at first, seem to be a sad story to many of you but**
21   **if you look deeper into it you will see the great message**
22   **of the Good News it carries: Christ was born to give us**
23   **the proof of everlasting life and eternal peace.** *(Fade up*
24   *lights.)*
25 **FATHER:**   **Do you tell me there is not so much as a crust of**
26   **bread in the house?**
27 **MOTHER:**   **You took the money to buy spirits.**
28 **FATHER:**   **A man has to keep warm some way.** *(Tries to find one*
29   *more drop in mug.)*
30 **MOTHER:**   **The rest of us are cold too.**
31 **FATHER:**   **Might as well burn this table if there's nothing to**
32   **put on it.**
33 **MOTHER:**   **You would be wiser to sell it.**
34 **FATHER:**   **It's the last day of the year. Isn't that one we sent**
35   **out to work supposed to bring us his wages?**

1   **MOTHER:**   The chimney sweep will not pay Charles until he
2   has worked six months. He says too many of his boys run
3   away. He wants to be sure to get his money's worth out of
4   Charles before he pays him.
5   **FATHER:**   Lazy brats! Afraid of a little work! At least a sweep's
6   boy has a nice warm place to work. *(Laughs nastily.*
7   *MOTHER coughs.)* Oh, don't pretend you're so sick. If you
8   don't feel like working, why don't you just say so instead
9   of lying there trying to look so weak and helpless.
10   **MOTHER:**   Do you think I would let my children starve if I
11   were able to go out and find work?
12   **FATHER:**   Why not? Let them starve. What kind of life do they
13   have to look forward to? More of this? Rags and cold and
14   hunger. What's the sense of trying? The rich get richer
15   and the poor get poorer. *(Looks around.)* There must be
16   something in this place that'll burn. *(Grabs CHILDREN's*
17   *toy. They cry out and reach for it.)* This will smell, but it'll
18   be better than nothing.
19   **MATCH GIRL:**   Please don't take the boys' ball. It's all they
20   have.
21   **FATHER:**   You can make them a new one in the spring from
22   the rags in the cracks.
23   **MATCH GIRL:**   Please give them their ball back. It won't burn
24   well. Really it won't. *(FATHER throws toy down; CHILDREN*
25   *pounce on it.)*
26   **FATHER:**   What are you doing home, anyhow? *(Grabs her and*
27   *lifts her by one arm.)* Why aren't you out selling your
28   matches? You can't make money sitting home. No wonder
29   there's no food on the table or wood for the fire.
30   **MATCH GIRL:**   It's New Year's Eve.
31   **FATHER:**   Right! And everyone will need matches to light
32   their ovens for the New Year's feast. Go on! Get moving!
33   And don't come back until you've sold enough so we can
34   eat too!
35   **MOTHER:**   It's so cold outside!

1 FATHER: I suppose you think it's warm in here. What's the
2   sense in having a brat old enough to work if she doesn't
3   bring in any money?
4 MOTHER: *(To GIRL)* Take my shawl.
5 MATCH GIRL: No, Mother, you need it more than I.
6 MOTHER: You can't go out there with nothing on your feet!
7   Put on my shoes. They'll be big for you but they're better
8   than nothing. I won't need them.
9 FATHER: No, you won't need them. You're not planning to
10   get up. *(To GIRL)* Well, what are you waiting for? And be
11   sure to bring that money back or I'll give you a whipping
12   you won't soon forget.
13   *(Fade down lights to black on scene. LITTLE MATCH GIRL,*
14   *barefoot and in rags, walks to place near the NARRATOR or*
15   *into a spotlighted area. She holds her apron up to carry the*
16   *matches. Spotlight up on NARRATOR.)*
17 NARRATOR: The poor little match girl went out into the cold
18   and dark. People were hurrying to their homes eagerly
19   looking forward to the next day's holiday. But no one
20   stopped to buy matches. As she started to cross a busy
21   street, two carts came along. Jumping out of their way,
22   the poor little girl lost both of her too-big shoes. One just
23   seemed to disappear. A boy grabbed the other and ran
24   off with it. The match girl walked on through the ice and
25   snow getting colder and colder. She couldn't go home.
26   She hadn't sold a single match. Actually, she felt more
27   peaceful out here under the clear sky. If only she weren't
28   so cold. In the corner formed by two buildings she
29   huddled down out of the wind. *(She sits down.)* There were
30   her matches. Surely it would be all right to light just one
31   of them to warm her hands. No one would miss just one
32   match. *(Pantomimes lighting match. Use pencil flashlight. She*
33   *keeps hands cupped around it.)* So the little match girl lit
34   just one match. And the most amazing thing happened.
35   A stove appeared. A warm, gaily burning, toasty stove.

1	Surely she was mistaken. No, it was definitely a stove.
2	*(Spotlight on NARRATOR fades to black.)*
3	*(Fade lights up for a middle-class home setting with large stove.*
4	*Enter well-dressed MOTHER and two small BOYS, one carrying*
5	*an armload of wood, the other a basket of coal.)*
6	**MOTHER: Build the fire up well, Albert. Father will be home**
7	**from work soon and he'll be chilled from his cold walk.**
8	*(ALBERT puts wood in holder next to stove. Other sets down*
9	*basket of coal.)*
10	**ALBERT:** *(Opening door of stove)* **There's a nice bed of coals**
11	**but I think I'll put a piece of wood on to get the flames**
12	**started again.**
13	**MOTHER: It's been so cold for so many days. We haven't had**
14	**such a bad winter in years.**
15	**WILLIAM:** *(Facing audience, mimes blowing hole in frost on*
16	*window, making the hole larger by rubbing with his fingers.)* **I**
17	**can see Father coming! He has his scarf around his ears**
18	**and his hands in his pockets.**
19	**MOTHER: A few minutes in front of our fire and a good hot**
20	**cup of coffee and he'll forget how cold it is out there.**
21	*(Enter FATHER, dressed for winter.)*
22	**FATHER: I finally made it! Who wants to knock the icicle off**
23	**my nose?**
24	**ALBERT:** *(Laughing)* **You don't have an icicle on your nose!**
25	**FATHER: I don't? Then my whole nose must be as frozen as**
26	**an icicle!**
27	**WILLIAM:** *(Looking out his hole that he must continually rub to*
28	*keep open)* **Father, there's a little girl outside with no coat**
29	**or shoes or mittens or anything. She must be *terribly* cold.**
30	**FATHER: No one would go out in weather like this without**
31	**the proper clothes, William.**
32	**MOTHER:** *(Goes to window and looks out.)* **Oh, Edward, it's the**
33	**little match girl. She must be nearly frozen! Albert, run**
34	**quickly and bring her into the house.** *(Fade lights to black.*
35	*Scene disappears.)*

1 *(The MATCH GIRL's match/flashlight goes out as she starts to*
2 *move toward the stove in the setting. Spotlight up again on*
3 *NARRATOR.)*
4 **NARRATOR:** **But just as the little match girl dreamed she**
5 **was about to warm herself at the nice, warm, toasty stove,**
6 **her match burned out and she found herself in the freezing**
7 **ice and snow. For a minute everything had seemed so**
8 **wonderful that she wanted to make believe again. So she**
9 **lit a second match.**
10 *(Spotlight on NARRATOR fades to dark. MATCH GIRL "lights"*
11 *another match/flashlight. Fade up main lights on home setting*
12 *once again. There is a table covered with a white cloth and set*
13 *for New Year's dinner. Four chairs are around the table.*
14 *MOTHER and WILLIAM Onstage.)*
15 **MOTHER:** **Now, let's see. Potatoes. Red cabbage. You can**
16 **call the others, William. Dinner is ready.**
17 **WILLIAM:** *(Running to Stage Right)* **Mother says to come.**
18 **Dinner is ready.** *(Enter FATHER and ALBERT. They each*
19 *stand behind his chair.)*
20 **FATHER:** **New Year's is such a wonderful time. Here we are,**
21 **gathered together in our own snug house about to eat**
22 **an elegant dinner and ready to start a new year. Let us**
23 **say grace. Dear Father in heaven, guide our steps in the**
24 **way thou wouldst have us go. Bless this food thou hast**
25 **set before us that we may be strengthened by it to serve**
26 **in thy kingdom. In this new year opening to us, help us**
27 **to draw closer to thee and save us from our sins. Amen.**
28 **OTHERS:** **Amen.** *(FATHER and BOYS sit down.)*
29 **ALBERT:** **Mother, where's the goose? You forgot the goose,**
30 **Mother.**
31 **MOTHER:** **The goose! Why so I did. Can you imagine New**
32 **Year's dinner without a goose? How silly of me.** *(Walks*
33 *right and returns with goose on platter.)* **Here's something I**
34 **found in the kitchen. What do you suppose it could be?**
35 **WILLIAM:** *(Clapping hands)* **It's the goose! My, but it looks good.**

1   FATHER: *(Taking up carving tools)* **And just which part of this**
2   **plump, juicy, golden brown goose would you like,**
3   **William?**
4   WILLIAM: **May I please have a leg?** *(As FATHER puts fork*
5   *into goose it slides off plate toward the little MATCH GIRL who*
6   *raises her arms to catch it. Lights out instantly except for spotlight*
7   *on NARRATOR.)*
8   NARRATOR: **The plump, juicy, golden brown goose went**
9   **flying right toward the outstretched arms of the little**
10   **match girl but just then the match burned out and once**
11   **more she found herself alone and shivering and hungry.**
12   **But now she knew just what to do. She lit a third match.**
13   *(NARRATOR spotlight fades.)*
14   *(Another actress the same size as the original MATCH GIRL*
15   *and dressed the same should now move into the exact same*
16   *position to replace the original actress so that the original*
17   *MATCH GIRL can move into the scene that follows for a speaking*
18   *part. When in position, replacement actress "lights" another*
19   *match. Main lights fade up to reveal a beautifully decorated*
20   *Christmas tree. Tree lights are not on. There are two chairs in*
21   *front of it and to the side. The family enters.)*
22 FATHER: **That was an excellent meal, Caroline.**
23 MOTHER: **Thank you.** *(They seat themselves.)*
24 WILLIAM: **May I have some candy?**
25 MOTHER: **I don't know how you can eat any more, but go**
26   **ahead if you want.**
27 ALBERT: **Me too?**
28 MOTHER: **Of course, dear.** *(Boys go behind tree and eat candy.)*
29 MATCH GIRL: *(Walks into the scene from the darkness.)* **May I**
30   **come closer and look at your tree?** *(They don't hear her.)*
31   **I've never seen anything so beautiful. How the tinsel**
32   **glitters! Oh, look! Here's a gingerbread boy! And there's**
33   **another!**
34 ALBERT: **May we eat the gingerbread boys, Mother? They're**
35   **a whole week old, already.**

1   MOTHER: Oh, Albert, won't you make yourself sick? Why
2   don't you wait until tomorrow? They'll taste better if
3   you're hungrier.
4   ALBERT: All right.
5   MATCH GIRL: I've wondered if you ate the gingerbread or
6   saved it from year to year. What pretty stars. And look
7   at the angel on top! Isn't it beautiful?
8   WILLIAM: Next year I'm going to make ornaments for the tree.
9   ALBERT: You're too little. What could you make?
10 WILLIAM: Next year I'll be a whole year older and then I'll
11   be able to do things better.
12 MATCH GIRL: What beautiful dolls! That one is just begging
13   me to take her.
14 ALBERT: May we light the tree, Father?
15 FATHER: Yes, but be careful. *(MATCH GIRL steps back outside*
16   *of scene into darkness.)*
17   *(Stage lights fade as tree lights up. Don't use candles. Fade up*
18   *spotlight on NARRATOR.)*
19 NARRATOR: As the tree was lighted it seemed to the little
20   match girl that the lights reached right up to the stars.
21   *(Slowly fade lights to black. Original MATCH GIRL gets back*
22   *into position. Show a moving flash of light. Swing a flashlight*
23   *across staging area in an arc. The flashlight is at the end of a*
24   *string suspended from the ceiling, if possible. Fade up spotlight*
25   *on MATCH GIRL.)*
26 MATCH GIRL: Oh, look. There's a falling star. That means
27   someone has died and that person's soul has gone to
28   heaven. Grandmother told me that before she went to
29   heaven herself. I miss Grandmother very much. I loved
30   her so. Oh, it's cold. It can't matter if I light just one more
31   match. *(She "lights" another match/flashlight. Spotlight on*
32   *GRANDMOTHER.)* Grandmother! Grandmother, I was
33   just thinking of you. Oh, please, don't go away. Don't go
34   away like the stove did, and the goose, and the Christmas
35   tree. Take me with you. Wait! I'll light all my matches and

1	then you can stay with me forever. *(MATCH GIRL lights*
2	*several matches. After the last match she drops shawl and walks*
3	*into the dark area. Spotlight on NARRATOR.)*
4	NARRATOR: The next morning, people on their way to
5	celebrate New Year's Day found the frozen body of the
6	little match girl with the burned matches in her hand.
7	"How dreadful," they said. "She must have tried to keep
8	warm. How pitiful." *(Spotlight on little MATCH GIRL and*
9	*her GRANDMOTHER.)*
10	MATCH GIRL: Grandmother, they don't understand. It
11	wasn't dreadful at all. It was wonderful! First, there was
12	a lovely warm stove with brass feet and brass decorations.
13	It made me feel warm. And then there was a New Year's
14	dinner with a plump goose stuffed with apples and
15	prunes. I almost got to eat as much as I wanted. After
16	that there was a beautiful Christmas tree, far more
17	splendid than the one I had seen through the glass doors
18	of the home of the rich merchant. And then you came. I
19	thought you would leave me but then you took me with
20	you after all.
21	GRANDMOTHER: Yes, and now we shall always be together
22	and you'll never be sad or cold or hungry again because
23	here in heaven we are with God. *(She embraces little*
24	*MATCH GIRL and kisses her as the spotlight fades to darkness.)*
25	*(If desired, an organ can begin playing under the MATCH GIRL's*
26	*last speech and after it a solo voice may sing the appropriate*
27	*lines, "And God shall wipe away all tears from their eyes. There*
28	*shall be no more death, neither sorrow nor crying; neither shall*
29	*there be any more pain," from Arthur Sullivan's song, "The Light*
30	*of the World," included in the book entitled "52 Sacred Songs*
31	*You Like to Sing" published by G. Schirmer, Inc.)*
32	
33	
34	
35	

How God Came to Us
by MICHAEL E. DIXON

CAST

MATTHEW

LUKE

ANGEL

MARY

CAESAR

JOSEPH

INNKEEPER

WISE MAN

HEROD

SCHOLAR

RHYTHM CHOIR

PRODUCTION NOTES

How God Came to Us is a narration of the Christmas story for a rhythm choir and solo readers. What's a rhythm choir? It's a group of children who talk — not sing — to a beat. They speak to a beat to keep the story moving, and they use changes in speed and volume to set moods and build anticipation. Why a rhythm choir? It's fun — fun to learn, fun to perform, fun to hear. The messages of the story attract the children's attention and stay in their memories longer. It's a good teaching device as well as a performing method. It involves all age ranges and abilities. Children too young or too shy or without musical ability can chant as part of a rhythm chorus.

Although participants can memorize lines if they want to, *How God Came to Us* was designed as a Readers Theatre production. That way, the group can emphasize delivery, not memorization. A bright, fast pace is necessary for an effective performance, and that's easier done without the pauses that often come from memorization.

The performance can be adapted for large or small groups. There are 10 characters, but only three (Matthew, Luke and the Angel), appear throughout the performance. Thus, with a use of identifying props (see later section on props), parts could be doubled for a group smaller than 10. In groups of 15 or less, the individual readers will also be part of the rhythm choir. Larger groups may want to separate solo readers on one side of a chancel or stage, and the rhythm choir on the other. This would free the solo readers for some simple movement and bodily interpretation (for example, Mary bowing to the angel; a magi processing to and from Herod). This is up to the initiative of the local director, though, and the performance works just fine with the children simply standing in rows on the chancel steps.

How do you direct a rhythm choir? Simple — just keep the beat with your hand and voice. Those with musical directing ability can expand from that. In the choir's speeches, lines to be emphasized are underlined. Say those louder and the other words softer, and the beat will be there. Most of the solo speeches are without beat, and should be interpreted in a normal way. The only exception is that some lines of the Angel's will pick up the beat from the rhythm choir and give it back to the choir, to build intensity and power. Two of the choir's speeches are designated for flowing rhythm or to be sung. These don't carry the heavy beat of the other speeches, but are more melodic. They could easily be adapted to simple tunes by a director with musical skills.

The production was designed as part of a longer Christmas program, with prayers, Scripture readings, carols and possibly another play or reading for older participants to go along with it. Such components can be added as your group's size and traditions warrant. This narration itself will last 20 to 25 minutes.

No props or costumes are necessary. A printed bulletin can provide identification of characters. The performance can be dressed up, however, by the addition of simple hand props or costume pieces. Here are some suggestions:

- Matthew and Luke: Large book covers over their scripts with their names in large letters, or symbols of the evangelists drawn on the covers.

- Angel: Halo or wings from the storage closet.

- Mary: A blue scarf.

- Caesar: A large paper crown or a plastic laurel wreath.

- Joseph: Carpenter's apron or a hand tool.

- Innkeeper: A "No Vacancy" sign around the neck or in hand.

- Wise Man: A wrapped gift.

- Herod: A smaller crown.

- Scholar: A book or a scroll, which can be two cardboard tubes with a strip of paper attached between.

The first performance of *How God Came to Us* communicated a reverent but joyous and humorous message. If the director fears that some lines might raise some eyebrows, they can be edited and rephrased as necessary.

1	RHYTHM CHOIR:
2	We wanna <u>te</u>lla 'bout the <u>birth</u> of
3	Jesus.
4	<u>This</u> is the <u>way</u> God <u>came</u> to <u>us</u>.
5	
6	MATTHEW: My name is Matthew.
7	LUKE: You can call me Luke.
8	MATTHEW & LUKE: We want you to know the news.
9	RHYTHM CHOIR: *(To the rhythm of "Shave and a Haircut")*
10	They're gonna <u>tell</u> you — <u>Good</u> <u>News</u>!
11	
12	MATTHEW: The best news you've ever heard.
13	LUKE: *(Nods.)* The very best.
14	MATTHEW: Now the birth of Jesus took place this way.
15	LUKE: The angel Gabriel was sent from God to a city of
16	Galilee named Nazareth, to a young woman who was
17	engaged to a man named Joseph.
18	RHYTHM CHOIR:
19	Now <u>Joseph</u> was de<u>scen</u>ded from
20	<u>Da</u>vid the king.
21	
22	LUKE: The young woman's name was Mary. Here's what the
23	angel told her.
24	ANGEL: Hail, O favored one, the Lord is with you!
25	LUKE: Mary was confused. Angels? Visiting her? What did
26	it all mean?
27	ANGEL: Don't be afraid, Mary, for God is with you. What do
28	you think about this? Within you will grow a baby, you
29	will give him birth, and you will name him Jesus.
30	RHYTHM CHOIR: *(Speaking with a flowing rhythm or singing)*
31	He will be great, he will be good,
32	He will be God's Son;
33	He will reign forever and ever,
34	In the kingdom to come.
35	

1 MARY: But how can this be, since I have no husband?
2 RHYTHM CHOIR: *(Whispers rhythmically, getting increasingly*
3   *louder.)*
4   The Holy Spirit, the Holy Spirit,
5   The Holy Spirit, the Holy Spirit,
6   The Holy Spirit!
7
8 ANGEL: *(Chanting)*
9   The Holy Spirit
10   will come upon you
11   and God's great power
12   will overshadow
13
14 RHYTHM CHOIR:
15   Will overshadow, will overshadow
16
17 ANGEL:
18   Will overshadow you,
19   for the child to be born will be holy.
20
21 LUKE: With God, nothing is impossible. Mary said,
22 MARY: Behold, I am the handmaiden of the Lord. Let it happen
23   as you have said. My soul magnifies the Lord, and my
24   spirit rejoices in God my savior. I was a nobody, and God
25   paid attention to me. People through all time will see
26   how happy I am, for my mighty God has done great things
27   for me, and God's name will be holy.
28 LUKE: And so it came to pass.
29 MATTHEW: When Mary was engaged to Joseph, before they
30   were married, she was found to be expecting the child.
31   Now Joseph was a kind man, and was willing to leave
32   without a lot of fuss, to break off the engagement in a
33   gentle sort of way. But then an angel came, and the angel
34   and Joseph had a little talk.
35 ANGEL: Joseph, son of David, don't be afraid. Take Mary as

your wife, and be proud of her. The child she bears is a gift of the Spirit. A son will be born, his name will be Jesus, and he'll save the world from sin.

MATTHEW: After Joseph woke up, he did what the angel said. The two got married, and thought they'd settle down.

LUKE: In those days, Caesar Augustus sent out an order that all the world should be taxed.

RHYTHM CHOIR:

Hear ye, hear ye, hear all about it!

Caesar Augustus is going to bust us!

CAESAR: I'm broke. I'm going to make me a tax. But how do I make sure that everybody pays? Hmmm. *(Brightens.)* I know! Everybody will go back to his old hometown, the place that he was born. We'll get them all on the records, and then they'll pay. *(Rubs hands.)* And pay and pay and pay.

LUKE: So Joseph also went up from Galilee, from the city of Nazareth, to travel to Judea, the city of David.

RHYTHM CHOIR:

Now Joseph was descended from

David the king.

LUKE: Mary his wife had to go along, though she was great with child.

RHYTHM CHOIR: *(Clipclopping hands on knees, as donkey hooves, saying in rhythm:)*

Poor tired Mary.

Poor tired Mary.

Poor tired Mary.

LUKE: The long, tiring journey came to an end as they entered Bethlehem. But where could they stay? The town was full of travelers.

JOSEPH: Sir, you are my last hope. Is there room? My wife

1   will have a baby soon, and we need shelter.

2   INNKEEPER: I'm sorry, but every room is full.

3   JOSEPH: Sir, we'll take any shelter at all!

4   INNKEEPER: The cave where we shelter the animals would

5   protect your wife from the wind. If there is no place else,

6   you may stay there.

7   JOSEPH: Thank you!

8   LUKE: And while they were there, the time came for her to

9   be delivered. She gave birth to her first-born son. Then

10   she wrapped him in warm cloth, and laid him in the straw

11   of the animals' feeding trough.

12   RHYTHM CHOIR: *(Normal, then softer)*

13   On the <u>hill</u>side <u>shep</u>herds <u>wait</u>ed.

14   On the <u>hill</u>side <u>shep</u>herds <u>wait</u>ed.

15   On the <u>hill</u>side <u>shep</u>herds <u>wait</u>ed.

16   On the <u>hill</u>side <u>shep</u>herds <u>wait</u>ed.

17

18   LUKE: Near the town, there were shepherds out in the fields,

19   keeping watch over their flock by night. And then God's

20   angel appeared to them, and the light of God's glory shone

21   around them, and they were filled with fear!

22   ANGEL: Don't be afraid!

23   RHYTHM CHOIR: *(Speaking with flowing rhythm or singing)*

24   Don't be afraid, don't be afraid,

25   Hear good news of great joy.

26   Don't be afraid, don't be afraid,

27   Come see Mary's baby boy.

28

29   ANGEL: This is good news for all the people; for to you is born

30   this day in David's hometown a Savior, who is Christ the

31   Lord. And here is a sign so you will recognize him: look

32   in an animal's feeding trough and find a newborn baby

33   there, wrapped in warm cloth.

34   LUKE: Many more angels suddenly appeared, and they all sang!

35

```
1    RHYTHM CHOIR & ANGEL:
2                        Glory, glory glory, glory, glory
3                            glory, glory!
4                        Glory, glory glory, glory, glory
5                            glory, glory!
6
7    ANGEL:   Glory to God in the highest! And peace be to you, for
8        God is pleased!
9    LUKE:   As soon as the angels left, the shepherds didn't waste
10       time.
11   RHYTHM CHOIR:   (Walking in time)
12                        Let's get going — let's get going —
13                        Let's get going — let's get going.
14
15   LUKE:   They hurried there and found Mary and Joseph, and
16       the baby lying in a manger. And when they saw the baby,
17       they told what the angel had said, so that all who had
18       gathered there were filled with wonder. But Mary kept
19       all these things, and pondered them in her heart. The
20       shepherds returned to work, praising God for all they
21       had heard and seen.
22   RHYTHM CHOIR:
23                        Glory, glory glory, glory, glory
24                            glory, glory!
25                        Glory, glory glory, glory, glory
26                            glory, glory!
27
28   MATTHEW:   After Jesus was born, wise leaders came from
29       the east. They came to Jerusalem, and began asking
30       questions.
31   WISE MAN:   Where is he born king of the Jews? For we have
32       seen his star in the east, and have come to worship him.
33   MATTHEW:   This made Herod the king and all the other leaders
34       in Jerusalem very nervous.
35   HEROD:   You are a great scholar. Can you tell me where the
```

1   Christ is to be born?

2 SCHOLAR: In Bethlehem of Judea, for a prophet has written,

3   And you, O Bethlehem, in the land of Judah, are not the

4   least among Judah's rulers; for from you shall come a

5   ruler who will govern my people Israel.

6 MATTHEW: Then Herod asked the wise men to a secret

7   meeting, to find when they had first started following

8   the star, and he gave them instructions.

9 HEROD: Go and search well for the child, and when you have

10   found him, let me know, so that I, too, may come and

11   worship.

12 MATTHEW: When the wise rulers heard the king, they went

13   on their way; and behold, the star which they had seen

14   in the east went before them, and led them to the very

15   place where the child was. When they saw the star, they

16   were filled with great joy. They saw the child with Mary

17   his mother, and they fell down and worshiped him. Then

18   they gave him precious gifts of gold and perfumes. But

19   they were warned in a dream not to return to Herod, and

20   they returned to their own countries by another route.

21 RHYTHM CHOIR: *(Slow, speeding up to fast, and soft becoming*

22   *loud)*

23   Be careful! Be careful! Be careful!

24   Be careful! Be careful! Be careful!

25   Be careful!

26

27 MATTHEW: Again, an angel appeared in Joseph's dream,

28   and warned him of Herod's cruel plans.

29 ANGEL: Rise, take the child and his mother, and flee to

30   Egypt, and remain there till I tell you, for Herod is about

31   to search for the child, to destroy him.

32 MATTHEW: Many babies were killed, and many mothers

33   were heartbroken. But Joseph and Mary escaped with

34   Jesus. They went to a foreign land, Egypt, where they

35   would be safe. After Herod had died, they returned to where

1   it all began — Nazareth.

2   **RHYTHM CHOIR:**

3   **And that's the story, the special story,**

4   **the story of how God came to us.**

5   **Peace be with you.**

6

7

8

9

10

11

12

13

14

15

16

17

18

19

20

21

22

23

24

25

26

27

28

29

30

31

32

33

34

35

Thank You, Santa
by ANNE L. NUNLEY

CAST

SANTA CLAUS

MRS. CLAUS

MAILMAN

ELVES:
Twinkletoes
Jingle
Happyeyes
Merrythought
Jangle
Starbright

DANCERS:
6 to 8 young girls

SMALL CHILD
Toddler — to be the "lifelike" doll

NOTE: A differentiation is made in this play between elves and brownies. The elves are the ones in the play — they help make the toys and are Santa's helpers. The brownies, who are only spoken of, are the actual workers.

Elves may be male or female, although most references to elves in the dialog are "she."

1	**Scene 1**
2	
3	*SETTING:* The North Pole in July.
4	
5	*AT RISE:* Before curtains open, lead into the play by playing a
6	bouncy, happy Christmas song. MR. and MRS. SANTA CLAUS
7	are in a brightly-lighted living room. A fully decorated
8	Christmas tree is in one corner, with wrapped boxes under the
9	tree. A picture of Santa is over the fireplace. Couch and
10	overstuffed or rocking chair; background music of Santa Claus
11	songs is playing. MRS. CLAUS is in chair doing handwork.
12	SANTA is on couch reading newspaper, but is very listless. He
13	reads for a minute, lays paper down and sighs loudly, picks
14	paper back up and reads for another minute, then lays paper
15	back down and sighs again.
16	
17	**MRS. CLAUS: Did Happyeyes tell you the elves are almost**
18	**out of red paint?**
19	**SANTA: Yes, she did.** *(Goes to the window and looks out.)* **Has the**
20	**mailman come yet?**
21	**MRS. CLAUS: I don't believe he has. Santa, have you seen**
22	**Twinkletoes' design for the new doll?**
23	**SANTA:** *(Goes back to the couch.)* **Yes, I've seen it.** *(Picks up the*
24	*paper again.)*
25	**MRS. CLAUS: Well, are you going to use the new design?**
26	**That doll looks so lifelike! It will make little girls and**
27	**boys so happy!**
28	**SANTA: Twinkletoes can do whatever she wants.** *(Goes to the*
29	*window again.)* **Are you sure the mail hasn't come yet?**
30	**MRS. CLAUS: It's a little early yet. Santa, what about**
31	**Happyeyes' idea for the wagon with the steering wheel?**
32	**Are you going to use that?**
33	**SANTA: I don't care — she can do whatever she wants. I just**
34	**don't care.**
35	**MRS. CLAUS: Santa! Whatever in the world is wrong? You are**

1   so restless. You aren't interested in any of the new toys.
2   You haven't been to the workshop for almost two weeks.
3   The elves are almost out of paint and you don't seem to
4   care. At the rate we're going, we won't have the toys done
5   by Christmas Eve. Whatever is wrong? *(ELVES burst in.)*
6   TWINKLETOES: Santa, come quickly.
7   JINGLE: The brownies are fighting!
8   HAPPYEYES: They're hitting each other!
9   MERRYTHOUGHT: I'm afraid they'll hurt each other!
10   SANTA: *(Crossly)* Don't bring your problems to me.
11   JANGLE: But Santa, they're throwing sawdust all over the
12   workshop!
13   STARBRIGHT: And they're making the reindeer really
14   nervous!
15   SANTA: Well, a few nervous reindeer won't hurt anything.
16   TWINKLETOES: Santa! What is wrong? The workshop is a
17   shambles, the brownies are fighting, the reindeer are
18   nervous, the toys aren't getting done — and you don't
19   seem to care! What is wrong?
20   SANTA: *(Growling)* Nothing is wrong — except I think it looks
21   silly to still have the Christmas tree up in July.
22   MRS. CLAUS: But, Santa, we've always —
23   SANTA: *(Interrupting)* And turn off that miserable music! I
24   can't stand to hear another Christmas song! And now you
25   elves come in with problems, problems, problems. Well,
26   solve your own problems! I'm going to see what is keeping
27   the mailman. *(He leaves.)*
28   MRS. CLAUS: *(Shocked)* I can't believe how Santa is acting!
29   TWINKLETOES: He's been like that for weeks.
30   JINGLE: He's been so cross.
31   MERRYTHOUGHT: He made us take down the Christmas
32   tree in the workshop, too.
33   STARBRIGHT: We're almost out of paint.
34   JANGLE: The soldiers and the dolls are only half done.
35   JINGLE: And we haven't even started the bikes and

1	wagons yet.
2	**ALL:** What's wrong with Santa? *(All sing:)*
3	
4	**WHAT'S WRONG WITH SANTA?**
5	
6	What's wrong with Santa? He's so sad!
7	When Santa's sad, it makes me feel bad.
8	What's wrong with Santa? He's so blue!
9	It makes me want to cry. Boo Hoo.
10	Santa is always full of Christmas cheer.
11	What has happened to him this year?
12	Let's get to work and find what's wrong.
13	We haven't much time; we can't take very long.
14	We want to hear Santa say, "Ho Ho!"
15	It's nearly Christmas Eve, you know.
16	
17	**MRS. CLAUS:** Maybe Santa has just been having a few bad
18	days. We all do now and then, you know.
19	**ELVES:** I don't know — I think it's more than that.
20	**MRS. CLAUS:** Well, I'll fix his favorite dinner tonight and
21	make sure he gets a good night's sleep. He'll probably
22	feel better tomorrow. Now, you elves get back to work.
23	Twinkletoes, come with me. I'll send some cookies to the
24	brownies. Maybe that will help make them stop fighting.
25	Things will be better tomorrow, you'll see. *(ELVES go out*
26	*the door; MRS. CLAUS and TWINKLETOES go to kitchen.*
27	*SANTA re-enters — dejected — and sits on the couch.)*
28	**SANTA:** Another day and still no letters. All I get is junk mail.
29	Here's a beautiful advertisement suggesting I come to
30	Hawaii. Looks like a beautiful place, all right. But no
31	letters from the children. Not one single child has written
32	to say thank you for the toys they got last Christmas. Not
33	one! *(Big sigh)* Maybe they didn't like their toys. *(Another*
34	*big sigh)* Maybe they don't like Christmas anymore. Maybe
35	they don't like *me* anymore. Maybe I'll just forget Christmas

1   this year. I feel so sad. And I've been so cross with Mrs.

2   Claus and the elves and brownies. I'm ashamed of myself.

3   I feel so bad! Maybe a nap will help.

4   *(SANTA lies down on the couch and starts snoring. Lights go*

5   *down. Hula music starts — hula DANCERS enter from*

6   *Downstage Left and start to dance. SANTA [part of a dream]*

7   *gets up and dances behind them until almost the end of the dance*

8   *when he goes back to the couch and lies down again.)*

9 MRS. CLAUS: *(From Offstage)* **Santa, dinner is almost ready.**

10   *(Hula music stops — DANCERS go Offstage, lights come back*

11   *up. SANTA wakes up as MRS. CLAUS comes Onstage.)* **Santa,**

12   **dinner is ready.**

13 SANTA: What a great dream! That's what we'll do. We'll

14   forget Christmas this year and go to Hawaii.

15 MRS. CLAUS: *(Shocked)* **Forget Christmas?! Go to Hawaii?!**

16   *(Curtains close.)*

17

18   Scene 2

19

20 *AT RISE:*   The Christmas tree is down and Hawaii posters are up.

21   SANTA is in his red Santa pants, but is wearing a wild Hawaiian

22   shirt, is Centerstage doing exercises to wild music. MRS.

23   CLAUS enters.

24

25 MRS. CLAUS: Santa, what in the world are you doing?

26 SANTA: If we're going to Hawaii, I need to get in shape so I

27   can hula. *(Music down)*

28 MRS. CLAUS: But, Santa —

29 SANTA: Besides, exercise is good for you.

30 MRS. CLAUS: Well, I don't know why you are so set on going

31   to Hawaii — you don't even like warm weather.

32 SANTA: Maybe if I get some of this weight off, I will.

33 MRS. CLAUS: And when you're in the sun you sneeze and

34   break out in a rash.

35 SANTA: That will go away when I learn to surf. *(Does a*

1   *little dance and sings a line of "Surfin' USA.")*
2   **MRS. CLAUS:** Surfing?! Santa, you don't even know how to
3   swim!
4   **SANTA:** I'll learn.
5   **MRS. CLAUS:** But Santa, what about Christmas — the elves,
6   the brownies, the reindeer, the toys — and the children?
7   **SANTA:** We're going to forget all that this year.
8   **MRS. CLAUS:** *(Goes to record player or radio and turns off music.*
9   *Leads SANTA to the couch.)* Santa, you simply must tell me
10   what this is all about. This isn't like you. Please, won't
11   you tell me what is happening?
12   **SANTA:** Yes, I guess I should. I don't think the children of the
13   world liked their toys last year. Maybe they don't like
14   Christmas anymore — maybe they don't even like *me*
15   anymore. Not one single child wrote me a letter to say
16   thank you for the toys last year.
17   **MRS. CLAUS:** But, I'm sure there must be an explanation.
18   **SANTA:** Not one single letter.
19   **MRS. CLAUS:** Usually you get bags full of letters saying
20   thank you. There has to be some reason.
21   **SANTA:** Maybe there is, but I'm not going to stick around to
22   find out what it is — we're going to Hawaii. I've got the
23   suitcases right here. *(Points behind the couch.)* Let's start
24   packing. *(ELVES enter.)*
25   **TWINKLETOES:** Hi, Santa.
26   **HAPPYEYES:** How are you today?
27   **STARBRIGHT:** Are you feeling better?
28   **JINGLE:** What kind of shirt is that, Santa?
29   **SANTA:** It's a Hawaiian shirt.
30   **JANGLE:** But why are you wearing it?
31   **SANTA:** Because Mrs. Claus and I are going to Hawaii.
32   **MERRYTHOUGHT:** But what about Christmas?
33   **SANTA:** We're going to forget Christmas this year.
34   **ELVES:** *(All)* Forget Christmas!
35   *(Doorbell rings. The MAILMAN enters with two big, full bags.*

1   *SANTA and the ELVES are on one side of the stage — MRS.*
2   *CLAUS and the MAILMAN on the other. What follows here is*
3   *a double conversation.)*
4   **MAILMAN:**   **Is this the mail you've been waiting for, Santa?**
5   **SANTA:**· *(To MAILMAN)* **Probably not. It's probably just a**
6   **bunch of children getting a head start on asking for stuff**
7   **for next year.** *(Turns to ELVES)* **Come here you elves.**
8   **MAILMAN:**   *(To MRS. CLAUS)* **What's he wearing that shirt for?**
9   **MRS. CLAUS:**   **He says he's going to forget Christmas and go**
10   **to Hawaii.**
11   **SANTA:**   **Now, I want you, Twinkletoes, to send the brownies**
12   **home.**
13   **MRS. CLAUS:**   *(Starts going through the mail.)* **Santa, this is a**
14   **thank you letter.**
15   **SANTA:**   *(Not listening to MRS. CLAUS)* **And, Jingle, you get all**
16   **the supplies put away.**
17   **MRS. SANTA:**   **And here's another thank you — and another!**
18   **SANTA:**   *(Still not listening)* **And Starbright, you take the**
19   **reindeer to a boarding stable until you can sell them.**
20   **MAILMAN:**   **Santa, these are all old letters. I just found them**
21   **when the snow started melting.**
22   **SANTA:**   *(Still to STARBRIGHT)* **You ought to be able to get a**
23   **good price for flying reindeer.** *(Finally hearing the*
24   *MAILMAN, SANTA turns to the MAILMAN and MRS.*
25   *CLAUS.)* **What's that you say?**
26   **MAILMAN:**   **These are all thank you letters from the children**
27   **— from last year.**
28   **SANTA:**   **What do you mean? How could that be?**
29   **MAILMAN:**   **Well, do you remember the fire we had at the post**
30   **office in January? Some of the firemen must have thrown**
31   **these sacks out behind the building when they were**
32   **fighting the fire. And they must have been covered with**
33   **snow when we had that big blizzard a couple of days**
34   **after the fire. Anyway, now that the snow is melting we**
35   **found them — and I brought them right out here to you.**

1   MRS. CLAUS: And they are all letters from children saying
2   how much they liked their toys — they all say thank you.
3   SANTA: You mean I was wrong? The children really did like
4   their gifts? They really do still like Christmas? They
5   really do still like me?
6   MRS. CLAUS and ELVES: Oh yes, Santa!
7   SANTA: I almost made a big mistake! *(To the MAILMAN)* **Thank**
8   you for making the special trip out here to bring these
9   bags — you've made me so happy. *(To ELVES)* **Forget**
10   what I said! Let's get to work!
11   ELVES: *Yea!* *(ELVES go out the door. SANTA and MAILMAN*
12   *start to follow.)*
13   MAILMAN: Hey, I'll take those tickets to Hawaii off your
14   hands for you, Santa. *(All leave except for MRS. CLAUS.)*
15   MRS. CLAUS: Well, I guess that shows how important it is to
16   remember to say thank you. *(Curtains close, but MRS.*
17   *CLAUS is now in front of curtains and sings:)*
18
19   **PLEASE REMEMBER TO SAY THANK YOU**
20
21   Please remember to say thank you
22   Each time a gift is given to you.
23   Please remember to say thank you
24   For ev'ry kindness, too.
25   It isn't very hard to do.
26   You open your mouth and say, "Thank you."
27   Please remember to say thank you.
28   It makes others happy when you do.
29
30   **Scene 3**
31
32   *AT RISE:*   Room is back to normal — Christmas tree, Christmas
33   background music, wrapped gifts, picture of Santa, etc. SANTA,
34   MRS. CLAUS, and all the ELVES except TWINKLETOES are
35   Onstage, finishing wrapping.

1   MRS. CLAUS: Is the sleigh packed?

2   SANTA: Almost.

3   HAPPYEYES: We really had to hurry to get everything
4   finished.

5   SANTA: But we made it.

6   STARBRIGHT: The brownies worked so hard. They were so
7   much happier when we put the Christmas tree back up
8   and turned the music back on.

9   SANTA: They also worked harder when I remembered to tell
10   them thank you for working so hard.

11   TWINKLETOES: *(Enters carrying TODDLER.)* Mrs. Claus, see
12   the new Christmas doll I've made. She's really lifelike.

13   HAPPYEYES: Some child is really going to love Santa.

14   MRS. CLAUS: Everyone loves Santa. *(There's a knock at the*
15   *door.)* Now who can that be? *(Goes to door. MAILMAN enters*
16   *in knee shorts, thongs, Hawaiian shirt, sunglasses, straw hat,*
17   *etc.)*

18   MAILMAN: Oh, hi, Santa, I see you're about ready to leave. I
19   just stopped in to say thanks for the tickets to Hawaii.
20   *(Does a little hula movement.)* We had a wonderful time!

21   SANTA: I'm glad you did. We got all the toys done and the
22   sleigh is packed. *(To ELVES)* And now let's get ready. It's
23   almost time to go. *(All sing:)*

24

25   SANTA'S COMING

26

27   Santa's coming, Santa's coming, Have a Happy Holiday.
28   Santa's coming, Santa's coming, Have a Merry Christmas
29   Day.
30   He will visit girls and boys,
31   Fill their stockings full of toys, for
32   Santa's coming, Santa's coming, Happy, Happy Christmas
33   Day.

34

35   SANTA: *(Spoken)* But please make sure your attitude is

1	always one of gratitude, for
2	
3	*(Singing again)*
4	Santa's coming, don't you know.
5	Santa's coming, Ho Ho Ho.
6	Santa's coming, he will say,
7	"Have a Merry Christmas Day. Have a Merry Christmas
8	Day."
9	*(Curtain closes.)*
10	
11	
12	
13	
14	
15	
16	
17	
18	
19	
20	
21	
22	
23	
24	
25	
26	
27	
28	
29	
30	
31	
32	
33	
34	
35	

What's Wrong with Santa?

What's wrong with San- ta? He's so sad, when San- ta's sad it makes me feel bad. What's wrong with San- ta? He's so blue, it makes me want to cry! Boo Hoo! San- ta is al- ways full of Christ- mas cheer; What has hap- p'n'd to him this year?

Let's get to work and find what's wrong; We have-n't much time we

can't take ver- y long. We want to hear San- ta say, "Ho, Ho." It's

near- ly Christ- mas Eve you know.

Please Remember to Say Thank You

© 1987 Anne Nunley

Please re-mem- ber to say "Thank you!" Each time a gift is gi- ven to

Santa's Coming

© 1986 Anne Nunley

San- ta's com- ing, San- ta's com- ing, have a hap- py hol- i- day!

San- ta's com- ing, San- ta's com- ing Have a Mer- ry Christ- mas Day!

He will vis- it girls and boys Fill their stock- ings full of toys, for

San- ta's com- ing, San- ta's com- ing, Hap- py, Hap- py Christ- mas Day! But

MIDDLE GRADES

An Animal's Christmas
by JANET MEILI

CAST

Non-Speaking Parts
MARY
JOSEPH
TWO INNKEEPERS
SHEPHERDS
THREE WISE MEN
ANGELS

Speaking Parts
DONKEY
ADA, the street dog
(beagle)
BRUTUS, the inn dog
(bull dog)
FORTA, the shepherd's dog
(collie)
TWO SHEEP
THREE CAMELS

PRODUCTION NOTES

One of the problems of a Christmas presentation is to have something for all the children to do and yet not have a production of such intricacy that it becomes a burden on the directing adults. Since the humans in this playlet have nonspeaking parts, there is considerable room for expansion without difficulties. You may add innkeepers' wives, camel attendants, shepherds and angels, as well as choirs.

The only carol which is an integral part of the plot is the angel choir in Scene Two. If you do not wish to use "It Came upon the Midnight Clear," you may use any carol with a "Peace on Earth" message. In Scene Four, a choir singing "What Child Is This?" before the naming of the child will prove a helpful transition. Other carols may be used as desired before and/or after each scene.

The questions about the child's name are taken from the Heidelberg Catechism.

The simplest staging is to drape the animals in rather shapeless garments and have them appear on stage on hands and knees while the humans remain standing. If this staging is not practical from the point of view of being seen and heard, they should remain upright.

For elaborate production, papier-mâché heads may be made for the animals. Make them as lightweight as possible and be sure to leave much open room around the nose and mouth so the speakers' words will not be muffled.

COSTUME SUGGESTIONS

Materials: Fabric (sheets will do); commercial ice cream cartons; quart-sized milk cartons; pint-sized milk cartons; chicken wire; wallpaper (wheat) paste; staples; paint; old newspapers.

Basic head and costume: Cut open area for mouth in commercial ice cream carton (bottom-side-up). Form chicken wire in round shape around carton and staple to carton. Form chicken wire in shapes around open-ended milk cartons for nose, mouth and ear pieces, and attach to head structure. Open-ended milk carton may act as megaphone for actor.

Cut newspapers into strips, soak in paste, and apply layer upon layer over chicken wire structure until a workable shape is built up. Then dry, mold for features, and paint. Lumps of pulp or cotton may be added while still moist and molded into features.

When dry, sand the heads down and paint as before.

Sheets may be dyed to match heads, pleated and stapled onto bottom rim of the head.

1   **SETTING:** Various scenes in or near Bethlehem: road, inn,
2   hillside, more distant road.
3   **NOTE:** Carols may be inserted where desired.
4
5   **SCENE ONE**
6
7   **AT RISE:** MARY and JOSEPH are walking beside DONKEY on
8   the road into Bethlehem.)
9
10   **DONKEY:** **What a beautiful night! The stars are so bright!**
11   **There's a big one over there that seems to be following**
12   **us.** *(Enter ADA, the street dog.)*
13   **ADA:** **Hello, Donkey. Welcome to Bethlehem. I'm Ada, the**
14   **street dog. Have you had a long journey?**
15   **DONKEY:** **We've come from Nazareth.**
16   **ADA:** **That's quite a trip. But you seem to have an easy job. Do**
17   **you always make your people walk?**
18   **DONKEY:** **No. Mary said she was tired of sitting and wanted**
19   **some exercise.** *(They stop. JOSEPH knocks at the door of an*
20   *inn. INNKEEPER ONE shakes his head "no" in pantomime*
21   *during ensuing speeches.)*
22   **ADA:** **It's late. I'm surprised your people didn't stop**
23   **someplace out of town.**
24   **DONKEY:** **We've been looking for a place but all the outlying**
25   **villages and huts have as many guests as they can handle.**
26   **Joseph thought there'd probably be fewer people in town**
27   **where rooms cost so much more.**
28   **ADA:** **I tell you, with this tax business, you'd never believe**
29   **the number of people who've come home to Bethlehem.**
30   **Rooms are really scarce.**
31   **DONKEY:** **We'll find a place. Mary is going to have a baby and**
32   **people are always kind to babies and their mothers.**
33   *(INNKEEPER closes door.)*
34   **ADA:** **She's going to have a baby? You're right. That will make**
35   **a difference. Let me think. There's one place we can try.**

1		It's the inn my brother-in-law lives at. He's a mean brute,
2		but the innkeeper is a nice man.
3	DONKEY:	Lead the way. This isn't just a plain baby we're
4		talking about, you know. This is the Prince of Peace.
5	ADA:	Royalty? Here in Bethlehem? Are you sure you've got
6		that straight?
7	DONKEY:	Not earthly royalty — heavenly royalty. An angel
8		told Mary so. This baby is the Son of God. The Savior
9		we've been waiting for.
10	ADA:	The Savior? The Messiah of the Jewish people? Why,
11		Bethlehem will be famous! Here's my brother-in-law's
12		inn. *(JOSEPH knocks. Door is opened by INNKEEPER TWO*
13		*and BRUTUS, his dog.)*
14	BRUTUS:	Ada, what are you doing here? I told you last time
15		we had no room and we've still got no room.
16	ADA:	You *have* to find room for these people.
17	BRUTUS:	Why are they any different from all the others
18		looking for a place to stay?
19	ADA:	Because Mary's going to have a baby. And it's not just
20		an ordinary baby. It's the Messiah! The Savior we've all
21		been waiting for.
22	BRUTUS:	*(Sarcastically)* Sure. A little baby is going to free
23		Palestine from the Romans. Real likely!
24	ADA:	But the man who does free us has to be a baby before
25		he grows up.
26	BRUTUS:	But he'll be the son of some important family in
27		Jerusalem, not the child of a couple of nobodies.
28	ADA:	He's going to be this baby.
29	BRUTUS:	Who told you all that foolishness?
30	ADA:	The donkey that brought them here.
31	BRUTUS:	Some dogs believe anything they hear. How would
32		the donkey know?
33	ADA:	An angel told his people so.
34	BRUTUS:	Oh, sure. Angels always talk to people.
35	ADA:	Brutus, please don't turn them away. Please!

1   BRUTUS: But there are no empty rooms.

2   ADA: Donkey, this is Brutus and he's going to find some place

3   for your people, aren't you, Brutus?

4   BRUTUS: I suppose so. They can stay in the stable.

5   ADA: The stable? You're just trying to be insulting.

6   BRUTUS: Where else would you put them? At least they'll

7   have a roof over their heads and it's warm.

8   DONKEY: And there won't be a lot of people around to disturb

9   the baby. Thank you. You're very kind.

10   ADA: I suppose it's better than nothing. I'll help you get them

11   settled and then I must go and tell the wonderful news

12   to my friend, Forta, the shepherd's dog. The Savior is

13   coming!

14

15   SCENE TWO

16

17   *AT RISE:*   FORTA, the shepherd's dog, and two SHEEP are Center

18   Stage. Shepherds and more sheep, if desired, are in the distance.

19   Enter BRUTUS.

20

21   BRUTUS: Brr, but it's cold up here.

22   FORTA: It may seem cold to an inn dog used to lying in front

23   of a fire. We think it's a pleasant evening.

24   SHEEP ONE: A pleasant evening.

25   SHEEP TWO: A very pleasant evening.

26   FORTA: And what brings the inn dog so far from his fire?

27   BRUTUS: I came to warn you about Ada.

28   FORTA: Warn us? Ada is our friend.

29   SHEEP ONE: Our good friend.

30   SHEEP TWO: Our very good friend.

31   BRUTUS: Ada heard a lot of foolishness from a traveling

32   donkey and now she's going around telling everyone

33   what she calls the good news.

34   FORTA: We'll be happy to hear Ada's news.

35   SHEEP ONE: Her good news.

1 SHEEP TWO: Her very good news.
2 BRUTUS: Wait until you hear it. You'll be glad to help me
3   keep her quiet. *(Enter ADA.)*
4 ADA: Oh, Forta. I've got such good news. Wait until you hear.
5   Hello, Sheep One, Sheep Two. Brutus, what are you doing
6   here?
7 BRUTUS: Just out for a walk.
8 ADA: You didn't spoil my surprise, did you?
9 BRUTUS: Who, me? I didn't say a word.
10 ADA: Oh, good. I did so want to be the one to spread the news.
11   Now listen, dear friends. A baby has been born down
12   there in Bethlehem. And do you know who he is? He's
13   the Savior we've all been waiting for. The Son of God.
14   The Messiah.
15 FORTA: Savior?
16 SHEEP ONE: Son of God?
17 SHEEP TWO: Messiah? *(BRUTUS' lines are ignored by the others*
18   *for the rest of the scene.)*
19 BRUTUS: Don't listen to her.
20 ADA: Oh, yes. It's the greatest day for the world since it was
21   created.
22 BRUTUS: Ignore her.
23 ADA: Now, you must tell your shepherds to go down to the
24   stable at the inn to worship our heavenly king.
25 BRUTUS: Don't pay any attention to her.
26 FORTA: You want us to tell the shepherds —
27 SHEEP ONE: Tell the shepherds.
28 SHEEP TWO: Tell the shepherds.
29 ADA: Oh, yes, everyone must be told and you can tell the
30   shepherds while I go find someone else to tell.
31 FORTA: Ada, with all these strangers coming to Bethlehem,
32   you've been working very hard lately.
33 BRUTUS: That's right, Forta. She's near a breakdown.
34 ADA: Oh, I don't mind carrying such glorious news.
35 FORTA: That's not what I meant. Your story is a little strange

1   and I wondered where you heard it.
2   BRUTUS: Why don't you come right out and say she's crazy?
3   ADA: Oh, the donkey told me and he heard it from the angels.
4   FORTA: Angels?
5   SHEEP ONE: Angels?
6   SHEEP TWO: Angels?
7   BRUTUS: I think she should stay with you guys tonight so
8   she doesn't get into any more trouble.
9   ADA: The angels told Mary, the baby's mother. Now please go
10   tell the shepherds. They'll be so happy to hear that the
11   Savior has come.
12   FORTA: Well, if he's here, I imagine he'll be around for a
13   while and there's no hurry. Have you had supper?
14   ADA: Forta, I don't think you believe me!
15   BRUTUS: Of course she doesn't. No one with any sense
16   would.
17   ADA: You're my best friend. I wanted you to be the first to
18   know. And you don't believe me.
19   FORTA: It's nice that you believe. It doesn't matter about
20   the rest of us.
21   ADA: It does matter. How can I convince you? *(ANGELS*
22   *appear before the SHEPHERDS who kneel while they sing, "It*
23   *Came upon the Midnight Clear.")*
24   FORTA: Ada, did you hear that? Peace on earth. The Prince
25   of Peace has come.
26   SHEEP ONE: Peace on earth.
27   SHEEP TWO: The Prince of Peace has come.
28   FORTA: I must tell the shepherds to go and worhship him.
29   They can leave. I'll guard the sheep.
30   BRUTUS: No, no, don't believe her. Don't listen. It's all a lot
31   of foolishness.
32
33
34
35

1

SCENE THREE
2
3   *AT RISE:* Three WISE MEN and THREE CAMELS on a road
4   outside Bethlehem.
5
6   CAMEL ONE: Where are we?
7   CAMEL TWO: Nobody knows.
8   CAMEL THREE: For wise men, they do some foolish things.
9   CAMEL ONE: Do you really think that star is moving?
10   CAMEL TWO: It doesn't matter what we think.
11   CAMEL THREE: If they say it's moving, it's moving.
12   CAMEL ONE: I'd certainly like to know how much longer
13   we're going to be walking. My feet are killing me.
14   CAMEL TWO: Until we get to where the star is leading us.
15   CAMEL THREE: Which is not Jerusalem. At least we've
16   learned that much. *(Enter ADA.)*
17   ADA: Welcome to Judea, strangers.
18   CAMEL ONE: Thank you.
19   CAMEL TWO: Do you know where we are?
20   CAMEL THREE: Do you know where that star is going?
21   ADA: You're outside the village of Bethlehem. I don't know
22   anything about the star. It's a big one, isn't it? Do stars
23   go places?
24   CAMEL ONE: Our wise men say the star is leading us.
25   CAMEL TWO: We have to follow it until it stops.
26   CAMEL THREE: It signifies a wonderful event, the birth of
27   the King of the Jews.
28   ADA: Is that so? I wonder how Herod managed to get a star
29   in the sky. Those mighty rulers can do anyting! I'm afraid
30   you've wandered off the route to Jerusalem.
31   CAMEL ONE: We've been to Jerusalem.
32   CAMEL TWO: It's not that kind of king.
33   CAMEL THREE: Herod's wise men said he'd be born in
34   Bethlehem of Judea.
35   ADA: Oh, you must mean *my* baby.

1   CAMELS: *Your* baby?
2   ADA: Yes. Well, not mine, of course. I just feel a little responsible
3   for him. Tonight, Donkey brought Mary and Joseph to
4   town. I found them a place at the inn and Mary had a
5   baby and the baby is our Savior, the Son of God. The
6   angels told Mary he would be.
7   CAMEL ONE: That must be the one.
8   CAMEL TWO: Odd that they'd travel by donkey. You'd think
9   they'd come in a camel train.
10 CAMEL THREE: Odd that Bethlehem would have an inn
11   large enough for their entire household.
12 ADA: They're very poor. Joseph is just starting business as a
13   carpenter. And there are just the two of them, no servants
14   or anything.
15 CAMEL ONE: Something's wrong.
16 CAMEL TWO: They don't sound like very special people.
17 CAMEL THREE: Maybe it's just the baby that's special.
18 ADA: Oh, he is. He's the sweetest thing!
19 CAMEL ONE: Is he dressed in silk and gold?
20 ADA: No, just wrapped in swaddling clothes.
21 CAMEL TWO: Does he prophesy?
22 ADA: He can't talk. He was just born tonight!
23 CAMEL THREE: Can he do miracles?
24 ADA: I don't think so. When I saw him, he was just sleeping.
25 CAMEL ONE: Something's wrong.
26 ADA: When you look at him, you have a feeling that everything's
27   going to be right.
28 CAMEL TWO: What did you call him? Your Savior? The Son
29   of God?
30 ADA: Yes. And that would explain the star, of course, Herod
31   might not be able to place a new star in the sky, but the
32   Creator can. *(Enter BRUTUS.)*
33 BRUTUS: I suppose Ada told you to pitch camp out here.
34   There's no room in town.
35 ADA: Brutus, what are you doing here?

1 BRUTUS: I came to get you. Good-bye fellas, hope you had a
2   nice journey.
3 ADA: Wait, Brutus, they're coming with us to see the baby.
4 BRUTUS: Look, fellas, don't pay attention to her. She's been
5   having hallucinations.
6 CAMEL THREE: You mean there is no baby?
7 BRUTUS: Sure, there's a baby. A plain, everyday baby. So
8   what?
9 CAMEL ONE: Would you say the place where the baby is is
10   right under that star?
11 BRUTUS: That star? Yeah, it looks like it's right over our
12   stable.
13 CAMEL TWO: Stable?
14 ADA: That's where they are. There was no room in the inn.
15 CAMEL THREE: I guess we've located the king. Let's go.
16
17   SCENE FOUR
18
19 *AT RISE:* Manger scene. MARY, JOSEPH, INNKEEPERS,
20   DONKEY and all ANGELS available. Enter SHEPHERDS,
21   FORTA and SHEEP ONE and TWO. SHEPHERDS go to crib.
22   DOG and SHEEP remain far right. Enter ADA and BRUTUS.
23   ADA crosses to FORTA. BRUTUS turns his back to manger.
24
25 ADA: Oh, Forta, you came, too. I'm so glad.
26 FORTA: Sheep and I were curious.
27 SHEEP ONE: Curious.
28 SHEEP TWO: Very curious.
29 ADA: Isn't he the sweetest baby?
30 FORTA: He's so calm and peaceful.
31 SHEEP ONE: Calm.
32 SHEEP TWO: Peaceful. *(Enter CAMELS and WISE MEN.*
33   *CAMELS remain far left. WISE MEN offer gifts.)*
34 CAMEL ONE: For this we traveled hundreds of miles?
35 CAMEL TWO: You could see a baby born to a poor couple

1   anywhere in our country.
2   CAMEL THREE: With a giant star over the stable and Magi
3   offering precious gifts?
4   CAMEL TWO: No, not exactly.
5   *NOTE:*   Carol "What Child Is This?" may be sung.
6   ADA: What's the baby's name?
7   DONKEY: Jesus Christ.
8   ADA: Why is he called Jesus?
9   DONKEY: It means Savior. He is the one who will save us
10   from our sins, and salvation is neither to be sought or
11   found in any other.
12   ADA: Why is he called Christ?
13   DONKEY: It means anointed. He has been anointed to be our
14   Chief Prophet and Teacher, our Only High Priest and
15   Our Eternal King. *(Just before lights dim or curtains are closed,*
16   *BRUTUS turns around and faces the manger.)*
17
18
19
20
21
22
23
24
25
26
27
28
29
30
31
32
33
34
35

Was It a Star?

by JOANNA EVANS

CAST

POLARIS
The King

MIZAR and ALCOR
Pages

BETELGEUSE and RIGEL
Ministers

GEMINII and GEMINEE
Twin Star

MARCO
A Star

FLASHER, FUZZY and DIMMER
Imperfect Stars

SIX PERFECT STARS

1	**SCENE ONE**
2	
3	*SETTING:* Throne room of POLARIS.
4	*AT RISE:* POLARIS is walking frantically from Stage Left to Right.
5	He looks at the audience with hand shadowing his eyes as if to
6	see far off in the distance. Then he shakes his head negatively
7	and begins pacing again, muttering to himself. He goes to the
8	calendar and starts counting the days with his finger in a great
9	gesture, turning to the twelfth month.
10	
11	**POLARIS:** *(Shouting)* **Time! Time!** *(Picks up the bell from the*
12	*table and rings it frantically while shouting.)* **Mizar,**
13	**Alcor . . . Mizar, Alcor!** *(Enter MIZAR and ALCOR, one from*
14	*each side of the stage. They rush in with head bowed and meet*
15	*at Center Stage, not seeing each other and bump heads. They*
16	*beg each other's pardon and then bow low before the throne not*
17	*noticing that POLARIS is not sitting there.)*
18	**MIZAR and ALCOR:** *(In unison)* **We are here, your greatness!**
19	**POLARIS:** *(Still standing by calendar)* **I'm over here!** *(MIZAR*
20	*and ALCOR see their mistake and immediately rush to*
21	*POLARIS, again falling over each other's feet. They bow.)*
22	**MIZAR:** **You yelled, er, I mean, you called, your greatness?**
23	**POLARIS:** *(Irritated)* **Where are my ministers? Did you call**
24	**them as I instructed?**
25	**ALCOR:** **Oh, yes sir, we called them. They should be here soon.**
26	**POLARIS:** **Go and see where they are — immediately!** *(MIZAR*
27	*and ALCOR quickly move back in fear and bow low. They become*
28	*confused as to which way to go, bump into each other, and fall*
29	*on the floor. POLARIS in disgust:)* **Of all the binary stars in**
30	**the universe to serve me, why did I choose the two of**
31	**you? Now** *you* *(Pointing to MIZAR)* **go in that direction,**
32	*(Points to Stage Right* **and** *you* *(Pointing to ALCOR)* **go in that**
33	**direction.** *(Pointing to Stage Left. MIZAR and ALCOR get set*
34	*and start bowing as they move in the direction they are told.)*
35	**And stop the bowing . . . *Just go!*** *(MIZAR and ALCOR run*

1	*in the direction they are told while POLARIS returns to his*
2	*throne, sighing. MIZAR goes out of the scene but ALCOR merely*
3	*puts his head behind the curtain while the rest of his body is*
4	*still visible to audience. After a second, he begins to jump up*
5	*and down and wiggle, his head still behind the curtain.*
6	*POLARIS sees him.)* **What are you doing? You look like a**
7	**spider with his head caught in its own web!**
8	**ALCOR:** *(Running toward POLARIS)* **The ministers are**
9	**coming!** *(Runs toward audience and shouts.)* **The ministers**
10	**are coming!** *(He stops suddenly, looks at the audience hesitantly,*
11	*and rushes back to POLARIS.)* **Commoners are here today,**
12	**your greatness. Did you wish to see them?**
13	**POLARIS:** **I have no time for anyone today except my ministers.**
14	**Where are they?**
15	**ALCOR:** *(To audience)* **Go home! Polaris does not have time**
16	**for you today. Go! Shoo! Go!** *(Waves his hand. Enter MIZAR*
17	*and two ministers, BETELGEUSE and RIGEL.)*
18	**MIZAR:** *(Rushing in breathless)* **I found them! I found them!**
19	*(Turning to ALCOR)* **I** *(Emphasizing himself)* **found them.**
20	**POLARIS:** *(Irritated)* **Sit down you two and** *shush!* *(To the*
21	*MINISTERS)* **Rigel, Betelgeuse, come here quickly.**
22	**BETELGEUSE:** *(Bows)* **Betelgeuse at your service, your grace.**
23	**RIGEL:** *(Bows)* **Yours to command.**
24	**POLARIS:** **A great happening is about to happen . . . er, I**
25	**mean a great happiness is about to happen . . . well, not**
26	**quite . . . I mean a great tragedy** *might* **happen before the**
27	**great happening. Do I make myself clear?** *(RIGEL and*
28	*BETELGEUSE look puzzled.)* **Let's start again. The birth of**
29	**a great prophet is to take place very soon and a star is**
30	**to guide the people of planet earth to the birthplace. It**
31	**is my task to choose the most brilliant star to be found.**
32	**But we must hurry because the time is almost here.**
33	*(Turning to MIZAR and ALCOR)* **Somebody forgot to remind**
34	**me.** *(MIZAR and ALCOR bury their heads in their hands and*
35	*tremble.)*

1   BETELGEUSE: Begging your pardon, sir, but perhaps you
2   are mistaken about the time.
3   POLARIS: There is the Book of Forecast on the desk *(Pointing*
4   *to it)* **and there is the day of time.** *(Pointing to the calendar)*
5   **See for yourself!**
6   BETELGEUSE: *(Goes to table, runs finger across a few lines,*
7   *looks at the calendar, then turns to RIGEL and speaks*
8   *alarmingly.)* **Polaris is right! There is little time left!**
9   POLARIS: We *must* choose a star, a beautifully brilliant star
10   and one who knows navigation well.
11   RIGEL: Your grace, may I suggest that you have both
12   qualities in abundance. Perhaps you should have this
13   great honor. *(MIZAR and ALCOR jump and clap their hands*
14   *in agreement.)*
15   POLARIS: *(Pretending embarrassment)* **That's very generous of**
16   **you. It is true that I am brilliant and well traveled.**
17   MIZAR: *(To audience)* **And humble, too.**
18   POLARIS: Ahem, yes humble, too. But I feel every star should
19   have the opportunity for this momentous occasion.
20   Therefore, I am sending you, my ministers, on a search.
21   Pass through every galaxy and every cluster. Tell them
22   the kind of star we need and urge them to come to my
23   kingdom. Then I will choose. If we are too late, I will be
24   shamed for all eternity. *(POLARIS hangs his head in shame*
25   *while MIZAR and ALCOR rush to his side to console him.)*
26   RIGAL: We will bring only the best stars, and soon, your
27   highness. *(The MINISTERS bow low and leave in a dramatic*
28   *flair of urgency. MIZAR and ALCOR wave good-bye but continue*
29   *to console POLARIS.)*
30
31   **SCENE TWO**
32
33   *SETTING:*   In front of curtain. Enter Stage Left a group of imperfect
34   stars including FLASHER, FUZZY and DIMMER led by
35   GEMINII and GEMINEE, the twin star. Other stars may be

added to form a bigger group. Each star has some problem with its form such as one point larger or smaller than should be; or, a three-point star; or, one half of the star very bright while the other half is very dull, etc. GEMINII and GEMINEE are one star.

(The group, in front of curtain, stops when nearly to Center Stage, some bumping into each other and looking around in bewilderment.)

GEMINEE: *(To GEMINII, in a voice ready to cry)* **See, I told you, we're lost.** *(His tone becomes angry.)* **You and your big ideas!** *(Tone changes to crying again.)* **How will we ever get back home?**

GEMINII: *(Sternly to GEMINEE)* **We're not going home! At least not until we have been to Polaris' court.**

GEMINEE: *(Depressed)* **It will never work, never work.**

DIMMER: **I hate to say this, Geminii, but I'm beginning to agree with Geminee. I don't think this is going to work either.**

GEMINII: *(Becoming irritated)* **Only if you think it isn't. Think positive!**

FLASHER: *(Blinking a flashlight on and off repeatedly)* **I'm thinking, Geminii,** *(Pause)* **and I think we're positively lost.**

FUZZY: *(In slow manner of speech)* **Do you think other stars are floating around like us looking for the castle? Maybe one of them will take us along.**

FLASHER: **Good, clear thought, Fuzzy.** *(Flashes light on and off again.)*

GEMINEE: *(Depressed)* **And how long will that be? The contest could be over by that time.**

DIMMER: **Flasher, why don't you keep flashing as hard as you can and maybe we'll attract somebody.**

GEMINII: **Now that's a good idea. In the meantime, we'll keep moving toward the galaxy over there.** *(Points to far right of audience.)* **It's so bright, it must be Polaris' castle.** *(The*

1	*group starts moving toward Stage Left. A voice is heard from*
2	*the direction behind curtain, Stage Left.)*
3	MARCO: *(Behind curtain)* **Hey, you over there! Can you turn**
4	**your light down a little? You're hurting my eyes.** *(Enter*
5	*MARCO wearing large sunglasses. He stops and shades his eyes*
6	*until FLASHER stops his light from blinking.)* **Oh, thanks.**
7	**My eyes are so sensitive to light. Thanks, a lot.** *(As he looks*
8	*up he is amazed to see the group.)* **Oh, there's more than one;**
9	**no wonder you were so bright.**
10	GEMINII: *(To others, excitedly)* **See, I told you. Together we're**
11	**brighter than only *one* star. Polaris will see that too and**
12	**we'll get the job!**
13	MARCO: **Polaris? Are you going to his castle?**
14	GEMINEE: **We *were* going — but who knows where we're**
15	**going now.**
16	MARCO: **I don't understand.**
17	ALL STARS: *(Except GEMINII)* **We're lost!**
18	MARCO: **No, you're not. The castle is around the bend of that**
19	**galaxy over there.** *(Points directly to audience, center aisle.)*
20	**You only have a little way to go.**
21	GEMINEE: *(In self-righteous tone)* **My illustrious brother, our**
22	**leader, was taking us to that galaxy.** *(Points far right.)*
23	GEMINII: **All right, all right. I was trying to do my best.**
24	FUZZY: **Yes, he was. Er, I think he was. Oh, yes, he was.**
25	MARCO: **Maybe I can help. My name is Marco and I love to**
26	**travel around finding new planets, asteroids, galaxies**
27	**and new friends. I hope you will be my new friends.**
28	GEMINII: **We'd like that Marco, but we have to get to the**
29	**castle as soon as possible.**
30	MARCO: **I assume all of you are going together.**
31	FUZZY: **Yes, we are. Er, I think we are. Oh, yes, we are.**
32	GEMINEE: **Aren't you, Marco? Aren't you entering the contest?**
33	MARCO: **Oh, no, my eyes are too sensitive to brightness.**
34	**That's why I wear these dark glasses most of the time. I**
35	**don't like brightness.**

1   GEMINII: *(Saddened)* **That's too bad. I thought you might**
2   **like to join us.**
3   MARCO: *(Slightly embarrassed)* **I don't mean to sound cruel,**
4   **but I heard Polaris is looking for a very beautiful, very**
5   **bright star. Er, um ... none of you really fit that**
6   **description,** *(Adds hurriedly)* **but I don't either. That's why**
7   **I'm not going.**
8   GEMINEE: **My brother had this less than brilliant idea that**
9   **if we all went together we could be brighter than one star.**
10   GEMINII: **Also, suppose the chosen star was to have a failure**
11   **of some kind — burn right out in the middle of the**
12   **journey — what would happen then? All of earth's history**
13   **might be changed. But with us, there's always back-up**
14   **power from the rest if one konks out.**
15   MARCO: **I must say, Geminii, I am impressed with that logic.**
16   **You might be able to convince Polaris on that idea. I**
17   **think it's worth a try.** *(All in group yell "Yeah" in approval*
18   *including GEMINEE . . . but he stops suddenly.)*
19   GEMINEE: **Hold everything! Hold everything! I've heard the**
20   **star is supposed to find some tiny little town on earth**
21   **called Bethlehem. If we can't find Polaris' castle, how are**
22   **we going to find that place?** *(All in group moan and nod in*
23   *agreement.)*
24   MARCO: **Umm, that is something to consider.** *(Pauses)* **Maybe**
25   **I can draw a map for you but I would need time to study**
26   **the earth. I don't know that planet too well.**
27   DIMMER: **Can you read maps?**
28   MARCO: **Oh, yes, quiet well. I recently graduated from**
29   **Stellar University. Here's my diploma.** *(Shows group.)*
30   FLASHER: *(Reading from diploma)* **It says here: To Marco, a**
31   **degree, capital S and capital N, Magna Cum Brighter.**
32   **What does that mean?**
33   MARCO: *(Shyly)* **That I was pretty good at my studies in**
34   **stellar navigation.**
35   GEMINII: **Pretty good! He was terrific! OK, that settles it.**

1   You lead us and we'll do the rest.
2   MARCO: Oh, I don't know about that. I haven't had that much
3   practice and besides too much light hurts my eyes,
4   remember? *(Group pleads with MARCO to join them.*
5   *Hesitantly:)* Well, OK, I guess it's worth the experience of
6   just going to the castle. And I do like all of you so much.
7   So, why not? Let's go! *(All cheer happily and move out into*
8   *audience, up center aisle to back of auditorium.)*
9
10   SCENE THREE
11
12   *SETTING:*   Same as Scene One.
13   *AT RISE:*   POLARIS is sitting in his chair with MIZAR and ALCOR
14   at his feet. All look sad. There is a great deal of noise from
15   behind the curtain, Stage Right.
16
17   POLARIS: *(To MIZAR and ALCOR, irritated)* See what's going
18   on out there — and tell them to be quiet!
19   MIZAR: *(Looking behind the curtain and then turns to POLARIS)*
20   They're here! Oh, boy! *(Then remembering his dignity, bows*
21   *low and says very dramatically.)* The stars have arrived, your
22   majesty.
23   POLARIS: Good! Bring them in. *(Enter RIGEL, BETELGEUSE*
24   *and six beautiful STARS. RIGEL motions STARS to stand in*
25   *front of POLARIS and all bow. RIGEL and BETELGEUSE*
26   *stand at each end of the row and proudly display their find.)*
27   BETELGEUSE: The finest stars, your grace.
28   POLARIS: Indeed they are. *(Very pleased)* Beautiful, every
29   one. This is going to be a difficult decision, to be sure.
30   Move to the sides so I may view you separately. *(STARS*
31   *separate to two sides making an aisle from throne toward Stage*
32   *Front. One STAR at a time steps in front of throne, bows to*
33   *POLARIS, walks to Center Front, returns down aisle and back*
34   *to original place. Other STARS follow same pattern. Soft*
35   *background music may be played during this display. When it is*

                          – 70 –

1 *over, POLARIS stands.)* **How will I choose just one star?**
2 **Each of you is truly magnificent. Perhaps I should test**
3 **your powers of navigation.** **It will be a most important . . .**
4 *(Pauses, hears commotion from rear of auditorium. POLARIS*
5 *looks to audience and shouts loudly.)* **What's that commotion?**
6 *(All on stage turn to look at back of auditorium. IMPERFECT*
7 *STARS, headed by MARCO, walk toward stage down center*
8 *aisle. As they near the stage, RIGEL speaks.)*
9 **RIGEL:** *(Angrily)* **Stop where you are!** *(The group stops shortly,*
10 *bumping into each other. RIGEL in angry tones.)* **What is the**
11 **meaning of this interruption? Do you know where you**
12 **are?**
13 **GEMINEE:** **Oh, sure! This is the kingdom of Polaris.** *(Pauses,*
14 *then continues in an unsure tone.)* **Isn't it?**
15 **RIGEL:** **It is indeed! All of you are trespassing. Leave at once!**
16 **FUZZY:** **Oh, we can't do that . . . er, can we? No, we can't do**
17 **that.**
18 **BETELGEUSE:** *(Also angry and yells even louder)* **Leave!** *(The*
19 *IMPERFECT STARS begin shaking in fear and start to walk*
20 *backward slowly. There is slight whimpering among them.)*
21 **POLARIS:** **Wait. Come closer!** *(IMPERFECT STARS walk onto*
22 *stage and stand near the throne. The MINISTERS and*
23 *PERFECT STARS grudgingly make room for them.)* **Who is**
24 **spokestar for this group?**
25 **GEMINEE:** *(Afraid)* **He is.** *(Points to GEMINII.)*
26 **GEMINII:** **Your grace!** *(Tries to bow, jerks GEMINEE to bow with*
27 *him. Other STARS bow when they see them bowing.)* **We heard**
28 **of your search for a star to announce the birth of the**
29 **prophet king on planet earth. We have come to enter the**
30 **contest.** *(MIZAR, ALCOR, RIGEL, BETELGEUSE and other*
31 *STARS begin laughing and pointing at the unfitness of the group.)*
32 **POLARIS:** *(Holds hand across his face to subdue a smile. His voice*
33 *becomes firm.)* **I appreciate the efforts you have taken, but**
34 **you will admit that you are not the magnificent looking**
35 **stars I had requested. See these that have come before you?**

1   *(Points to PERFECT STARS.)* **Each is brilliant! Each is**
2   **beautiful!**
3 GEMINII: **Indeed they are beautiful, your grace. But how**
4   **long will their brilliance last?**
5 POLARIS: *(Quizzingly)* **What?**
6 GEMINII: *(Continuing thought)* **Suppose** ... *(Pauses, then*
7   *continues with geat drama.)* **Suppose, at the most crucial**
8   **moment, they lose their power, then get dim, dim, and**
9   **yet dimmer. Or, suppose** *(Pauses again)* **the chosen one is**
10   **hit by a meteor and shattered into a million pieces?**
11 POLARIS: **Why are you supposing all these unfortunate**
12   **accidents?**
13 GEMINII: **We stars of the galaxies have a great pride in this**
14   **blessed event and we don't want anything to go wrong.**
15   **I have an idea, your grace. Would you like to hear about**
16   **it?**
17 MIZAR and ALCOR: *(Jump up and say in delight:)* **We would.**
18   *(Then realizing they have talked out of place, sit down quickly*
19   *after POLARIS has given them a stern look.)*
20 POLARIS: **Very well, go on.**
21 GEMINII: **My friends and I, when joined together, look like**
22   *one* **ever brilliant, ever glowing star. If one part is**
23   **dimmed, the others remain bright.** *(Seeing that POLARIS*
24   *is not convinced, motions to others to get together to show how*
25   *it could be done. All IMPERFECT stars form in Center Stage,*
26   *except MARCO, so that their best parts are showing. FLASH*
27   *blinks as bright and as hard as he can.)*
28 GEMINEE: **Even our friend Marco thought we were just one**
29   **when he first saw us.**
30 MARCO: **Oh, yes, your grace, that's true. I had to put on my**
31   **sunglasses, it was so bright.**
32 POLARIS: **Hmmm.** *(Looks into large book on desk.)* **It doesn't**
33   **say just** *one* **star is to be used. And I suppose from a**
34   **distance you could all look like one star. That is something**
35   **to consider.** *(POLARIS cups his chin in his hand, continues to*

1   *look at book while drumming his fingers.)*
2   **BETELGEUSE: Tell me now, how did you bump into each**
3   **other?** *(Laughs slightly with RIGEL.)*
4   **GEMINEE: Just that way!**
5   **BETELGEUSE: What do you mean?**
6   **GEMINII: After we heard about the search for the star, we**
7   **decided to try and enter the contest, too. As we glided**
8   **along in the sky, we met some of these others looking for**
9   **your kingdom.**
10   **GEMINEE: We got lost and I started yelling,** *(In singing tone)*
11   **"Polaris, oh Polaris, where are you?"**
12   **POLARIS:** *(Unaware of the previous conversation and still reading*
13   *in the book answers without thinking also in a singing tone.)*
14   **Here I am.** *(He abruptly catches his mistake and quickly motions*
15   *GEMINEE to go on with the story. MIZAR and ALCOR start*
16   *to giggle but quickly stop as POLARIS slinks back in his chair*
17   *while looking at everyone to see that they are not laughing at*
18   *him too.)*
19   **GEMINII: To go on with the story, your grace, we were**
20   **watching some of those beautiful stars go by and thought**
21   **they were surely going to the contest so we thought we**
22   **would follow them. We lost them somehow but soon**
23   **bumped into Marco coming our way and we persuaded**
24   **him to join our illustrious group.**
25   **RIGEL: Illustrious group? Ha!**
26   **POLARIS: Your story points up one factor, my friends. You**
27   **do not know navigation very well, and we do need a star**
28   **who can find Bethlehem without trouble.**
29   **GEMINEE: I thought if we just looked for a crowd of people**
30   **that would surely be it, because people always gather**
31   **when a king is born.**
32   **POLARIS: That is not to be the case this time, my boy. I'm**
33   **sorry, but you will not be able to compete in this contest.**
34   **GEMINII: Wait, please. I did say that Marco brought us here.**
35   **He is a recent graduate from Stellar University and has a**

1   degree in stellar navigation. He was top star in his class.

2 **FLASHER:** *(Flashes light in RIGEL's face who quickly moves away.)*

3   **And he graduated Magna Cum Brighter!**

4 **POLARIS:** *(Impressed)* **Well, well. Let's see this scholar.**

5   *(MARCO steps forward but hesitantly; shows bashfulness.)*

6   **Congratulations, my boy! Let us see that diploma.**

7   *(MARCO holds it up for all to see. POLARIS turns to PERFECT*

8   *STARS.)* **Do any of you possess a degree in stellar**

9   **navigation?**

10 **PERFECT STARS:**   No, sir. No, sir.

11 **POLARIS:**   **Well, then, the contest is settled.** *(Walks toward*

12   *group of IMPERFECT STARS.)* **Band together my glowing**

13   **friends and make the most brilliant light your efforts can**

14   **achieve. Here is the map of direction.** *(Hands paper to*

15   *MARCO.)* **With Marco leading you, go and announce the**

16   **birth of the prophet king. Leave now, for there is little**

17   **time left!** *(IMPERFECT STARS line up, MARCO first, followed*

18   *by GEMINII and GEMINEE and others, going back by the center*

19   *aisle in audience.)*

20 **POLARIS:** *(Shouting as they leave.)* **Blessings of the stellar**

21   **universe be with you.** *(All on stage wave good-bye — could*

22   *sing appropriate Christmas carol. Group waves good-bye to those*

23   *on stage and those in audience as they leave.)*

24

25

26

27

28

29

30

31

32

33

34

35

Santa Goes on Strike
by ROBERT A. MAURO

CAST

SANTA

MRS. CLAUS

TINKER

KATRINKA

WINKER

BIXBY

TV NEWSCASTER

CAMERA PERSON

REPORTERS
(Extras as desired)

PRODUCTION NOTES

PLAYING TIME:

About fifteen minutes.

COSTUMES:

Santa and Mrs. Claus — Santa-type costumes.
Tinker, Winker, Katrinka and Bixby — red long johns with baggy pockets and floppy red hats.
TV Newscaster and Reporters — suits.

PROPERTIES:

Long, long rolled up letter, pad and pencil, mailbags, letters, hammer, wrench, five hand microphones, old mimeograph machine on rolling typewriter table, eyeglasses, mock TV camera, pocket watch, six picket signs saying, for example, the following:

> **"Christmas — Bah, Humbug!"**
>
> **"It's More Blessed to Give than to Receive!"**
>
> **"Strike Christmas — Not White Christmas!"**
>
> **"Ho Ho! No No Christmas!"**
>
> **"Christmas Cancelled!"**
>
> **"We're Not Opened to Christmas!"**

SETTING:

SCENE 1: Santa's workshop. Toys and games, dolls and bicycles stand around stage and on shelves of backdrop. Table with pile of mail sits Center Stage.

SCENE 2: Santa's workshop. No toys, but piles of mimeograph paper stand around stage. Podium with cluster of microphones stands Center Stage.

SOUND EFFECTS:

"Jingle Bells" and "Deck the Halls" are played. Christmas carols can be played between Scenes 1 and 2 while stage is reset.

LIGHTING EFFECTS:

Lights dim out at the end of Scene 1.

NOTE: The mailbag, microphones and mimeograph machine can be made from any materials at hand. It is not necessary that they be actual items.

SCENE 1

TIME: The night before the night before Christmas.

SETTING: SANTA's workshop. Toys and games, dolls and bicycles stand around the stage and on shelves of backdrop. Table with pile of mail sits Center Stage.

AT RISE: SANTA and MRS. CLAUS read letters as TINKER, KATRINKA, WINKER and BIXBY (also referred to as HELPERS) work on toys.

SANTA: *(Speaks sadly as he shakes his head.)* **Another one. They're all the same. Listen to this letter.** *(He reads it.)* **"Dear Santa: Please bring me a sailboat, a ten-speed bike, a new skateboard, a video game, two dogs, one cat and a new deluxe set of trains. And"** — he underlines — **"don't forget the video game."**

TINKER: **These children will have us working overtime.**

MRS. CLAUS: **True, Tinker.**

SANTA: **Yes. And all year I get letters from children asking for more and more toys. I just don't have enough helpers to make all these things.**

WINKER: **And every year we work night and day to make them.**

KATRINKA: **Yes, Winker. I make dolls, bicycles, video games ...**

WINKER: **I make toy soldiers, trains, boats and cars.**

BIXBY: **And I make swings, sliding ponds, seesaws and monkey bars.**

TINKER: **And I make baseball gloves, kittens and puppies — the stuffed ones, I mean.**

KATRINKA: **Anyway, by the time Christmas comes, Winker, Tinker, Bixby and I are too tired to even open our own presents.**

BIXBY: **We have to sleep until the reindeer come home!**

MRS. CLAUS: **Listen to this letter. "Dear Santa: Please bring me a portable, battery operated color TV; a new tape recorder — stereo — and a moped. I'll also need a helmet,**

1 boots, gloves and a year's supply of gas! And don't forget
2 an extra set of batteries for the TV!" My, oh my. Whatever
3 happened to those nice Christmas cards we used to get,
4 Santa?
5 SANTA: I don't know, Mrs. Claus. I guess people can't afford
6 the postage anymore.
7 KATRINKA: Except to ask for toys!
8 MRS. CLAUS: And now with radio, TV, movies and those
9 reindeer-less carriages, people are too busy to take time
10 to wish us a Merry Christmas.
11 SANTA: By the way, have we fed the reindeer, dear?
12 MRS. CLAUS: Yes. They're all ready to go.
13 SANTA: How are all those toys coming, helpers?
14 HELPERS: Fine, Santa.
15 BIXBY: *(Wipes his brow.)* But we're all so tired.
16 KATRINKA: The children have us working so hard.
17 TINKER: I can hardly make another gift.
18 WINKER: And we have millions to wrap yet!
19 SANTA: *(Picking up another letter)* I know. And listen to this.
20 "Dear Santa: I want a new sled, a new pair of skis, a new
21 camera, a hang glider, a surfboard, and" — it goes on and
22 on! *(Lets the long, long letter unroll and stretch across the floor.)*
23 For miles! *(SANTA throws the letter on the table and picks up*
24 *one after another and reads them to himself.)* They're all the
25 same! *(Checks another letter.)* Everyone wants so much!
26 *(Suddenly BIXBY faints.)*
27 ALL: Bixby!
28 SANTA: Are you all right? *(SANTA runs over to BIXBY as*
29 *remaining HELPERS hold BIXBY up. SANTA and MRS.*
30 *CLAUS help BIXBY onto table.)* Bixby! Say something!
31 MRS. CLAUS: Bixby, oh, poor Bixby!
32 BIXBY: Where am I?
33 WINKER: You're in Santa's workshop.
34 BIXBY: Oh. I guess I passed out from overwork. Sorry, Santa.
35 I haven't had much sleep since last Christmas.

1   KATRINKA: And we haven't had sugarplums dancing in our
2   heads for ages!
3   MRS. CLAUS: None of us has.
4   SANTA: Right. We've all been working too hard! Well, I've
5   had enough of this! There'll be no Christmas this year —
6   and I mean it. We're going on strike! Winker.
7   WINKER: *(Stands at attention.)* Yes, Santa?
8   SANTA: You and Tinker go unhitch the reindeer.
9   WINKER: *(Saluting)* Yes, Santa. Come on, Tink.
10   TINKER: Here I am. *(TINKER and WINKER exit.)*
11   KATRINKA: What'll Bixby and I do, Santa?
12   SANTA: You and Bixby can help Mrs. Claus and I put together a
13   press release. We're going to let the world know that there'll
14   be no Christmas this year. Come on, let's put these letters
15   away. *(KATRINKA, BIXBY, MRS. CLAUS and SANTA put*
16   *letters in bag.)* There. Now, Katrinka, you go fetch our
17   mimeograph machine — and lots of paper! We have to
18   get out billions of these strike notices by midnight!
19   KATRINKA: Right, Santa! We'll use all that white wrapping
20   paper we were going to wrap some of the presents in!
21   SANTA: Excellent idea! Bixby!
22   BIXBY: *(Standing at attention)* Yes, Santa?
23   SANTA: You can help Mrs. Claus and me put together that
24   notice. Got your pad and pencil handy?
25   BIXBY: *(Takes out a pad and pencil from his baggy pockets.)* Got
26   them, Santa. Just tell me what you'd like me to write.
27   Writing is what I do best.
28   SANTA: We know, Bixby. After all, you're the one who
29   addresses all those "To and From" labels on all the gifts.
30   MRS. CLAUS: An excellent idea. It's so much less confusing
31   for Santa.
32   SANTA: At least now I know who gets what and from whom
33   they get it.
34   BIXBY: Yep. That was the idea. Efficiency in Christmas gift
35   giving! That's my motto.

1   MRS. CLAUS: And a very good one, too. It helps to make the
2   season-that should be jolly just a bit more jolly.
3   SANTA: I'll say. So . . . ready, Bixby?
4   BIXBY: Ready, Santa. Now . . . what are you going to say?
5   SANTA: Good question. *(Strokes his beard as he thinks and paces,*
6   *then)* Ah! I have it! Take this down, Bixby. 'Twas the night
7   before Christmas and all through the workshop . . .
8   *(BIXBY writes as SANTA thinks again.)*
9   BIXBY: Got it! And?
10   MRS. CLAUS: Tell them of all those letters about wanting to
11   get, get, get.
12   SANTA: Ho, ho. Yes. *(As SANTA paces)* Take this down, Bixby.
13   BIXBY: Go ahead, Santa.
14   SANTA: We receive millions and millions of letters — all
15   asking for gifts, gifts, gifts. Everyone wants, wants,
16   wants. Therefore, as of Christmas Eve, Santa Claus is
17   going on strike!
18   BIXBY and MRS. CLAUS: Strike?!
19   SANTA: Yes.
20   MRS. CLAUS: Oh, dear. That gives us only twenty-four hours
21   to deliver all those notices.
22   BIXBY: We have to run them all off on the mimeograph first!
23   *(WINKER, TINKER and KATRINKA enter with beat-up old*
24   *mimeograph machine.)*
25   SANTA: Ah, here's Winker and Tinker and Katrinka with our
26   old mimeograph.
27   BIXBY and MRS. CLAUS: *(Looking over the machine)* It's a mess!
28   WINKER: I'll say. Needs a bit of fixing up. *(Takes out his hammer*
29   *and is about to pound mimeograph.)*
30   TINKER: Wait! I'll tinker with it, Winker. *(TINKER takes out a*
31   *big wrench and is about to pound machine with it.)*
32   KATRINKA: Hold it! Let me clean it up first. Where's that
33   garden hose?
34   SANTA: Stop! We'll take the message down to Santa's Quick
35   and Speedy Print Shoppe. There, where we make up all

1	of the address labels for the gifts, we'll be able to print
2	up all the strike notices we need! Come on, we have no
3	time to waste. Tinker, you go get the reindeer ready. It's
4	nearly Christmas Eve! *(All exit as lights dim. Christmas carols*
5	*can be played as stage is set for next scene.)*
6	
7	**SCENE 2**
8	
9	*TIME:* The night before Christmas.
10	*SETTING:* Santa's workshop. All toys are gone. They've been
11	replaced with stacks of mimeograph paper. A cluster of
12	microphones stands at a podium Center Stage.
13	*AT RISE:* TV NEWSCASTER taps his microphone and says
14	"testing, testing" as CAMERA PERSON aims mock TV camera
15	at him.
16	
17	NEWSCASTER: Are you ready with that North Pole to
18	network feed?
19	CAMERA PERSON: All set. Satellite is locked on us. But our
20	microwave dish is full of snow.
21	NEWSCASTER: Hope we don't send back a snowy picture.
22	CAMERA PERSON: Hope not.
23	NEWSCASTER: *(Checks watch.)* Five seconds to air time —
24	two, one! *(Big smile)* Hello ladies and gentlemen and
25	children of all ages. As you know, last night Santa and
26	his reindeer dropped nearly a billion and a half strike
27	notices down chimneys all over the world. It seems there
28	will be no Christmas this year. And that's why we're here
29	this Christmas Eve. Santa has decided to hold a press
30	conference and we're going to bring it to you live from
31	the North Pole. *(SANTA enters with MRS. CLAUS and*
32	*HELPERS. They're each carrying a picket sign.)* And here he
33	comes now! *("Jingle Bells" is being played.)* With him is the
34	lovely Mrs. Claus and four of Santa's chief helpers.
35	*(HELPERS nod their heads as they are introduced. Music fades.)*

1   Tinker, Winker, Bixby and Katrinka. *(Suddenly all*
2   *REPORTERS rush on stage and up to SANTA.)* **Hold it! Hold**
3   **it! Ladies and gentlemen, it would appear that reporters**
4   **from all over the world are here to ask Santa questions.**
5   **Let's listen.**
6 REPORTER 1: Santa, I'm Jackie Smith from the *African*
7   *Times.* And I'd like to know if it's true that you are
8   refusing to deliver Christmas presents tonight?
9 SANTA: *(Nods as he stands behind podium and places his picket*
10   *sign against podium so all can see it.)* **Yes. You see, so many**
11   **people are asking for gifts — and so far not one person**
12   **has asked me to help them give a gift to someone.**
13   **Therefore, I've decided to go on strike. Christmas has**
14   **been cancelled.**
15 MRS. CLAUS and HELPERS: Strike! Strike! Strike! Strike!
16 REPORTER 2: Sandy McGee here from the *London Times.*
17   You mean there won't be any Christmas at all this year,
18   Santa?
19 SANTA: No, no. There'll always be a Christmas. But my
20   reindeer and I won't be delivering any gifts.
21 REPORTER 3: Red Jones from the *Boston Globe.* No gifts?
22   But what kind of Christmas is that going to be?
23 MRS. CLAUS: A sad one I'd suppose.
24 MRS. CLAUS and HELPERS: Strike! Strike! Strike! Strike!
25 REPORTER 4: Flash Valdez from the *South American Daily.*
26   Señora Claus, can I ask you a personal question?
27 MRS. CLAUS: *(Stepping up to podium)* **That depends on what**
28   **it is. Ask and we'll see.**
29 NEWSCASTER: *(To camera)* **Hold it, ladies and gentlemen!**
30   **Mrs. Claus will now answer a personal question!**
31 REPORTER 4: Señora Claus, has your husband been feeling
32   ill lately?
33 ALL: *(Except REPORTER asking question)* **Ill?**
34 REPORTER 4: Si, ill. What I mean is . . . is Santa Claus getting
35   too old for the stress and strain of the Christmas rush?

1   MRS. CLAUS and SANTA: No! Of course not!
2   MRS. CLAUS: True, Santa is nearly two thousand years old —
3   SANTA: But I feel more like twenty! *(Flexes his muscles.)*
4   REPORTER 5:   Jade Ling from the *Oriental Gazette*. So then
5   you are striking because of all those letters from people
6   asking for gifts. Is that correct?
7   SANTA: Correct. And until at least one person asks me to
8   help them give a gift to someone, I refuse to go out this
9   Christmas Eve. *(Folds his arms.)*
10   NEWSCASTER: Well, there you have it, ladies and
11   gentlemen and children of all ages. There'll be no gifts
12   this Christmas. *(Checks his watch.)* However, we still have
13   a few hours left before Christmas Day actually
14   commences. And possibly we'll get more mail. Maybe even
15   a letter asking Santa to help someone give someone a
16   present.
17   MRS. CLAUS: That's possible.
18   SANTA: Right. We do have special deliveries right down to
19   midnight.
20   NEWSCASTER: Well, Mrs. Claus and Santa, let's hope a child
21   or two has already written that letter and mailed it. If
22   we do receive one, folks, we'll let you know right away!
23   Right, Santa?
24   SANTA: Certainly, but until then —
25   MRS. CLAUS, SANTA and HELPERS: *(Holding up their picket*
26   *signs)* Strike! Strike! Strike! Strike! Strike! Strike! *(A few*
27   *notes of "Jingle Bells" is heard.)*
28   NEWSCASTER: What's that?
29   SANTA: My doorbell.
30   KATRINKA: I'll get it! *(She exits.)*
31   SANTA: *(Sighs)* This is a sad Christmas for my reindeer and
32   me. We do enjoy giving gifts, but — *(KATRINKA runs in*
33   *waving a letter.)*
34   KATRINKA: Santa! Santa! A letter! A letter! Special delivery!
35   *(KATRINKA hands the letter to SANTA.)*

1   SANTA: Let's see what it says. *(He looks at envelope.)*
2   NEWSCASTER: It's a tense moment up here at the North
3   Pole, folks. Santa is looking at a special delivery letter.
4   It seems Santa just received it. *(SANTA opens letter.)* And
5   he's now opening it! Who's it from, Santa?
6   SANTA: A child!
7   REPORTERS: *(Together)* What's in it? What's it say? The
8   world wants to know!
9   NEWSCASTER: Could this be the letter we've all been
10   waiting for? What's it say, Santa?
11   SANTA: I can't believe what I see!
12   MRS. CLAUS: *(Hands him his glasses.)* Your glasses, Santa.
13   SANTA: *(Puts glasses on and reads letter.)* It says ... "Dear
14   Santa: Please give!" It says give! *(SANTA mumbles the rest
15   of the letter to himself, then)* This little child has asked for
16   something for someone else! For someone less fortunate.
17   Therefore, because of the generosity and thoughtfulness
18   of this one little child, Christmas is on again! *(All cheer
19   as MRS. CLAUS, SANTA and HELPERS put down their picket
20   signs.)* Christmas, after all, should be a time of giving each
21   to the other. For giving to one another, not getting, is
22   what Christmas is all about.
23   REPORTERS: What about next year, Santa? Will there be a
24   Christmas next year?
25   NEWSCASTER: Will there, Santa?
26   SANTA: Well, if I don't get more of this here sort of letter —
27   and next year I want at least two of them — I'll cancel
28   Christmas again. But for now, Katrinka and Bixby, get
29   my sack ready! And put the automatic, electronic gift
30   packer on high!
31   KATRINKA and BIXBY: Will do, Santa! *(THEY run off.)*
32   SANTA: And Tinker and Winker, hitch up the reindeer! Take
33   off is in ... *(Checks his pocket watch)* thirty-five minutes!
34   TINKER and WINKER: *(Saluting)* Roger, Santa! *(They run off
35   in opposite direction of BIXBY and KATRINKA.)*

1   SANTA: Now we're ready to once again spread joy and good
2   will all over the world! *(All cheer and dance around as "Deck*
3   *the Halls" is heard in the background.)*
4   KATRINKA and BIXBY: *(Running on stage)* OK, Santa, your
5   sack is being automatically packed. So, we're all set. *(More*
6   *dancing)*
7   TINKER and WINKER: *(Run on stage in a panic.)* Santa! Santa!
8   Oh, Santa!
9   SANTA and MRS. CLAUS: What's wrong? *(Dancing ends.)*
10   NEWSCASTER: Hold it, folks! Something wrong is developing
11   up here at the North Pole. Stand by!
12   SANTA: *(To WINKER and TINKER)* What's the problem?
13   WINKER: *(Catching breath)* The reindeer! It's the reindeer!
14   NEWSCASTER: It's the reindeer, folks. The reindeer!
15   REPORTERS: What's wrong with the reindeer? Are they
16   ill? Tell us! The whole world wants to know!
17   SANTA: *(To WINKER and TINKER)* What is the matter with
18   my reindeer?
19   TINKER: The reindeer are on strike!
20   ALL: What?
21   SANTA: On strike?
22   WINKER and TINKER: Yes! Yes!
23   WINKER: They refuse to deliver any gifts!
24   MRS. CLAUS, REPORTERS and NEWSCASTER: And what do
25   they want?
26   SANTA: Yeah! What do they want?
27   TINKER: One holiday off a year!
28   ALL: *(Together)* Which one?
29   WINKER: This one!
30   TINKER: Christmas Eve!
31   ALL: Oh, no! *(Quick curtain)*
32
33
34
35

A Most Memorable Christmas
by JANET MEILI

CAST

ANGELS

MICHAEL (A)

GABRIEL (A)

SERENA (US)

TERRA (US)

STELLA (US)

CHORA (US)

IRANIA (US)

ROMANUS (A)

TARDIA (US)

(The angels may be either sex.

Add letters to change name.)

ANGEL CHORUS

EARTHLINGS

MARY

JOSEPH

OLD WOMAN

SMALL CHILD

MAGI *(any number)*

SHEPHERDS *(any number)*

HOMEOWNER

INNKEEPERS *(2)*

ROMAN SOLDIER

HEROD

OTHER TOWNSPEOPLE

(as desired)

SETTING

This playlet is intended to be performed in the church chancel so no scenery is required. The later scenes would benefit from spotlights.

Carols may be sung within and between scenes if desired.

1

SCENE I

2

3   *AT RISE:*   MICHAEL is on stage. Flourish of trumpets — can be

4   played on organ. ANGELS come from all directions, down the

5   aisles, through all the doors. There may be more ANGELS than

6   there are speaking parts.

7   MICHAEL: Are all the angels present?

8   CHORA: We're all here, Michael.

9   SERENA: I don't see Tardia.

10   GABRIEL: Tardia will be late. She's visiting Elizabeth, the

11   mother of John, who will be the Baptist.

12   TERRA: Today? The baby is already three months old!

13   GABRIEL: Tardia finds so many things to do, she's always

14   a little behind. But she'll get here eventually.

15   MICHAEL: We'll begin without her. I have news of the

16   greatest importance. It has been decided that now is the

17   time to bring Christmas to earth.

18   TERRA: Christmas! That's the most important event in

19   human history!

20   MICHAEL: Yes, it is. And we angels are responsible to see

21   that the world realizes this is so. Now, what can we do

22   to accomplish this?

23   TERRA: The Christ Child must be born in the palace of the

24   Caesars in Rome!

25   SERENA: I hardly think that will be appropriate, Terra.

26   Jesus is going to earth as the Messiah of the Chosen

27   People, the Jews.

28   TERRA: Oh, I'm sorry. I forgot. Still, Jerusalem is a notable

29   city, too.

30   IRANIA: Terra, I'm surprised at you! Have you forgotten

31   Micah's prophecy? "But thou, Bethlehem Ephratah,

32   though thou be little among the thousands of Judah, yet

33   out of thee shall he come forth unto me that is to be ruler

34   in Israel."

35   TERRA: We've been waiting for Christmas to come for so

1   long that I just forgot some of the details.

2   MICHAEL: That's a poor excuse. You had better set aside a

3   few minutes each day to read the prophets.

4   TERRA: I will, Michael.

5   MICHAEL: Now, you all remember that Joseph and Mary

6   have been chosen to be the earthly parents of the baby.

7   ROMANUS: Joseph of Nazareth?

8   MICHAEL: Yes, Romanus. Gabriel, will you explain to

9   Mary — and Joseph — the importance of this child?

10   GABRIEL: Gladly.

11   ROMANUS: I'm confused. If Joseph lives in Nazareth, why

12   are they going to be in Bethlehem when the baby is born?

13   STELLA: Yes, Joseph has no close relatives living there

14   anymore.

15   CHORA: And people always want their babies to be born at

16   home.

17   MICHAEL: The prophecy foretold that Bethlehem would be

18   honored by the baby's birth. Is there anything that can

19   be done to fulfill the prophecy?

20   ROMANUS: There is one thing that will take Joseph to

21   Bethlehem.

22   MICHAEL: Good. What is it?

23   ROMANUS: The power of Rome.

24   TERRA: Rome doesn't care about a country village like

25   Bethlehem or a simple carpenter like Joseph.

26   IRANIA: And when Rome does pay attention to you, it means

27   you're in trouble.

28   ROMANUS: I have a plan. It will take Mary and Joseph to

29   Bethlehem and yet see that they are in no danger from

30   the Roman government.

31   MICHAEL: Will you tell us about your plan?

32   ROMANUS: No. I won't need any help.

33   MICHAEL: All right. What can we do to herald the baby's

34   birth?

35   STELLA: I'll provide a sign in nature that everyone will notice.

1	MICHAEL: That's an excellent idea, Stella. Do you have
2	something in mind?
3	STELLA: What would you say to an earthquake?
4	CHORA: Isn't that a little frightening for a child?
5	STELLA: Do you think so? It's something everyone will notice.
6	SERENA: Let's try to find something they'll notice that won't
7	scare the baby, too. Let me see —
8	STELLA: I'll think of something. You don't have to help me.
9	But I still like the idea of an earthquake.
10	CHORA: An earthquake would drown out my music. I am in
11	charge of the music, aren't I, Michael?
12	MICHAEL: If you want to be, Chora, you certainly may.
13	CHORA: I already know what I'm going to use. I've been
14	practicing a new "Gloria in Excelsis" that will be just
15	right.
16	MICHAEL: Is it an arrangement for full chorus?
17	CHORA: No, it's a solo. The others can choose something by
18	themselves.
19	MICHAEL: Very well. What else can we do to mark this day?
20	IRANIA: There must be some earthly sign.
21	MICHAEL: Do you have a suggestion?
22	IRANIA: Yes, indeed. Will you all be surprised when you find
23	out what it is!
24	SERENA: Will you need any help?
25	IRANIA: No, thank you. I don't expect to have any problems.
26	MICHAEL: You all seem to have such excellent ideas, this
27	should be a night the world will never forget. Serena,
28	have you anything to add?
29	SERENA: No. I'll just try to bring a sense of peace and calmness
30	to the night.
31	MICHAEL: *(As TARDIA rushes in, breathless)* Are there any
32	questions?
33	TARDIA: Am I late? Will you forgive me? Have I missed
34	anything? What is the meeting about?
35	MICHAEL: So, Tardia, you finally arrived. The answers to

1   your questions are three yeses and Christmas.

2 TARDIA: Christmas? You mean it's finally time to bring
3   Christmas to earth? How wonderful!

4 TERRA: We've been deciding what each of us can do to make
5   the night a memorable one.

6 TARDIA: Fine! What do you want me to do?

7 MICHAEL: I don't know, exactly. Gabriel will explain the
8   importance of the child to Mary and Joseph, Romanus
9   will lead them to Bethlehem and guard them from the
10   power of Rome, Chora will provide the music, Stella will
11   create a sign in nature, Irania has an idea for an earthly
12   sign and Serena will keep things calm.

13 TARDIA: There doesn't seem to be anything left for me to do.

14 SERENA: Tardia, since you spend so much time on earth,
15   perhaps you could take charge of the physical
16   arrangements — find a place in Bethlehem for the child
17   to be born.

18 TARDIA: Certainly. Although there won't be anything very
19   memorable about any place in Bethlehem where they can
20   stay. But I'll do the best I can. Are you sure that's all I
21   can do to help?

22 SERENA: Yes. And we'll be here in case anyone has any
23   problems.

24

25   **SCENE II**

26

27 *AT RISE:* Spotlight focuses on each ANGEL as he/she comes
28   center. TARDIA holds the hand of a small child.

29 TARDIA: Now, there's nothing to cry about. Your father and
30   the sheep can't be far away. We'll just look until we find
31   them.

32 SMALL CHILD: I'm afraid when I'm alone.

33 TARDIA: You aren't alone. I'm here with you and I'll stay
34   with you until we find your father.

35   * * *

1   *(HEROD holding an open scroll speaks to ROMAN SOLDIER.*

2   *ROMANUS stands in the background.)*

3   **HEROD:**   I have been expecting some such directive as this.

4   **All the people are to be taxed.**

5   **SOLDIER:**   This area is lucky to have evaded the Roman tax

6   **this long.**

7   **HEROD:**   Well, the sooner we do it, the happier Caesar will

8   **be. Before we can tax them, we have to know who they**

9   **are. Publish this notice: "There will be a census of all the**

10   **people. Each one will go to the city of his fathers for this**

11   **census. This will be done immediately."**

12   **SOLDIER:**   Yes, sire.

13   *   *   *

14   *(CHORA practices arpeggios and perhaps a snatch of her solo.)*

15   *   *   *

16   *(STELLA talking to TERRA)*

17   **STELLA:**   Maybe I could have the greatest volcano the world

18   **has ever known erupt.**

19   **TERRA:**   A volcano is so dangerous. We're celebrating the birth

20   **of the *Savior* of the world.**

21   **STELLA:**   But an erupting volcano is such a spectacular

22   **sight! Especially at night.**

23   **TERRA:**   I think you should choose a spectacular sight that's

24   **quiet.**

25   **STELLA:**   All right. I'll try to think of one.

26   *   *   *

27   *(IRANIA talking to THREE MAGI sitting on stools and holding*

28   *scrolls)*

29   **IRANIA:**   A great king is to be born in a country to the west.

30   **It would be a gracious gesture if you went to pay him**

31   **homage.**

32   **MAGI #1:**   There is no country to the west important enough

33   **to have a great king.**

34   **MAGI #2:**   Unless she means Rome. And I for one do not care

35   **to risk Caesar's anger by going to do homage to his successor.**

1   MAGI #3:   We are old men. Rome is far away. We would never
2   live long enough to make the journey.
3   IRANIA: Oh, no, not Rome. He will be born in Judea and
4   Judea is only half as far away as Rome. Surely the birth
5   of this king has been foretold in your books of wisdom.
6   Won't you search them and when you find such a
7   prophecy, go to do him honor?
8   MAGI #1:   We will search our books.
9   MAGI #2:   That is our duty.
10   MAGI #3:   If we find the prophecy, we will make the journey.
11   * * *
12   *(The annunciation to MARY — MARY and GABRIEL.)*
13   GABRIEL: Hail, O favored one, the Lord is with you. Do not
14   be afraid, Mary, for you have found favor with God. And,
15   behold, you will conceive and bear a son and you shall
16   call his name Jesus. He will be great and will be called
17   the Son of the Most High and the Lord God will give to
18   him the throne of his father, David, and he will reign
19   over the house of Jacob forever and of his kingdom there
20   will be no end.
21   MARY: I am the Lord's servant. May it happen to me as you
22   have said.
23   * * *
24   *(TARDIA to OLD WOMAN sweeping her house)*
25   TARDIA: You've lost your last coin? Let me help you look for it.
26   OLD WOMAN: There are such shadows in the corners. I need
27   a lamp to be able to see, but I can't hold the lamp and
28   sweep at the same time.
29   TARDIA: You hold the lamp and I'll do the looking.
30
31   SCENE III
32
33   *AT RISE:*   TARDIA at door of house in Bethlehem.
34   TARDIA: You have such a large home, the largest in
35   Bethlehem. Would you have room for a weary couple who

1   have traveled many miles —
2 HOMEOWNER: I have no room. My home is filled with my
3   relatives and friends — ask at the inn.
4   *(TARDIA to INNKEEPER)*
5 TARDIA: I'd like to reserve a room.
6 INNKEEPER #1: You're too late. I have no room.
7 TARDIA: No room? But I must have one! Oh dear, oh dear.
8   *(Goes to next inn.)* I'd like to reserve a room. It doesn't have
9   to be a large room —
10 INNKEEPER #2: No room.
11 TARDIA: *(Firmly)* Now, that just can't be!
12   * * *
13   *(GABRIEL with MARY and JOSEPH. They stop their journey*
14   *and take a drink from a water bottle.)*
15 MARY: Joseph, I'm so tired.
16 JOSEPH: Have courage, Mary. That is Bethlehem just
17   ahead. In a little while you can rest.
18   * * *
19   *(IRANIA, TERRA, MAGI)*
20 IRANIA: Terra, what am I going to do? The Magi are going
21   to Jerusalem!
22 TERRA: Didn't you tell them about Bethlehem?
23 IRANIA: Not specifically.
24 TERRA: Then they'd naturally go to the capital city.
25 IRANIA: I thought they would do such honor to the baby by
26   their presence and now they not only won't be there, but
27   they've put his life into danger by telling Herod of his
28   birth.
29   * * *
30   *(CHORA and the SHEPHERDS. CHORA sings her solo to the*
31   *SHEPHERDS who sit around the fire and never look up or give*
32   *any sign they hear anything.)*
33 CHORA: Didn't you hear me? I bring you good news.
34 SHEPHERD #1: The sky is very clear tonight. That means
35   it will be cold.

1   SHEPHERD #2: I had better gather more fuel for the fire.

2   CHORA: Listen to what I have to tell you! It's Christmas!

3   Oh, why can't they hear me?

4

5   SCENE IV

6

7   *AT RISE:* On stage: MICHAEL, SERENA, GABRIEL, CHORA,

8   STELLA, IRANIA, TERRA, ROMANUS.

9   MICHAEL: It is almost time for the birth of the Christ Child

10   and all is peaceful and quiet, eh, Serena?

11   SERENA: All is quiet, but not peaceful. In fact, I feel a sense

12   of great unrest. Do any of you need help?

13   ROMANUS: The Magi came to Jerusalem. Herod is

14   violently jealous at the news of the birth of a rival.

15   IRANIA: There is no earthly sign at Bethlehem because the

16   Wise Men went to Jerusalem.

17   STELLA: I placed a great star in the sky, but it is so quiet,

18   no one sees it.

19   CHORA: I sang my best, but the shepherds didn't hear me.

20   GABRIEL: Tardia was too late to find a room at the inn. Mary

21   and Joseph are housed in a stable.

22   SERENA: What a long list of troubles! But each of you wanted

23   to work alone and get all the credit for your ideas. If you

24   would be willing to work together, all these problems

25   could be easily solved.

26   MICHAEL: Will you work together?

27   ALL: *(Chorus of agreement)*

28   SERENA: Irania, it's all right for the Magi to travel by way of

29   Jerusalem. Romanus, will you please go there and help

30   Herod's priests find the Bethlehem prophecy?

31   ROMANUS: Certainly.

32   SERENA: And then warn the Wise Men and Joseph of Herod's

33   jealousy. *(ROMANUS exits.)* Stella, you make the Wise Men

34   look up. They are astronomers and will recognize the

35   import of your star and will follow it. You see, Irania, with

1   the help of Romanus and Stella, your Wise Men will get
2   to Bethlehem on time.
3 STELLA: Oh, thank you, Serena. *(She exits along with IRANIA.)*
4 SERENA: Chora — shepherds need a lot of persuading to
5   leave their sheep. Maybe it's too big a job for a single
6   angel. Why don't you have your whole chorus sing?
7 CHORA: Oh, yes! I'm sure they'd hear if we all sang together.
8   *(Exits.)*
9 SERENA: And Gabriel, even though Tardia was too late to
10   get a room at the inn, it wasn't because she was selfish,
11   but because she was so unselfish with her time. I think
12   the stable's a perfect place. How could you crowd
13   shepherds and Wise Men and townspeople and angels all
14   into one little room in an inn? You're going to need all
15   the space you can find.
16 GABRIEL: Of course, Serena. I should have realized that
17   myself. *(Exits)*
18 SERENA: Well, Michael, *now* I think we're ready for the
19   Prince of Peace to come.
20
21   SCENE V
22
23 *AT RISE:*   The manger tableau with MARY, JOSEPH, BABY,
24   MICHAEL, GABRIEL, SERENA, STELLA and TERRA. The
25   ANGEL CHORUS and CHORA sing. The SHEPHERDS arrive.
26   If desired, there can be another song after which the WISE
27   MEN and IRANIA come. ROMANUS, the INNKEEPERS,
28   HOUSEOWNER and any other TOWNSPEOPLE can also come.
29   After everyone else is set, TARDIA enters with the OLD
30   WOMAN and SMALL CHILD.
31 TARDIA: My, aren't there a lot of people! But you mustn't
32   be frightened. It's perfectly all right for you to be here.
33   After all, he's your Savior, too.
34
35

PROGRAMS FOR TEENS AND ADULTS

Angels, Please Come to Order
by ALEXANDER T. COYLE

CAST

GABRIEL

MICHAEL

URIEL

JOPHIEL

RAPHAEL

ZADKIEL

PASTOR
or Program Chairman

PRODUCTION NOTES

This is a play of words and character. Staging can be simple and direct. A large, conference-type table, chairs and a few well-placed lights should provide a most suitable setting in a chancel area of your church. Though chancels vary widely in design, each offers its own unique theatre setting suggestive of some celestial meeting place.

If your program requires presentation in a proscenium stage or in a hall, a simple background flat suggesting a gothic doorway will quickly and simply say, with the dialog, that the place is some heavenly sphere. The remainder of the setting would be the same.

Our players are all angels. There are no class distinctions in heaven so they are all dressed alike. White robes, if they are available, certainly would be appropriate. If you choose to be a little more theatrical, you might dress all the angels in white suits with white shirt, tie and shoes, or white dresses (there's no reason that ladies can't be angels, too). This sort of costume can be quite striking.

Though there is not much support for the idea in the Bible, most of us think of angels as having wings. This, too, is a costuming option. If younger children are performing the play, angel wings seem to fit them more than with adults. Only the director can properly make these decisions, for he/she is the one who knows the mood and feeling he/she wants to communicate.

Character portrayal presents a unique problem to both the author and the actors in a play like this where all the players are angels and hence angelic. Nonetheless, there are some differences in the personalities of our angels. Gabriel is the most mature and so the most easygoing. He speaks with some deliberation and, of course, with courtesy. Michael, on the other hand, is rather impatient and aggressive. He will speak more rapidly and is always anxious to get things done at all costs. Uriel is the secretary-of-the-organization type. Jophiel is a little irresponsible but makes up for this with a large supply of initiative. Raphael is a loyal follower who finds satisfaction in reflecting his hero's (Michael) opinions and will glow for days under the light of an occasional kind word from him.

These angels never really show disrespect toward God or toward one another and do not become contentious in their meeting.

There are no petty, personal animosities between them because, as angels, they are incapable of these feelings. They are, however, divided by honest differences on the matter of respect for human freedom.

It is not required that the players memorize their lines, for the "field reports" given by the angels provide some excuse for them to be reading from a manuscript. Still, the best performances will be those in which everyone knows his/her part from memory and can pick up his/her cues crisply and with assurance.

Your own church director of music may well choose Christmas music other than the selections indicated in the script. It is important that he does review the music recommended in consideration of the total program or service of which this play is a part. Our own feeling is that the music between the acts should be bright and cheerful carols in keeping with the light spirit of the play.

The most important contribution to the success of this presentation will be yours. You know your audience, your players, and the mood you want to create. Don't hesitate to amend or add according to your judgment until everything "feels" right. When this happens, you may be sure you will have an appreciative audience as the reward for your effort.

Alexander T. Coyle

LIGHTING DIAGRAM

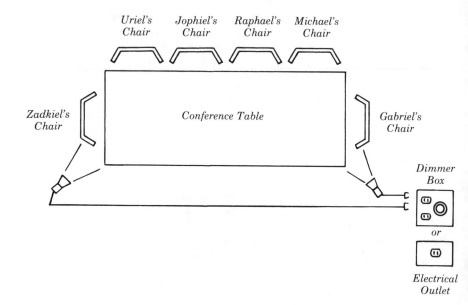

This play can be effectively lighted with as few as two spotlights as diagrammed above. They may be plugged directly into an electrical outlet or used with a dimmer box to fade in and out of each scene for that professional transitional touch. Lights should be at least five feet high so that their beams are not obstructed by the corners of the conference table.

MUSIC CUE NOTES

It is recommended that music be used to reinforce the mood of the entire presentation. It should be used preceding, following, and for bridging transitions as indicated in the script. Inasmuch as this is a Nativity story, Christmas music is most in order. Some of the selections that seem most appropriate to the subject matter include: *Oh, Little Town of Bethlehem, Away in a Manger,*

Joy to the World, We Three Kings of Orient Are, What Child Is This?

Each minister of music and each church may have other selections that they feel would be more appropriate to their presentation and congregation.

ACT ONE

(Organ prelude into brief organ introduction of "Hark, the Herald Angels Sing." Fade after first refrain.)

PASTOR: *(Or Program Chairman at rostrum or pulpit)* **In these years of new time and space dimensions everywhere about us, the participation we ask of you now should stretch your imagination hardly at all. Of course, we cannot vouch for the authenticity of the re-created celestial meetings you will soon witness, but we do know that the earthly events in discussion did most certainly occur almost two thousand years ago.**

(Lights fade up on empty table in center of chancel area. Six ANGELS file in crisply and stand for a moment at their places at the table. GABRIEL, in position of chairman, nods a cue and they all sit in unison except GABRIEL himself, who remains standing.)

GABRIEL: *(With gavel)* **Angels of the heavenly host, let the meeting come to order! We are meeting today for the purpose of briefing you on certain plans of the Almighty which will have far-reaching effects on the future of humans. However, before I say more, I wish to have you understand that, while the Almighty is very anxious to have his plans succeed, he is not willing to have you act in any capacity except as messengers and while ...**

MICHAEL: *(Interrupting)* **But, Gabriel, sir, I wish to enter a complaint and to remind you that we used to be allowed to take things into our own hands and not act like a lot of messenger boys.**

GABRIEL: **I can well understand, Michael. I know it isn't easy to stand by and watch humans make up their own minds.**

MICHAEL: **Well, then, if he wants his plans to succeed, why can't we just wade in and do it right?**

GABRIEL: **You must not be so impatient, Michael ...**

MICHAEL: **But it's agonizing to me to see humans make so**

1	many mistakes. Most of the time they do just the wrong
2	things and mess up the plans of the Almighty.
3	RAPHAEL: Mr. Chairman, I am with Michael and I call for a
4	vote.
5	GABRIEL: Now, just wait a minute! There will be no more
6	discussion — let alone a vote. We are meeting to hear the
7	Almighty's plan and his orders. I will now pass out your
8	messenger assignments. Uriel will now read God's message
9	to us.
10	URIEL: *(Reading)* "Angels of the heavenly host: I, the Almighty,
11	have now come to the point of setting plans in motion
12	which will make possible a new beginning for humans
13	and may result in their deliverance from evil. My plan is
14	that a baby boy will be born to a woman of Israel. He will
15	grow up and become the Savior of those people and finally
16	of the world. Humans will be free to accept his wise
17	counsel or reject it — and to accept or to reject him. If
18	they freely accept him, all will be well. If they reject him,
19	perhaps I will have to try again. My orders to you then
20	are these: Michael is to take a message to the temple
21	priest in Jerusalem, Zechariah, that he is to be the father
22	of a baby boy who will in his manhood be the forerunner
23	of Israel's Savior."
24	MICHAEL: Sir, if I may be free to refuse an assignment, I wish
25	to decline and ask permission to state my reasons at the
26	proper time.
27	GABRIEL: Since I am sure that the Almighty wants only willing
28	messengers in his service, I will release you, Michael, and
29	will notify Zechariah myself. Continue, Uriel, please.
30	URIEL: "Gabriel is ordered to take a message to a young
31	maiden by the name of Mary that she is to give birth to
32	a son who will be the long-expected Savior of Israel. And
33	finally, Jophiel is to carry the news of the birth of this
34	baby at the proper time to some of the most lowly
35	peasants in the neighborood that the common people may

1	first know of his arrival. These assignments are to be
2	carried out without interfering in any way with human
3	freedom and with no devices or tricks to control their
4	actions. So be it!"
5	GABRIEL: Are there any questions?
6	JOPHIEL: I would like to ask a question.
7	GABRIEL: Proceed, Jophiel.
8	JOPHIEL: Where will the baby be born and to whom in
9	particular am I to carry the message?
10	GABRIEL: I assume that you are to be on the alert to discover
11	the place of his birth and the time. Then you must choose
12	for yourself the audience of your announcement.
13	JOPHIEL: Thank you, sir.
14	GABRIEL: If there are no further questions, the meeting —
15	MICHAEL: *(Cutting in)* Mr. Chairman. If you please, I would
16	like to give my reasons for refusing my assignment.
17	GABRIEL: Go right ahead, Michael.
18	MICHAEL: Well, sir, it is not that I am in any degree rebelling
19	against the authority of the Almighty, but it is simply
20	that I object to the attitude of permissiveness toward
21	these humans. He seems to hold their freedom so sacred
22	that he is never willing to give them direct orders or to
23	force them into obedience.
24	GABRIEL: I'm sure the Almighty has good reason for this
25	approach, Michael.
26	MICHAEL: Maybe he does, Gabriel, but remember how
27	quickly we used to get things done. Remember when we
28	told Abraham what to do? We scared the living daylights
29	out of his boy, Isaac, when he thought he was going to
30	be a human sacrifice. And then what a stroke of genius
31	when he whomped up a goat to take the boy's place on
32	the altar! Those were the good old days when we could
33	push people around a little and make them do things.
34	And besides, if the Almighty wants to get things done
35	and wants this salvation business to succeed, he'd better not

be so all-fired gentle about it.

GABRIEL: I think you've made your point, Michael, but I still think that God knows his business better than you or me, or any of us. After all, he's had a lot more experience. I'm certain he knows what he wants to accomplish. Meeting adjourned. *(Gavel)*

MUSIC: "It Came upon the Midnight Clear," sung as an interlude.

ACT TWO

PASTOR: Four weeks later, as angels measure time, the meeting of angels convened again. Jesus had been born and each of the angels had done as ordered. They were all eager to give their reports.

(As lights fade up, ANGELS are busily chattering the news to each other.)

GABRIEL: *(Pounding with gavel)* **Fellow angels, let our meeting come to order.** *(Hammers with gavel and shouts to get attention.)* **Angels, Angels, please come to order!** *(Finally gets their attention.)* **I am pleased that you are so glad to see one another again, but let us proceed quickly to our business. It is time for your reports concerning your actions with reference to the Messiah's birth. Michael, will you please take the chair while I make two reports.**

MICHAEL: *(Taking the chair)* **Let us now hear Gabriel's report of taking God's message to Zechariah. He did this, as you know, because I had declined.**

GABRIEL: **Mr. Chairman, I went almost immediately after our last meeting to the temple in Jerusalem. Finding Zechariah performing his priestly duties there, I gave him my message while he was offering incense. Afterward, I realized that it was a stupid thing for me to do and that I should have waited. But I was so anxious to tell him the good news that I didn't think about what I was doing. You see, he and his wife were quite old. I**

- 107 -

1	thought it would give him reason for rejoicing, but
2	instead, hearing that his wife would have a son came to
3	him as a terrible shock. In fact, he obviously couldn't
4	believe his ears. When he told me that he didn't believe
5	me, I struck him dumb to prove my point. I am sure that
6	the Almighty will not approve of my action. Fortunately,
7	I did promise him that his speech would return when
8	their son was born.
9	MICHAEL: Thank you for your report, Gabriel. Frankly, I
10	regret that I turned over the assignment to you. You went
11	beyond your authority in striking Zechariah dumb. I
12	shall certainly report this to the Almighty when he
13	lectures me for refusing to go.
14	GABRIEL: I think that's hardly fair, Michael.
15	MICHAEL: You must admit that you acted as foolishly as a
16	human.
17	GABRIEL: And you were as stubborn as a human.
18	MICHAEL: That may be true. But this is a business meeting.
19	Let us proceed with decorum. Now, Gabriel, give us your
20	report concerning your visit to the young woman, Mary.
21	GABRIEL: I have a written report on this mission containing
22	a copy of a beautiful hymn of praise and thanksgiving
23	which expressed the feelings of Mary when she knew
24	that she was to be the mother of the Chosen One of God.
25	For now I will simply say that it was a source of great
26	joy to be the messenger of glad tidings to this sweet and
27	humble girl. Unlike Zechariah, she believed me. Her final
28	words were simply: "Behold, I am the handmaiden of the
29	Lord; let it be to me according to your word." Therefore,
30	Mr. Chairman, I was not even tempted to take any action
31	beyond the delivery of the message. I did better in this
32	mission.
33	MICHAEL: Indeed you did, Gabriel. The Almighty will be
34	pleased. I now gladly surrender the chair back to you.
35	GABRIEL: Thank you, Michael. Now, there is one more report.

1	Jophiel was assigned to make the announcement of the
2	baby's birth to some common folk as he chose. Please
3	proceed, Jophiel, if you will.
4	JOPHIEL: Mr. Chairman, my assignment turned into a real
5	adventure. I did a bit of investigating and I guessed the
6	time of the baby's birth pretty close. I decided then to
7	deliver the message to some fishermen on the Sea of
8	Galilee. But then, when the time of the birth came, I sure
9	had to speed around the country to find out exactly where
10	he was actually born. I should have consulted prophecies
11	but I was so sure that Mary and Joseph would remain in
12	Nazareth that it never occurred to me to expect anything
13	else. Well, there I was just arriving in Bethlehem when
14	the birth was already taking place in a stable. How that
15	ever came to pass I didn't find out at the time! I really
16	was on the spot and I flashed around the countryside to
17	locate some likely peasants. Of course, as my luck would
18	have it, it was nighttime and everybody seemed to be in
19	bed. *(Pause)*
20	RAPHAEL: Well, tell us, what did you do?
21	JOPHIEL: The truth is that I was desperate. But then I
22	happened to see the flickering of a campfire on a hillside
23	outside the village. And there were exactly the people I
24	wanted — a group of shepherds watching their sheep
25	nearby.
26	URIEL: How did you deliver the message?
27	JOPHIEL: Well, you know me, I sometimes rush in where
28	archangels fear to tread. So, of course, I flew in with a
29	rush and a blaze of light and scared them silly before I
30	even opened my mouth. As quickly as possible I tried to
31	reassure them and told them that I had "good news of a
32	great joy to all the people," and I announced the birth
33	right then and there. I wasn't sure that they believed me
34	so I called in our best choir to add a little inspirational
35	music to my message. You all would have been proud how

1   beautifully their voices filled the heavens with glorious
2   symphony of joyful music. So it turned out well in the end.
3   GABRIEL: Very ingenious, Jophiel. Did you stay around
4   long enough to see what happened?
5   JOPHIEL: Yes, sir, and it all worked out just fine. Those
6   bashful men and boys were so reassured that they went
7   to Bethlehem to see the child for themselves. They also
8   reported to Mary and Joseph what they had heard, which
9   was, of course, as good as a direct message from us. They
10   went back to their sheep in a bit of a daze I assure you,
11   but I don't think they will ever forget the occasion.
12   GABRIEL: Excellent, Jophiel! These reports will be turned
13   over to the Almighty and I am sure you will hear from
14   him. Is there anything more? *(Suddenly an ANGEL enters*
15   *the meeting. He is very much in a hurry and blurts out his urgent*
16   *message.)*
17   ZADKIEL: Gabriel, please, I have something to say that
18   cannot wait. Herod has given orders for soldiers to go to
19   Bethlehem and kill the baby Jesus. You had better do
20   something in a hurry.
21   GABRIEL: Now, just a minute, Zadkiel. This matter may not
22   be all that urgent. Even Roman soldiers require some
23   little time to get going. It is, after all, a day's trip to
24   Bethlehem from Jerusalem. Have you reported this
25   situation to the Almighty?
26   ZADKIEL: No, I haven't. I thought that you would know
27   what to do. I didn't think that God should be bothered
28   with this crisis.
29   GABRIEL: Perhaps we can handle this business without
30   special orders from the Almighty. Will you please brief
31   us on what happened before Herod gave this order?
32   MICHAEL: Mr. Chairman, I think that this is a time for
33   immediate action. We ought to stop talking right now
34   and act. My suggestion is that we go directly to the palace
35   and kill Herod.

1 GABRIEL: Just a minute, Michael. If I may say so, you often
2 talk before you think. You criticized me for striking
3 Zechariah dumb, but now you are suggesting we kill a
4 king. You know that the Almighty has said that we are
5 not to interfere directly.
6 MICHAEL: That may be so, but I say that if Herod has any
7 idea of laying his filthy hands on that baby — or any baby
8 for that matter — I am in favor of eliminating him entirely
9 — and now!
10 RAPHAEL: (Vigorously) I agree, sir, and call for a vote. (All
11 ANGELS catch the spirit of rebellion.)
12 GABRIEL: (Pounding) Angels, Angels! Order please! (Now
13 quietly) Raphael, must you always be calling for a vote?
14 I am chairman here. We are going to discuss this crisis
15 with some degree of sanity. We must obey the Almighty's
16 directive that we are to be only messengers and not to
17 take matters into our own hands! Now, let us hear the
18 rest of the story from Zadkiel — and please, no more
19 interrupting. Zadkiel, how did Herod come to give this
20 order to his soldiers?
21 ZADKIEL: What happened was that some men who make a
22 study of the stars and how they affect human destiny,
23 came the other day to Jerusalem. They had lost contact
24 with a star they were following and wanted help. Since
25 they believed the star was leading them to the presence
26 of a new-born king, they went to Herod's place. Since
27 there was no recent birth there, they were sent to
28 Bethlehem where the Messiah's birth was prophesied.
29 They were requested by Herod to report back to the
30 palace what they had found. When they did not, Herod
31 then gave orders for a legion of soldiers to go to
32 Bethlehem immediately. Their command was to kill all
33 boy children that no newborn king might survive.
34 GABRIEL: This Herod is a most evil king. We must find a way
35 to stop him.

1   URIEL: *(Quickly)* I would like to suggest, Mr. Chairman, that
2   someone be sent to Herod to tell him that this baby is no
3   threat to his throne. Maybe then he will call off those
4   soldiers.
5   MICHAEL: That's silly — he won't listen to that! *(Another*
6   *snap idea)* I suggest that we call for an epidemic of measles
7   or smallpox. Let's scare the soldiers right out of town.
8   GABRIEL: Come now, Michael, you know Herod would get
9   more soldiers from Caeserea.
10   MICHAEL: Well, let's get Herod himself. Give him leprosy
11   maybe. Or start a revolution in Jericho. Come on, let's
12   do something!
13   RAPHAEL: Mr. Chairman, I call for a vote.
14   GABRIEL: You are acting like humans — always trying to
15   use force and always threatening to destroy free-will
16   decisions. Let's remember the wishes of the Almighty and
17   be what we are, messengers — no more, no less.
18   JOPHIEL: From my experience in Bethlehem, I have developed
19   a lot of faith in following the Almighty's orders. I think
20   we should simply let these astrologers and the young
21   parents know what has happened. I feel sure that they
22   will act wisely and that all will be well. If we take things
23   into our own hands, humans will never be able to decide
24   anything on their own. They will always be nothing more
25   than puppets on a string.
26   GABRIEL: Absolutely right! I will take the responsibility for
27   ordering you to do the job. You have proven yourself
28   resourceful and I am sure that the Almighty would
29   approve. Is this generally agreed?
30   ALL ANGELS: *(Except MICHAEL)* Agreed!
31   MICHAEL: I still think we should clobber Herod. But since I
32   am outvoted, I will agree.
33   GABRIEL: This meeting is then adjourned, but we will
34   meet again as soon as Jophiel does his job. *(Lights fade.)*
35   *MUSIC:*   "Angels, We Have Heard on High" as an interlude.

ACT THREE

PASTOR: Jophiel did the job requested of him. And as he gave his report he had some surprises. The news he brought was both good and bad... *(Lights fade on as JOPHIEL is speaking.)*

JOPHIEL: Well, the good news is that Joseph and Mary have taken Jesus out of the country far from harm's reach. The bad news is that Herod did send soldiers to Bethlehem. They killed many babies hoping to get rid of any possible newborn king.

URIEL: I think that we should have informed Herod that Jesus would be no threat to his position. Perhaps we could have saved those babies.

ZADKIEL: Uriel, do not feel badly about this. Herod is a heartless and obstinate man who even killed a son of his own to avoid competition. I am sure that nothing short of assassination would have stopped him and the Almighty would not have permitted that.

JOPHIEL: Surely Zadkiel is right — and this sort of thing is the price of human freedom so dear to the heart of the Almighty.

GABRIEL: How did you deliver the message, if I may ask?

JOPHIEL: Well, I did it in the quietest possible way. You know that these people believe in dreams — so I simply slipped one of the astrologers and Joseph the word in their dreams. The wise men, as they are called, gave Herod the slip and made a detour around Jerusalem on their way home. Joseph, with the valued aid of gifts from the wise men, took off with his little family for Egypt. So the messages did the trick and Jesus is safe for a while.

GABRIEL: Thank you, Jophiel, for a good job. Anything else before we adjourn?

MICHAEL: Yes, Mr. Chairman. I still think that we could have saved some innocent lives by taking direct action.

1   **GABRIEL:**   Michael, I respect your right to your opinions.
2   However, our own ideas must not interfere with doing
3   our jobs. The Almighty will not allow anything to
4   interfere with human freedom. He has given men the
5   right to choose between good and evil knowing that they
6   will often choose evil and that innocent people will get
7   hurt. It is to win people to the good, not to force them
8   into doing good, that he has sent his son into the world.
9   So let us be messengers and trust in the Almighty.
10   **RAPHAEL:**   I call for a vote.
11   **GABRIEL:**   *(Amused at RAPHAEL)* **All right. All in favor of**
12   **adjourning say aye.** *(Large number of ayes)* **Opposed, no.**
13   *(MICHAEL and RAPHAEL feebly vote no.)* **Meeting**
14   **adjourned.** *(Lights fade out slowly.)*
15   *MUSIC:*   "God Rest Ye Merry Gentlemen"
16
17
18
19
20
21
22
23
24
25
26
27
28
29
30
31
32
33
34
35

Dateline: Bethlehem
by MARIAN DEAN EKIN

CAST

NARRATOR
THREE INTERVIEWERS
CAESAR
JOSEPH
MARY
SAMUEL
ABIGAIL
TWO SHEPHERDS
MELCHIOR
CASPAR
BALTHAZAR

PRODUCTION NOTES

This presentation can be staged either as a radio or TV news show. If produced as a radio news event, no costumes are needed. If staged as written, a few simple costume suggestions are included in the script. The "celebrities in costume" appear to be members of the audience, but it would be more effective to have the actors be "planted" in the audience beforehand. The feeling of audience participation will heighten the improvisational style of the script.

1   *(NARRATOR appears in front of chancel and picks up mike.)*

2 **NARRATOR:**   Good evening. **This is** *(Anchorman's name),* **and**

3   **we are leaving the twentieth century and through a**

4   **special device are taking you back in history to the year**

5   **six B.C. We have special correspondents here who are**

6   **going to help tell again the age-old story of the birth**

7   **of Christ. In order to tell this fascinating story,**

8   **members of the audience will be called on for several**

9   **parts.**

10   **First, let me set the scenes:**

11   **This is Bethlehem Central and our special**

12   **correspondent,** *(Newsperson's name).*

13   **This is Rome TV, for Octavius Augustus Caesar and**

14   **our Rome news correspondent** *(Newsperson's name).*

15   **This is the Voice of the Far East, and our**

16   **correspondent in residence** *(Newsperson's name).*

17   *(Pointing)* **This is a road outside Bethlehem. Later it**

18   **will become a hillside.**

19   *(Pointing)* **This is a motel run by Sam and his wife,**

20   **Abbie.**

21   *(Pointing)* **This is a garage or stable.**

22   **Now we need our actors for the production.**

23   **Throughout the sanctuary there are props for tonight's**

24   **drama. We will be asking some of the people near those**

25   **props to assume the character and help us.**

26   **The first character needed for the play is Caesar.**

27   **There is a red sash in the sanctuary. Who is nearest it?**

28   **Will you put it on and come to the studio in Rome? Thank**

29   **you.**

30   **We will need a couple to play the part of Joseph and**

31   **Mary. There's a couple just coming in. Pardon me, you two …**

32   **yes, you two … we need a couple for our play. I wonder**

33   **if you'd be willing to come down here and take these**

34   **parts? Thank you so much.** *(When couple comes forward, give*

35   *JOSEPH the robe and MARY the headdress to put on.)*

(*NARRATOR looks around again.*) **I see three men sitting together clear at the very back. You thought you'd get out of being in the play by sitting in the back pew, but I believe you'd be perfect for the parts of the wise men.** (*When they come forward, give them robes, crowns and gifts.*)

(*NARRATOR looks at paper for list of players.*) **Some gentleman who came in had the name "Sam" written on his program. Who was that? Oh, there you are. Well, you are Samuel, the motel keeper, and you'll need a wife for the play. Could you pick out a girl who could be your wife for thirty minutes or so?** (*MAN does, comes forward; fez put on him, scarf on wife.*)

We're just about ready to start our play. We need some shepherds. There's a large striped cane on one pew. Good. And there are two young men sitting there by it. You lucky boys will be our shepherds. (*They come forward and are given robes and crooks.*)

Now, ladies and gentlemen, boys and girls, you have met our cast. On with the play. This is (*Anchorman*) **of** (*Name of network*)**.**

The year is six B.C. What kind of a year has it been? Many events have taken place.

The Jews have pulled down the Roman Eagle from the temple gate. Although Herod has kept the peace for thirty years, tortures, executions, and murders are common. More than two thousand Jews have been slain by Roman soldiers for insurrection.

The king of the Jews in Jerusalem is Herod, who is not a Jew but an Arab from Askhelon.

Octavius August Caesar has just decreed that the people should be enrolled. We are covering that story from Bethlehem as people have been traveling here to be enrolled in the house of David. What kind of a day is it? A day like all days with events that alter and illuminate our times.

1   Bethlehem, Judea, six B.C.

2   In the studio in Rome, Augustus Caesar, the emperor,

3   has agreed to an interview. We turn to *(Newsperson)*, our

4   correspondent in Rome.

5 INTERVIEWER ONE: This is *(Newsperson)* in Rome. I have

6   here the great emperor, Augustus Caesar. Caesar, why

7   are you having so many people travel to Bethlehem?

8 CAESAR: As you probably are aware, not only are people

9   traveling to Bethlehem, but throughout the empire.

10   People are traveling to the town of their birth to register.

11   Under my leadership we shall become the greatest

12   empire in the world and this is a major advance in

13   history.

14 INTERVIEWER ONE: You are having this registration take

15   place in all parts of the Roman Empire?

16 CAESAR: Oh, yes. This will be a correct census. It will make a

17   most impressive listing of people. Persia to the east and

18   Egypt to the south are bound to take note of this great

19   undertaking.

20 INTERVIEWER ONE: Could you tell us just exactly what your

21   edict says?

22 CAESAR: Certainly. All people living in the empire under the

23   Emperor Augustus Caesar shall return to the place of

24   their birth for a registration. Each male head of a

25   household with the members of that household shall

26   appear in person before January first.

27 INTERVIEWER ONE: Why must this be done in person?

28 CAESAR: We want an accurate count. If each male head of a

29   household with his wife and children are actually there,

30   no one is going to escape being counted.

31 INTERVIEWER ONE: Isn't this a little rough on families with

32   little children making this trip, especially this time of

33   year?

34 CAESAR: Perhaps it is somewhat of a problem for a few

35   people, but it is a small sacrifice for such a great step

1	forward for the empire. On the whole, I think most of the
2	people are approaching the trip with a festive attitude.
3	After all, it has been a long time since most of them have
4	had the chance to return to their hometown.
5	INTERVIEWER ONE: Is is true, as some have reported, that
6	you want to register the people so you can establish a
7	method of taxing them?
8	CAESAR: I think the news media has blown this all out of
9	proportion. Do you know of any other kingdom or
10	empire in history that has attempted such a momentous
11	task as to register every man, woman, and child? Why,
12	the fact that we will be able to state the actual number
13	of people in our empire staggers the imagination and will
14	enhance our prestige among the other peoples of the
15	world. Of course, the knowledge we gain from this
16	registration will allow us to tax more fairly than we have
17	in the past, but taxing is a secondary function of this
18	project.
19	NARRATOR: Thank you, Caesar, for your time. So you have
20	heard the denial by Caesar that the primary purpose of
21	this registration is to form a tax base. I have just been
22	notified that we have a reporter stationed outside
23	Bethlehem and he has been talking to the travelers as
24	they approach the city limits. Are you there, *(Newsperson)*?
25	INTERVIEWER TWO: Yes. I am standing here on a road
26	outside Bethlehem. There has been a steady stream of
27	people going toward the city. Most are traveling by foot
28	or by donkey. There is a couple approaching now. Let's
29	see if they will stop for a moment and talk to us. Excuse
30	me, sir. Could you tell us your name and where you are
31	from?
32	JOSEPH: My name is Joseph Ben Jacob Ben Matthan. This
33	is my wife, Mary. We are from Nazareth in northern
34	Judea.
35	INTERVIEWER TWO: Are there others in your household?

1   JOSEPH: No. As you can see, we are expecting our first child.
2   INTERVIEWER TWO: You've made quite a journey coming
3   from Nazareth. That's almost one hundred miles. And the
4   weather has been quite chilly lately. Why are you coming
5   to Bethlehem?
6   JOSEPH: My ancestry goes back many generations. I am of
7   the great house of David so we had to come here to
8   register.
9   INTERVIEWER TWO: What are your feelings on coming to
10   Bethlehem?
11 JOSEPH: We're not really sure what to think. I've never heard
12   of this type of request before. I'm a little skeptical. It
13   sounds like just the beginning. First, they take a census
14   and then they'll levy a tax. Besides, it's a hard trip for
15   Mary.
16 INTERVIEWER TWO: Wasn't there any way that she could
17   have remained in Nazareth?
18 JOSEPH: I talked with some higher-ups and they couldn't
19   be bothered with exceptions. They said they had to treat
20   everyone the same.
21 MARY: I really haven't minded the trip, although after three
22   days on the road, I'm looking forward to a nice soft bed.
23   And it was cold camping out.
24 INTERVIEWER TWO: Do you have friends or relatives to
25   stay with?
26 JOSEPH: No, we're going to try to get a room at an inn but
27   we don't have reservations anywhere. We weren't sure
28   how long it would take us to get here. We've traveled
29   farther today because Mary is not feeling too well. I hate
30   to stop talking with you, but we must find that room.
31   We'd like to get settled very soon.
32 INTERVIEWER TWO: Thank you. We wish you luck in
33   finding accommodations. With the numbers we've seen
34   here you might experience some difficulties. OK,
35   *(Anchorman)*, back to you.

1   NARRATOR: Thank you *(Newsperson)*. **We're back at Bethlehem**
2   **Central. It is a great concern how all the people are going**
3   **to be accommodated.** I've asked Samuel Ben Amos, a
4   **prominent businessman who runs an inn in Bethlehem**
5   **and who is also an active Chamber of Commerce member,**
6   **to discuss arrangements the city has made for housing**
7   **the influx of people.** *(SAMUEL and ABIGAIL come up front*
8   *to talk to NARRATOR.)*
9   SAMUEL: *(After a pause, he makes an "official statement.")* **As you**
10   **are well aware, Bethlehem is a great city. A great place**
11   **to live and raise children. It also has some of the finest**
12   **inns in the country. In fact, my inn is, I can say without**
13   **bragging, one of the finest in the country. I had our inn**
14   **redecorated last summer and added four more units. It's**
15   **beautiful — really beautiful.**
16   ABIGAIL: **I'm sure anyone watching on TV will want to stay**
17   **at our inn if they come to Bethlehem. We're even talking**
18   **about putting in a swimming pool next year, aren't we,**
19   **Samuel?**
20   SAMUEL: **Yes, indeed we are.**
21   NARRATOR: **I appreciate your enthusiasm for your city and**
22   **your inn, but will you and your fellow innkeepers be able**
23   **to accommodate as many as you expect?**
24   SAMUEL: **Well, I certainly don't foresee any difficulties.**
25   NARRATOR: **Is there any truth to the rumor that the prices**
26   **have been inflated?**
27   SAMUEL: **Sir, you can't deny a businessman a profit. At my**
28   **inn we serve the finest quality food and offer attractively**
29   **decorated rooms. I have made quite an investment in the**
30   **best for high-quality patronage. We accept Bank Rom-a-**
31   **Card and Rome Express travelers checks.**
32   NARRATOR: **Thank you for appearing here at our studio.**
33   **We know how busy you must be at this time. We shall**
34   **talk with you again at your place of business.**
35   *MUSIC BRIDGE:*   "O Little Town of Bethlehem" *(CHOIR)*

1   JOSEPH: *(At inn setting)* **Sir, my wife and I are desperately in**
2   **need of a room. Our first child is about to be born. Do**
3   **you still have a vacancy?**
4   SAMUEL: **You should have made a reservation before you**
5   **came. Especially if you thought a baby was going to be**
6   **born. Your situation can't be my concern. I have nothing**
7   **available. Try up the street.**
8   MARY: **But we already tried there.**
9   ABIGAIL: *(Pulls SAMUEL aside.)* **Samuel, have you no heart?**
10   **His wife — can't you see she's in labor?**
11   SAMUEL: **Look at the small size of their donkey. Look at**
12   **their cheap clothes. You know we must make a lot of**
13   **money during this registration. There are rumors at the**
14   **chamber that the new chain outfits might be moving in**
15   **on us.**
16   ABIGAIL: **Can't we at least offer them some of our stable**
17   **space? They are warm and they would be out of the cold.**
18   **We could charge a few dollars for that shed space and**
19   **you could still rent the rooms for more money.**
20   SAMUEL: **Excellent idea, Abigail!** *(Turns back to others.)* **We**
21   **can give you a warm dry stable space for half the price**
22   **of a room.**
23   MARY: **We'd better take it, Joseph. I don't think I have much**
24   **more time.** *(MARY, JOSEPH, INNKEEPER and ABIGAIL*
25   *go off to side.)*
26   *MUSIC BRIDGE:*   "Birthday of a King" or "Infant Holy, Infant
27   Lowly" *(CHOIR will briefly hum a verse of either.)*
28   NARRATOR: **This special coverage from Bethlehem is being**
29   **brought to you through the world-wide network of**
30   **International Broadcasting and** *(Your church name).* **Our**
31   **staff of correspondents are on the scene with first-hand**
32   **glimpses of what is really occurring in Bethlehem this**
33   **day that may change history. Now back to** *(Newsperson)*
34   **who is covering the human interest events of this giant**
35   **census undertaking.**

1   INTERVIEWER TWO: This is *(Newsperson)* back on the streets
2   of Bethlehem. Large numbers of people continue to arrive
3   in this overcrowded city but there are no groups or
4   individuals that demonstrate, for me, the strength and
5   character of these people as much as the couple from
6   Nazareth: Joseph and Mary. The young wife, Mary,
7   arrived here about two hours ago in considerable
8   discomfort for she was about to give birth to a child.
9   There was no place for her anywhere. All we know is that
10   they gratefully accepted some space in a stable. There
11   have been no further reports on her condition. Back now
12   to Bethlehem Central.
13   NARRATOR: This is *(Anchorman)* at Bethlehem Central.
14   Something unaccounted for has occurred over this city
15   within the past half hour. The sky is suddenly bright with
16   an unusually bright star. We are checking the national
17   astrological observatory but we have not as yet received
18   a statement from them. Many of the religious folks here
19   are saying that the occurrence has symbolic meaning.
20   Some are suggesting that it may have some tie-in with
21   an infant boy said to have been born in the stable to the
22   young woman, Mary.
23   Choirs have been singing "Alleluia" throughout the
24   city of Bethlehem since the birth was announced. Crowds
25   are gathering around the stable area of the inn in the
26   north part of the city. Let's talk to *(Newsperson)*. People
27   everywhere would like to hear your story about the new
28   baby. Is it a boy or a girl?
29   INTERVIEWER TWO: This is *(Newsperson)* at the stable
30   beneath the main building belonging to Samuel, the
31   innkeeper. This man standing beside me is Joseph who
32   arrived in this city with his wife, Mary, earlier this
33   evening. Tell me, Joseph, something of the child born to
34   your wife, Mary.
35   JOSEPH: The child is a boy as was foretold in the prophecy

1 of Isaiah which has come true this night!

2 INTERVIEWER TWO: What is this prophecy that you speak of?

3 JOSEPH: Our prophet Isaiah said that a virgin would have a
4 son. At first, I didn't believe Mary when she said that she
5 was with child before our marriage. Then in a dream a
6 spirit came to me and said not to be afraid. So we went
7 ahead with our plans and were married. I am glad that
8 we did. Mary is such a good wife, so pure and kind.

9 INTERVIEWER TWO: What name have you chosen for the baby?

10 JOSEPH: He shall be called Jesus . . . Emmanuel . . . That is
11 the name I was told to give to the babe who will be the
12 Savior.

13 INTERVIEWER TWO: There is a large crowd gathering and
14 the star is unusually bright. It's as light as day here in
15 this area. Why do you believe so many people are coming
16 here?

17 JOSEPH: The people who believe in the God of Judea are
18 well versed in the prophecies. They know that Micah
19 wrote that Bethlehem would be the city where the ruler
20 of Israel would be born. Those with great faith have been
21 awaiting the fulfillment of this prophecy. We all pray that
22 this child will be the king of all kings and will rule by
23 love and righteousness.

24 INTERVIEWER TWO: Thank you, Joseph. I am moving now
25 to the side of the young mother, Mary. Mary, we know
26 you aren't very strong yet, but will you answer just one or
27 two questions? All the world is interested in your infant
28 son. Could you tell us why this baby boy is so special?

29 MARY: Yes. Some nine months ago I was all alone and an
30 angel came to me saying, "Peace be with you! The Lord
31 is with you and has greatly blessed you!" You can imagine
32 how astonished and frightened I was. I was even more
33 astonished when the angel told me I would bear a son. I
34 didn't see how that could be because I had no husband.
35 But the angel assured me the Holy Spirit would come to

1   me and my son would be the Son of God.

2   INTERVIEWER TWO: You were already engaged to Joseph

3   at this time. How did he react to your news?

4   MARY: Many of his friends warned him not to marry me, but

5   Joseph's faith is strong and we were married. Joseph has

6   been very good to me.

7   INTERVIEWER TWO: Your husband is a carpenter. Do you

8   hope the boy will follow in Joseph's footsteps?

9   MARY: We'll go back home to Nazareth and I imagine when

10   Jesus grows to manhood, he'll be able to help Joseph in

11   the carpenter's shop. But he is the Son of God and he

12   may choose to serve his Heavenly Father.

13   INTERVIEWER TWO: Thank you, Mary. Now back to

14   Bethlehem Central.

15   NARRATOR: We have had many requests from our audience

16   for more information. Many want to sing praises to this

17   child in Bethlehem. We pause briefly now so that you

18   may participate with us in this expression of musical

19   praise.

20   *MUSIC:* "Joy to the World" *(Congregation sings.)*

21   NARRATOR: *(Newsperson)* has just notified us of another news

22   event on the outskirts of Bethlehem. Please come in

23   *(Newsperson).*

24   INTERVIEWER TWO: This is *(Newsperson).* From this location

25   we have just learned of a spectacular happening in the

26   sky. For an eyewitness account I have a sheepherder here

27   who will tell us what he saw. Sir, what did happen?

28   SHEPHERD 1: At first there was this big flash of light in the

29   sky. We saw that it was a star . . . a superstar. Then a

30   voice seemed to come out of nowhere. I was afraid that

31   I was hearing strange noises or that being out here with

32   the sheep was finally getting to me, but the voice kept

33   repeating the same thing over and over. You can still

34   hear it . . . listen . . . *(CHOIR singing softly: "Alleluia.")*

35   INTERVIEWER TWO: Yes, I hear it, too. It is amazing! It sounds

1   like angels singing! Surely this *is* an unusual night!

2 SHEPHERD ONE: The prophecy has come true!

3 SHEPHERD TWO: I have never known such things to happen
4   before! I think we should go immediately to where the
5   star shines most brightly!

6 SHEPHERD ONE: Yes, let's go there!

7 INTERVIEWER TWO: Can you leave your flocks and go into
8   Bethlehem at this time of night?

9 SHEPHERD ONE: The sheep are all bedded down; nothing
10   will approach them with such a bright light; it's almost
11   like day! Bethlehem isn't very far.

12 INTERVIEWER TWO: This is *(Newsperson)* returning you now
13   to Bethlehem Central.

14 *MUSIC:* "While Shepherds Watched Their Flocks by Night" *(CHOIR)*

15 NARRATOR: For those of you who may have just tuned in,
16   this is the International Broadcasting Network. We have
17   been on the spot with our correspondents in far-off
18   Bethlehem where very unusual events are taking place
19   tonight. A child has been born to a peasant family,
20   followed by a series of unexplained events. Most
21   astounding of all is an extremely bright star which hovers
22   over the site of the birth. We return you now to our on-the-
23   street reporter. Come in *(Newsperson)*.

24 INTERVIEWER TWO: This is *(Newsperson)* in Bethlehem at the
25   stable. I am with the two shepherds who left their flocks
26   and came to where the star hovers. What have you
27   shepherds found here?

28 SHEPHERD ONE: We found a baby wrapped in swaddling
29   clothes and lying in a manger!

30 SHEPHERD TWO: This is our proof! The Savior has been born!

31 SHEPHERD ONE: He looked so tiny to be a Savior of the
32   whole world!

33 INTERVIEWER TWO: What do you plan to do now?

34 SHEPHERD TWO: We will return to our flocks and we will
35   tell all we meet of the events of this marvelous night!

1   INTERVIEWER TWO: Thank you. Now back to Bethlehem Central.
2   NARRATOR: Bethlehem Central reporting. Our network
3   executive producer has been contacted by our
4   correspondent from the Orient. He is quite excited about
5   developments there. It seems there are some related
6   events in far off Persia which have a bearing on this
7   story. We take you now to *(Newsperson)* in Persia.
8   INTERVIEWER THREE: This is *(Newsperson)* in Persia. Yes, I
9   have just been talking to three wise men here. Very
10   learned men. They spend their time studying the stars.
11   Let us talk with these astrologers from the East. What
12   are your names?
13 MELCHIOR: I am Melchior and I have never seen such a
14   meeting of the stars as in the horoscope of the newborn
15   child in Judea.
16 CASPAR: Caspar is my name. And it is my belief that it is
17   written in the stars that this child will have a kingdom
18   much larger than Caesar's.
19 BALTHAZAR: Balthazar's my name. They say power and love
20   will live together. That doesn't seem possible. But we're
21   going to follow these western stars and invesitgate for
22   ourselves.
23 INTERVIEWER THREE: How long have you been observing
24   this new revelation?
25 MELCHIOR: They have been visible for two years. It took a
26   year to calculate their significance.
27 CASPAR: The constellations Orion and Great Bear have
28   never before been in this position.
29 BALTHAZAR: The new star is the brightest yet to appear,
30   anywhere.
31 INTERVIEWER THREE: Tell me about this new star.
32 MELCHIOR: For the past days it has been so bright we can't
33   use our telescopes. And it was moving westward. Now it
34   has stopped moving.
35 CASPAR: We have studied many ancient writings, including

1   the Hebrew. We believe that it is in fulfillment of the
2   prophecies made by Isaiah centuries ago. We think it is
3   shining over where a baby is born who will prove to be
4   a man who will change our world.
5 INTERVIEWER THREE: I see that you are ready for a trip.
6   Apparently you plan to follow this star. Surely your
7   journey will take days?
8 MELCHIOR: We're certain that the stars are over Judea.
9   When we get to that land, we'll make an appointment
10   with Herod and he should be able to give us a map of the
11   territory. That should speed our trip.
12 BALTHAZAR: We shall proceed with all haste possible.
13 INTERVIEWER THREE: I see that you all have gifts. Are
14   they for Herod?
15 CASPAR: No, we see Herod only as a means of getting
16   information. Our gifts are for the child.
17 MELCHIOR: And because we really believe this child is
18   greatly significant to mankind, we chose great gifts. We
19   are taking gold, frankincense, and myrrh to the baby.
20 INTERVIEWER THREE: Well, I certianly don't want to
21   stand in your way. Good luck on your trip. I hope you do
22   find this baby. Now back to Bethlehem Central.
23 *MUSIC:*   "We Three Kings" *(CHOIR)*
24 NARRATOR: As the day has passed, the story of registration
25   for Caesar's census has grown into a story of a birth that
26   fulfills prophecies. We will now ask our correspondents
27   to briefly sum up what they have seen today.
28 INTERVIEWER TWO: A child has been born in Bethlehem
29   tonight. I have talked with the parents who know the
30   child is someone special. There is an extremely bright
31   star shining over the city causing excitement and awe. I
32   also talked to two shepherds who feel this event is the
33   fulfillment of prophecy. I have heard angel voices singing
34   "Alleluia."
35   We are not sure how to explain these events but there

1   most certainly is great expectation and exitement in the
2   air.
3   INTERVIEWER THREE: I have interviewed three very wise
4   men from Persia. They study the stars continually. As a
5   result of their study, they are convinced that the new
6   star shining over Bethlehem in Judea is the sign of the
7   birthday of a king. They are taking precious gifts of gold
8   and frankincense and myrrh to the infant. They, too, are
9   full of great wonder and awe. Now back to Bethlehem
10   Central.
11   NARRATOR: You have just heard a special broadcast from
12   far off parts of the world, including Bethlehem, Judea
13   and Persia. We are convinced that the Savior of the World
14   was born this night, six B.C. *(All sing: "Go Tell It on the*
15   *Mountain.)*
16
17
18
19
20
21
22
23
24
25
26
27
28
29
30
31
32
33
34
35

The Promised King

a dance liturgy for Christmas

by JANET LITHERLAND

General outline for printed program:

(Names of individual participants and the hymn numbers may
be inserted)
Asterisks* indicate congregation stands.

Prelude

Solo: "O Holy Night" .... Soloist

*Invocation .... Pastor

*Carol: "It Came Upon the Midnight
    Clear ....

The Promise

Isaiah 40:1-5 .... Choir

"Lo, How a Rose E'er Blooming" ...... Dancers and Choir

Isaiah 9:2-4 .... Dancers and Reader

Isaiah 9:6-7 .... Choir

Dialogue .... Readers

The Anticipation

"O Come, O Come, Emmanuel" .... Soloist, Dancers
    Solo Dancer and Choir

"I Heard the Bells on Christmas Day" .. Instrumental with
    Dancers

Dialogue .... Readers

"Silent Night," Luke 2:1-14 .... Instrumental with
    Dancers and Choir

Dialogue .... Readers

The Fulfillment

*Carol: "What Child is This?" ....

"Bring a Torch, Jeanette Isabella" .... Dancers and Choir

"Do You Hear What I Hear?" .... Choir

Sermon: "What Kind of King? .... Pastor

*Carol: "Joy to the World" ....

*Benediction .... Pastor

PRODUCTION NOTES

Setting

Sanctuary is in candlelight, decorated with evergreen. Chancel area is cleared of furniture and lit softly, but fully, to illuminate dancers. A small lectern for pastor stands Down Right, off chancel platform behind altar.

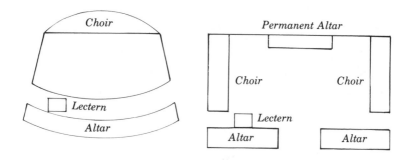

Center pulpit chancel   Split chancel

Participants

Dancers (four or more) may be both men and women, ages teen to adult. Costume: Black leotards — long sleeves and long legs with feet — covered by a sleeveless, below-the-knees tunic (purple to represent the Advent/Christmas season; may be trimmed in gold). If such costuming is not possible, dancers may wear calf-length robes. Stocking feet; no shoes. Women's hair should be fastened so it will not fall over the face in forward movement.

Basics for Dancers*

1. Begin with warm-up exercises and group meditation to establish the mood.
2. Follow the movement with the eyes; be expressive.

Basics for Dancers reprinted from "Let's Move Again," by Janet Litherland, © MCMLXXX Contemporary Drama Service.

3. Keep the mouth closed — interpretation is silent.
4. Move in slow motion, using entire phrases to complete the patterns.
5. Liturgical dance is worship, not entertainment.

Robed Choir is positioned in choir loft(s) as on preceding page. Carols and choral readings are performed by the same choir divided by the following designations: CHOIR, all members; MALES, male choir members; FEMALES, female choir members; READER 1, first reader; READER 2, second reader, etc.

SOLOIST is a member of the Robed Choir.

DIALOG READERS (3) may be members of the Robed Choir or actors who stand near the choir. Dialog is spoken to one another as in a play.

Resources

The carols chosen for this dance liturgy are found in most standard carol books and any hymnals. One carol book containing all the suggested music (except the special arrangement of "Do You Hear What I Hear?") is *Christmas in Song,* compiled and arranged for mixed voices (S.A.T.B.) by Theo Preuss, Rubank, Inc., Chicago. The same music is also available for unison singers with easy piano accompaniment in *International Christmas* by Ada Richter, Theodore Presser Co., Bryn Mawr, Pa. Many of the carols are found in *Fifty Christmas Carols of All Nations,* arr. Marzo, Willis Music Co., Florence, Ky.

"Do You Hear What I Hear?" — Suggested arrangement (words and music by Noel Regney and Gloria Shayne) is that of Harry Simeone for mixed voices (S.A.T.B.). It is from Shawnee Press, Inc., Delaware Water Gap, Pa. (Code A708). Another strong, uplifting Christmas anthem may be substituted if desired.

Scripture quotations are from the *Good News Bible, Old Testament:* Copyright © American Bible Society 1976; *New Testament:* Copyright © American Bible Society 1966, 1971, 1976.

1	PRELUDE
2	**SOLO:** "O Holy Night"
3	**One verse, chorus repeated as written. Dancers enter**
4	**sanctuary from all directions, each timing his entry so**
5	**that he may kneel at the altar on the first "Fall on your**
6	**knees." Sit up straight on knees, arms on altar, right hand**
7	**crossed over left. Focus straight ahead. Remain. When**
8	**chorus repeats,**
9	Oh, hear the angel voices
10	**Raise arms slowly overhead. Focus up.**
11	O night divine
12	**Hold position.**
13	O night when Christ was born
14	**Lower arms slowly.**
15	O night
16	**Hands in prayer position.**
17	O holy night, O night divine
18	**Lower head and hands** *(still in prayer position)* **to altar.**
19	*(PASTOR rises congregation for invocation and carol.*
20	*DANCERS rise, face congregation, arms at sides, until carol*
21	*ends.)*
22	***INVOCATION:** *(Pastor)*
23	**In a spirit of quiet joy, O Lord, we stand before you,**
24	**waiting to renew within us the unfolding mystery of your**
25	**birth. Through the beauty of music, the peace of**
26	**Scripture, and the grace of interpretation, may we**
27	**understand and appreciate our heritage in Jesus Christ,**
28	**our Lord . . . our King! Amen.**
29	***CAROL:** "It Came Upon the Midnight Clear"
30	**Isaiah 40:1-5** *(Choir)*
31	**As Choir speaks, dancers divide and enter chancel**
32	**platform from both sides, arriving in a circle, facing**
33	**inward. Drop slowly to full kneel, sitting on heels, hands**
34	**on knees. Lower the body until head rests on floor. This**
35	**should be timed to finish as the reading finishes.**

1	CHOIR: *(All)* "Comfort my people," says our God. "Comfort
2	them!"
3	FEMALES: Encourage the people of Jerusalem. Tell them
4	they have suffered long enough and their sins are now
5	forgiven.
6	CHOIR: *(All)* A voice cries out,
7	READER 1: Prepare in the wilderness a road for the Lord!
8	READER 2: Clear the way in the desert for our God!
9	READER 3: Fill every valley; level every mountain.
10	FEMALES: The hills will become a plain, and the rough
11	country will be made smooth.
12	MALES: Then the glory of the Lord will be revealed, and all
13	mankind will see it.
14	CHOIR: The Lord himself has promised this.
15	CHOIR: "Lo, How a Rose E'er Blooming"
16	Lo, how a rose e'er blooming from tender stem hath sprung
17	**Dancers rise to full kneel, arms at sides, focus toward**
18	**center of circle.**
19	Of Jesse's lineage coming as men of old have sung
20	**Raise arms overhead. Focus up.**
21	It came, a flow'ret bright
22	**Arms remain up but widen to clasp hands with person**
23	**on each side. Focus up.**
24	Amid the cold of winter
25	**Right foot smoothly on floor, preparing to rise. Hands**
26	**remain up and clasped to help brace the rise.**
27	When half-spent was the night
28	**Rise to feet, arms and hands in same position.**
29	Isaiah 'twas foretold it, the rose I have in mind
30	**Lower arms and circle slowly right.**
31	With Mary we behold it
32	**Release hands. Face center and walk toward it, forming**
33	**a close circle.**
34	The Virgin Mother kind
35	**Hold position. Hands slowly rise upward from center.**

1   To shew God's love aright

2   **Turn in place. Close circle now faces outward, hands still**

3   **up high.**

4   She bore to men a Saviour

5   **Widen the circle with four steps outward as arms lower**

6   **to waist level, outstretched, palms up.**

7   When half-spent was the night

8   **Arms slowly to sides as head bows.**

9   **Isaiah 9:2-4** *(Solo Reader)*

10   *(NOTE TO READER: Do not watch the dancers or wait for their*

11   *movements. They must conform to your expressive reading.)*

12   The people who walked in darkness have seen a great light.

13   **Dancers hands move up to cover eyes.**

14   They lived in a land of shadows,

15   **Head up toward "light," hands still over eyes.**

16   But now light is shining on them.

17   **Open arms to expose face.**

18   You have given them great joy, Lord.

19   **Hands out, around, and down, ending in a clap after the**

20   **word, "Lord."**

21   You have made them happy.

22   **Repeat above motion, ending in clap after "happy."**

23   They rejoice in what you have done,

24   **Hands still together from clap; raise them upward.**

25   As people rejoice when they harvest grain or when they divide

26   captured wealth.

27   **Arms lower to waist level. Turn in place, arms gracefully**

28   **following.**

29   For you have broken the yoke that burdened them and the rod that

30   beat their shoulders.

31   **With arms at sides, move into two lines, staggered so that**

32   **all are visible, backs to congregation. Remain in this**

33   **position until choir finishes reading and dialogue is**

34   **complete.**

35

1   **Isaiah 9:6-7** *(Choir)*

2   **FEMALES:** A child is born to us!

3   **MALES:** A son is given to us!

4   **CHOIR:** And he will be our ruler. He will be called Wonderful
5   Counselor,

6   **MALES:** Mighty God,

7   **CHOIR:** Eternal Father,

8   **FEMALES:** Prince of Peace.

9   **CHOIR:** His royal power will continue to grow; his kingdom
10   will always be at peace. He will rule as King David's
11   successor, basing his power on right and justice, from
12   now until the end of time.

13   **Dialogue:** *(Readers)*

14   **READER 1:** Did you hear that? We've been promised a king!
15   What kind of king do you suppose he will be?

16   **READER 2:** A great political leader, of course. You heard the
17   the Scripture. ". . . basing his power on right and justice,
18   from now until the end of time." Just think — a king to
19   restore our nation to its former glory!

20   **READER 3:** Not that kind of king! Our Messiah will be a
21   wonderful counselor, a mighty God. He will have power
22   to relieve us of this terrible famine we find ourselves in,
23   and, no doubt, he will bring the Romans to their knees
24   for the miserable tax burden they've placed upon us.

25   **READER 1:** I think you're both right, but I see our new king
26   as being even more powerful. I look for a miracle worker,
27   a king who will solve all injustice. No more poverty, no
28   more disease, no more —

29   **READER 2:** *(Interrupting)* Sorry, but I must disagree. After all,
30   a king is only a king. He will have power, sure. But
31   miracles? *(Sarcastically)* That's a bit much.

32   **READER 1:** Guess we'll just have to wait and see, won't we?

33   **CHOIR:** "O Come, O Come, Emmanuel"

34   *(SUGGESTIONS FOR CHOIR DIRECTOR: Have a soloist sing*
35   *the verses as a chant, unaccompanied. Choir sings only the refrain,*

1   *in parts. This song should move along smoothly and not too*
2   *slowly.)*
3   **A Solo Dancer turns, steps forward, and freely interprets**
4   **the words of Verse 1, using imaginative arm and body**
5   **movement. Dancers remain with backs to congregation.**
6   **On refrain, Solo Dancer faces other dancers, back to**
7   **congregation, and remain still.**
8 Rejoice
9   **Dancers face front, arms up.**
10 Rejoice
11   **"Reinforce" the arms-up gesture by dipping arms just**
12   **slightly and stretching high again.**
13 Emmanuel shall come to thee
14   **Arms lower slowly to sides, then rise to waist level, palms**
15   **up on "come."**
16 O Israel
17   **Arms cross over chest, head bowed.**
18   **Dancers hold position as Solo Dancer interprets another**
19   **verse. Repeat refrain beginning with "arms up." Solo**
20   **Dancer returns to place, joining other dancers during**
21   **final refrain.** *(Use as many verses as desired.)*
22 **INSTRUMENTAL WITH DANCERS:** "I Heard the Bells on
23   Christmas Day"
24   *(If the church has a handbell choir, this would be most effective.*
25   *Bells could be positioned on sanctuary floor at one side, or*
26   *divided — one table one each side. Organ, piano, or flute may be*
27   *substituted for handbells. Two verses.)*
28   *NOTE: Interpretation would be more dramatic if each row of*
29   *dancers performed in opposing directions, one row as printed*
30   *below, the other in reverse. Words, though not sung, are printed*
31   *to aid dancers in learning:*
32 I heard the bells on Christmas day their old familiar carols play
33   **Raise head very slowly. Focus out with increasing**
34   **awareness and wonder.**
35 And wild and sweet

1	**Step right on "wild," right hand to right ear on "sweet,"**
2	**left arm at side.**
3	The words repeat
4	**Reverse above movement.**
5	Of peace on earth
6	**Right hand meets left, high up left. Together they sweep**
7	**up, right, out, and around to down left.**
8	Good will to men
9	**Right hand moves right at waist level, palm down, ending**
10	**down right.**
11	Then pealed the bells more loud and deep: God is not dead, nor doth
12	he sleep
13	**Step left on "pealed" with arms up left, hands together**
14	**as if grasping a bell rope. Bring arms down right on**
15	**"bells," rocking weight back onto right leg. Repeat the**
16	**pulling motion: up left on "loud," down right on "deep,"**
17	**up left on "is," down right on "dead," up left on "doth,"**
18	**down right on "sleep."**
19	The wrong shall fail
20	**Turn the face left, placing right hand against right cheek,**
21	**palm out.**
22	The right prevail
23	**Face out, arms down and out at sides, fists clenched in**
24	**strong position.**
25	With peace on earth
26	**Right hand meets left, high up left. Together they sweep**
27	**up, right, out, and around to down left.**
28	Good will to men
29	**Right hand moves right at waist level, palm down, ending**
30	**down right.**
31	*(During next dialog, dancers divide, moving quietly to sides of*
32	*stage, where they sit, listening.)*
33	**Dialog:** *(Readers)*
34	**READER 1: Listen to everyone! I have more news about the**
35	**promised king.**

1   READER 2:   What is it?

2   READER 1:   Something I heard in the marketplace. It goes

3   like this: "Fling wide the gates, open the ancient doors,

4   and the great king will come in. Who is this great king?

5   He is the Lord, strong and mighty, the Lord, victorious

6   in battle."

7   READER 2:   What did I tell you! A political leader!

8   READER 3:   I heard something similar. Folks were talking

9   about the "triumphant" Lord. But to me that means

10   economic relief. As far as I'm concerned, there won't be

11   any "battles" until there are soldiers who are physically

12   able.

13   *("Silent Night" begins here.)*

14   READER 1:   Be quiet. Something's happening. Perhaps there

15   will be more news. Shhh!

16   INSTRUMENTAL WITH DANCERS AND CHOIR: "Silent Night"

17   Luke 2:1-14   *(Choir)*

18   Music plays softly on organ or piano and continues under

19   Scripture reading. Two dancers from one side of stage rise

20   and move center, pantomiming the parts of Mary and

21   Joseph. They form a tableau — Joseph standing; Mary

22   kneeling, cradling imaginary baby in her arms. She may

23   gently rock the baby. Joseph should be attentive —

24   pat Mary's shoulder, touch baby's cheek, etc. He may even

25   take baby from Mary for a few seconds, cuddle him gently,

26   then return him. As Scripture finishes, Mary and Joseph

27   remain in place. *(NOTE: Joseph does not have to be a male*

28   *dancer. Expression of idea is more important than actual*

29   *representation.)*

30   READER 1:   At that time Emperor Augustus ordered a census

31   to be taken throughout the Roman Empire. When this first

32   census took place, Quirinius was the governor of Syria.

33   Everyone, then, went to register himself, each to his own

34   home town.

35   READER 2:   Joseph went from the town of Nazareth in Galilee

to the town of Bethlehem in Judea, the birthplace of King David. Joseph went there because he was a descendant of David. He went to register with Mary, who was promised in marriage to him.

READER 3: She was pregnant, and while they were in Bethlehem, the time came for her to have her baby. She gave birth to her first son, wrapped him in cloths and laid him in a manger — there was no room for them to stay in the inn.

READER 4: There were some shepherds in that part of the country who were spending the night in the fields, taking care of their flocks. An angel of the Lord appeared to them, and the glory of the Lord shone over them. They were terribly afraid, but the angel said to them:

READER 5: Don't be afraid! I am here with good news for you, which will bring great joy to all the people. This very day in David's town your Savior was born — Christ the Lord! And this is what will prove it to you: you will find a baby wrapped in cloths and lying in a manger.

READER 6: Suddenly a great army of heaven's angels appeared with the angel, singing praises to God.

CHOIR: Glory to God in the highest heaven, and peace on earth to those with whom he is pleased!

Dialogue: *(Readers)*

READER 3: Wait! This can't be right. We were promised a king!

READER 2: And we were given a baby. In a manger, no less. I thought we'd be restored to our former glory. This certainly isn't glorious!

READER 3: And I thought we'd be given a king to lift our burdens. With any luck, our burdens will have disappeared long before this baby grows up!

READER 1: And I expected a miracle worker . . . Who is this child, anyway?

(CHOIR rises, their director indicating that congregation rise.)

1   ***CAROL:**   "What Child Is This?" *(Congregation is seated after carol*
2   *is sung.)*
3   **CHOIR:**   "Bring a Torch, Jeanette Isabella"
4   *(NOTE: Words to this carol may vary from book to book, but the*
5   *ideas are essentially the same.)*
6   **Two dancers from side of stage rise and pantomime first**
7   **phrases. One is Jeanette Isabella with a lantern. They**
8   **move center to see baby, motioning other dancers ("good**
9   **folk of the village") to join them. They admire the baby.**
10   **Dancers pantomime last verse, sitting quietly around**
11   **tableau as song ends. Joseph and Mary sit also. Remain**
12   **in place through sermon.**
13   **CHOIR:**   "Do You Hear What I Hear?"
14   **SERMON:**   "What Kind of King?" *(Pastor)*
15   **Young boys everywhere look forward to Saturday,**
16   **especially when Saturday promises a fishing trip with**
17   **Dad. For one such boy, the wait seemed endless. Each**
18   **night during the week he took out his fishing pole and**
19   **practiced imaginary casts — into his toy box, to the**
20   **bottom of the closet door, and behind the chair in the**
21   **corner. He would then pull the tackle box out from under**
22   **his bed, and, while inspecting each piece of fishing tackle,**
23   **he would dream about the fun and triumphs of the day**
24   **that was approaching much too slowly.**
25   **But when Saturday finally came, a fierce**
26   **thunderstorm came with it, ending a long, hot, dry spell.**
27   **The father tried to make the most of a rainy morning by**
28   **doing little household chores that never seemed to get**
29   **done during the week, but the boy could not contain his**
30   **disappointment. He prodded his father with questions:**
31   **Why? Why did it have to rain today?**
32   **"We needed the rain," the father answered, patiently**
33   **attempting to appease his son. "God is blessing us with**
34   **the wonders of his creation."**
35   **But the boy refused to allow anything to ease his**

disappointment. "If God is as good as you say he is," he replied, "he should have known how important today was and held off the rain until after our fishing trip."

At midday the storm ended as abruptly as it began, and the sun came out so strong as to boil the water on the pavement into mist. The fishing gear was quickly packed!

Because so much love was compressed into so short a time, the boy's afternoon of fun and fishing with his father exceeded his expectations, and, when they returned home, his joy and excitement bubbled out, sparing his mother no details.

That evening as the family bowed their heads in thanks, the boy added a P.S.: "Lord, I'm sorry if I was a little grumpy this morning. I just couldn't see far enough ahead."

The boy's experience is not uncommon to humanity, as we often dream of future events. Expectations arising out of either need or desire determine how we view the experiences of our lives, and the tragedy of the situation is that we all too often don't seek or expect the things that are best for us. We either don't have the ability to "see far enough ahead" or we are so wrapped up in the events of the moment that we don't want to look ahead. Such was the situation faced by mankind as the zero hour of history dawned and God intervened. When God sent his son, he was not accepted by many as the Messiah, the King of the Jews, because he was not the kind of king they expected.

There were those who were looking for a political leader, a king who could throw off the yoke of foreign oppression by driving out the Romans. Israel had historically been caught and tormented by the emerging empires of Africa and Eastern Asia. Only under David and Solomon was the nation politically strong enough to

develop a national personality that a patriot could point
to with pride. They lived each day in the hope that their
Messiah would be a political savior who would restore
the glory of Israel.

Unfortunately, they missed the true point of their
history. Their identity was not to be found as the political
"tough guys" but rather as God's chosen people, the
medium through which he would deliver his Truth and
Light.

Another segment of the Hopeful were looking for
relief from the desperate economic state in which they
were ensnared. The land of milk and honey given by God
into the hands of Joshua was no longer a land of
abundance. The past six centuries of struggle had taken
a devastating toll on the land, and what goods could still
be produced were so heavily drained under the Roman
system of taxation that the children of Israel were
surviving only by the barest of margins. Poverty was the
norm for the largest portion of society, but there was a
wealthy class who had, for the most part, aligned
themselves with their Roman rulers. This situation
embittered the political activists and provided fuel for
their revolutionary zeal, but the larger portion of the
populace had lost their will to fight, hoping only for an
economic savior who would deliver them from their
desperation.

Still others were looking for the God of the Exodus to
deliver a "Worker of Miracles" savior who would solve
all their problems and again allow them to experience a
promised land flowing with milk and honey. Their
problems covered the whole spectrum of human
experience and many believers felt that their only hope
of deliverance was for the nation to rediscover the
religious experience of their forefathers. They were
convinced that God, on seeing their repentance, would

send another Moses to deliver them from their oppressors and provide them with all the joys of the promised land.

The tragedy of these people lay not in the fact that they looked for a Messiah to provide relief from current problems, but rather that their current problems obscured their understanding of what "deliverance" meant, causing them to miss the Messiah sent by God. He didn't fit their expectations; therefore, he couldn't be the real Messiah. They could not see far enough ahead to recognize that the deliverance offered by Jesus of Nazareth would transcend current problems and provide a state of peace and wholeness lasting to the end of the age. Solutions to the current political and economic problems would provide only a temporary deliverance. In succeeding years the political oppression and economic depravity could return. The interpretation of God's self-disclosure through the nation's history had been misunderstood by the religious leaders of the day. There was need for a new understanding, evidenced later by Jesus' teachings. To look to a former age — the "good old days" — as a solution to contemporary problems, is to ignore the fact that time changes all earthly situations and that God's progressive revelation in Jesus provides an experience to sustain mankind for all time in a way that no understanding of an earlier age could do.

God in Jesus had provided the means through which man could be forgiven the sins of the past and, through his grace, begin as a new child of God. Under the ministry of the Holy Spirit this new creation could discover the contentment that would transcend political, economic, or social circumstances. God had sent a Spiritual King who provided an answer beyond the expectations of his people. But they were "a little grumpy" that day. They were disappointed that God didn't understand their situation.

And they missed God's greatest gift — his only son.

They couldn't see far enough ahead to understand what it was that God had done for them, and their relationship with their creator was too distant to allow them to recognize and accept his son on faith.

They missed the king because he didn't fit their expectations.

They missed the Gift of Life because they longed for power, money, and spectacular answers.

Their fate was determined by the kind of king they sought.

What kind of king do you seek?

(PASTOR rises congregation. CHOIR rises. DANCERS [including Mary and Joseph] rise.)

*CAROL: "Joy to the World"

As congregation sings verse 1, dancers join hands and circle right (two steps per measure or sixteen steps), raising clasped hands on "king." With clasped hands still up, circle left for sixteen more steps. On last phrase (last eight steps) release hands and twirl individually in place, hands still up. Stand facing congregation, arms down, if verses 2 and 3 are sung. Exit down center aisle during last verse.

*BENEDICTION: *(Pastor)*

May the blessed peace of our Promised King, the Lord Jesus Christ, fill your souls to overflowing, not only during this, the Christmas season . . . but forever. Amen.

Recollections of a Birthday
by JANET MEILI

CAST

NARRATOR *(Older Mary)*
MIME ACTORS

SECTION II
YOUNG MARY
MEN IN CARAVAN
YOUNG JESUS
SCRIBES & PRIESTS

SECTION III
YOUNG MARY
ANGEL

SECTION IV
YOUNG MARY
ELIZABETH

SECTION V
ZECHARIAH *(older man)*
ANGEL

SECTION VI
JOSEPH
ANGEL
MARY

SECTION VII
JOSEPH
MARY
INNKEEPER
SHEPHERDS
WISEMEN

PRODUCTION NOTES

This script is written as a modified tableau-type program. It may also be described as a mime-presentation with narrator.

This Christmas worship service dramatization is structured so that only minimum rehearsal is required. It also permits the participation of many church members of various ages.

Each of the recollections that comprise this program is titled. It is suggested that these titles be included in the worship program together with the carol selections that serve as a bridge between each recollection. It will help the congregation follow the action and interpret the mimes.

The mimes should be staged as a prologue to each section. The mimes are meant only to set a mood — to challenge the imagination of the audience to participate. If available, use a spotlight to direct attention to the mime actors immediately after each carol is sung. After their brief mime has been enacted, the spotlight fades as another spotlight directs attention to the narrator.

Do not try to mime the continuous scene in each of the sections. This will become ludicrous very quickly. If the actors want more than brief mime participation they should then speak the lines themselves.

The readings are from *Good News for Modern Man*. The citations are listed to allow you to use any version of the Bible you wish. The general tone of this program presupposes a modern translation.

The narrator is a woman portraying Mary's recollections.

The carols that bridge the sections may be sung by the church choir or the total congregation.

These staging directions may be modified according to your needs and limitations.

— Contemporary Drama Service

1 **OPENING CAROL:** *(Choir or congregation sings:)* "The First
2 Nowell" [traditional English carol] or "Unto Us A Boy Is Born"
3 [Latin carol 15th century].

4
5   **SECTION I (Jesus departs Nazareth)**
6
7 *(No mime lead-in. Spotlight on MARY at lectern.)*
8 **MARY:** *(Narrates)* **Today is my son's birthday. He is thirty**
9 **years old. This is an important milestone in our lives**
10 **because he is going to leave Nazareth to become a**
11 **traveling teacher. He won't be just my son anymore, but**
12 **someone of importance to the world. I don't know just**
13 **what that importance will be. I only know he was brought**
14 **into the world for a special purpose of the Lord's.**
15   **That's Jesus, my son, over there. You say he's very**
16 **handsome? Thank you. I think so, too, but what mother**
17 **doesn't say the same? He also has a very pleasing way**
18 **about him. People like him. He will be a success in**
19 **whatever he does. I can't really complain about his**
20 **wanting to leave Nazareth and become a teacher. Jesus**
21 **has always been a very good son. Up until now, he has**
22 **stayed home and worked in the carpenter shop**
23 **supporting me and the others in the family since Joseph,**
24 **my husband, died.**
25   **You may think it's only right and proper that he do**
26 **so, but some of our young Jewish men do not feel such**
27 **a sense of family responsibility. There are some young**
28 **hot bloods who hide in the hills and take part in the**
29 **insurrection against the Romans. They say that they do**
30 **this from their great sense of patriotism, to free our**
31 **country from Roman rule. That may be, but they are so**
32 **unlikely to succeed I personally think they are just giving**
33 **in to violence for its own sake.**
34   **But at least, they are doing something. Perhaps**
35 **some good can come of it. You can't say that about what**

– 149 –

1   certain others are doing. Those of a different type betray
2   their Jewish blood. They actually work with the Romans
3   and accept their money. And there are those who form
4   a middle group and have adopted some of the Roman
5   beliefs and rules to suit themselves. Jesus has been a
6   perfect Jewish son all his life. He was a very good student
7   of the law and attended the synagogue regularly. Jesus
8   has very strong opinions about what is right and wrong,
9   but somehow he never judges those others who are so
10   different from him. He's been waiting and preparing for
11   this time as I have too. He is leaving us with enough to
12   care for ourselves. He is ready now to do everything he's
13   been storing up inside himself. I'm not sure what this
14   will be but I do know it will be good and worthy.
15   *2ND CAROL:*   *(Choir or congregation sings:)* "Good Christian Men
16   Rejoice" [German-Latin carol, 14th century].
17
18   SECTION II
19   (The boy Jesus with the scribes and priests)
20
21   *SUGGESTED MIME:*   A different young actress portraying young
22   mother Mary is very distressed. She appears to be looking
23   everywhere for her lost son. Many men portraying a passing
24   caravan cross the stage area. Mary seems confused as they
25   indicate that they have not seen a lost boy. Mary returns to
26   Jerusalem and finds the boy Jesus standing among a group of
27   scribes and priests. The priests are in rapt attention listening
28   to boy Jesus.
29   **MARY:**   *(Narrates)* I remember the first time we took him with
30   us on our annual pilgrimage to Jerusalem for the festival
31   of the Passover. He was twelve. We had been on the road
32   for home a whole day before I realized Jesus was nowhere
33   in the caravan. I was just frantic. Joseph and I went back
34   to Jerusalem although all our friends and relatives said
35   we were foolish. They said if Jesus was so stupid as not to

1 be there when he knew we were leaving, we should let
2 him find his own way home. They said we'd never find
3 him in the crowds. But I insisted on going back.
4   Do you know where we finally found him? In the
5 temple, discussing the law, if you please, with the scribes
6 and priests. And the amazing thing was that those
7 learned and elderly gentlemen were taking the time to
8 talk to him, a twelve-year-old boy, seriously. They were
9 very impressed with his knowledge and attitude.
10   I couldn't help but scold a little. *(Luke 2:48)* "Son,
11 why have you done this to us? Your father and I have
12 been terribly worried trying to find you." Do you know
13 what he answered? *(Luke 2:49)* "Why did you have to look
14 for me? Didn't you know that I had to be in my Father's
15 house?" And he meant the Lord's house. Up until then,
16 Jesus had been such a normal son, it had been a long
17 time since anything had happened to remind me that he
18 was a very special person. But I had known he was, from
19 the very beginning.
20 **3RD CAROL:** *(Choir or congregation sings:)* "Angels, We Have
21   Heard on High" [traditional French melody].
22
23   **SECTION III**
24   (An angel of the Lord appears to Mary)
25
26 **SUGGESTED MIME:** Mary is asleep. Suddenly she is awakened
27   by a bright light. An angel appears. She is frightened at first,
28   then falls to her knees and listens as the angel speaks. She nods
29   acceptance of the message then looks upward briefly, then down
30   as her hands cross at rest at her waist.
31 **MARY:** *(Narrates)* **To help you understand, let me tell you the**
32   **story of his birth. Joseph and I were engaged but not yet**
33   **married when a strange and wonderful thing happened.**
34   **An angel of the Lord appeared suddenly one night and**
35   **spoke to me:** *(Luke 1:28)* **"Peace be with you! The Lord is**

with you and has greatly blessed you." Naturally, I did not understand. The angel then said *(Luke 1:30-33)* "Don't be afraid, Mary; God has been gracious to you. You will give birth to a son and you will name him Jesus. He will be great and will be called the Son of the Most High God. The Lord God will make him a king, as his ancestor David was, and he will be the king of the descendants of Jacob forever; his kingdom will never end."

I was astonished and replied *(Luke 1:34)* "I am a virgin. How, then, can this be?" The angel answered *(Luke 1:35-37)* "The Holy Spirit will come on you and God's power will rest upon you. For this reason the holy child will be called the Son of God. Remember your relative Elizabeth? It is said that she cannot have children, but she herself is now six months with child, even though she is very old. For there is nothing that God cannot do." *(Luke 1:38)* "I am the Lord's servant," I replied; "may it happen to me as you have said."

4TH CAROL: *(Choir or congregation sings:)* "Angels We Have Heard on High" [traditional French carol].

SECTION IV (Mary visits cousin Elizabeth)

SUGGESTED MIME: Mary and Elizabeth appear at opposite sides of the staging area. They stop when they see each other. After a moment's thoughtful pause, they open their arms and run to each other and embrace in great love and compassion.

MARY: *(Narrates)* **The news that my relative Elizabeth was to have a baby in her old age was very surprising to us all and, thinking she might need some help, I traveled to see her. She was very happy but not quite in the way I had expected. Her greeting to me was** *(Luke 1:42-45)* **"You are the most blessed of all women and blessed is the child you will bear! Why should this great thing happen to me, that my Lord's mother comes to visit me? For as soon as I**

1   **heard your greeting, the baby within me jumped with**
2   **gladness. How happy you are to believe that the Lord's**
3   **message to you will come true!"**
4   **I was very moved by her words which confirmed**
5   **what the angel had said and made clear to me that I had**
6   **not dreamed his coming. I sang a psalm of praise then.**
7   *(Luke 1:46-55)* **"My heart praises the Lord; my soul is glad**
8   **because of God my Savior, for he has remembered me,**
9   **his lowly servant! From now on all people will call me**
10   **happy, because of the great things the Mighty God has**
11   **done for me. His name is holy; from one generation to**
12   **another he shows mercy to those who honor him. He has**
13   **stretched out his mighty arm and scattered the proud**
14   **with all their plans. He has brought down mighty kings**
15   **from their thrones, and lifted up the lowly. He has filled**
16   **the hungry with good things, and sent the rich away with**
17   **empty hands. He has kept the promise he made to our**
18   **ancestors, and has come to the help of his servant, Israel.**
19   **He has remembered to show mercy to Abraham and to**
20   **all his descendants forever!"**
21   ***5TH MUSICAL INTERLUDE:*** *(A brief instrumental bridge is*
22   *suggested here in place of a carol.)*
23
24   **SECTION V (Zechariah refuses to believe)**
25
26   ***SUGGESTED MIME:*** An older man portraying Zechariah is
27   reading a scroll when an angel appears before him gesturing
28   that he will become a father. Angel "cradles" invisible infant
29   in his arms. Zechariah shakes his head in disbelief. The angel
30   stands back and points dramatically to Zechariah's mouth.
31   Suddenly Zechariah realizes that he cannot speak.
32   **MARY:** *(Narrates)* **I stayed with Elizabeth until just before**
33   **her baby was born. It was a strange time for her because**
34   **her husband Zechariah had been struck dumb in the**
35   **temple many months before. It was not until after their**

baby was born that we heard the whole story. Zechariah had been serving in the temple when an angel appeared to him and told him that Elizabeth would bear him a son. *(Luke 1:13-17)* "Don't be afraid, Zechariah! God has heard your prayer, and your wife Elizabeth will bear you a son. You are to name him John. How glad and happy you will be, and how happy many others will be when he is born! He will be a great man in the Lord's sight.

He must not drink any wine or strong drink. From his very birth he will be filled with the Holy Spirit, and he will bring back many of the people of Israel to the Lord their God. He will go ahead of the Lord, strong and mighty like the prophet Elijah. He will bring fathers and children together again; he will turn disobedient people back to the way of thinking of the righteous; he will get the Lord's people ready for him." *(Luke 1:18-20)*

Zechariah said to the angel, "How shall I know if this is so? I am an old man, and my wife is old also." "I am Gabriel," the angel answered. "I stand in the presence of God who sent me to speak to you and tell you this good news. But you have not believed my message, which will come true at the right time. Because you have not believed, you will be unable to speak; you will remain silent until the day my promise comes true." And Zechariah became mute until the day came to name the baby.

When he wrote that the baby was to be given the name of John instead of his own name, he was able to speak again and his words of praise were: *(Luke 1:68-79)* "Let us praise the Lord, the God of Israel! He has come to the help of his people and has set them free. He has provided for us a mighty Savior, a descendant of his servant David. He promised through his holy prophets long ago that he would save us from our enemies, from the power of all those who hate us. He said he would show mercy to our ancestors and remember his sacred covenant. With a solemn oath to our ancestor Abraham he promised to rescue us from our enemies and allow us to serve him without fear, so that we might be holy and righteous before him all the days of our life. You, my child, will be called a prophet of the Most High God. You will go ahead of the Lord to prepare his road for him, to tell his people that they will be saved by having their sins forgiven. Our God is merciful and tender. He will cause the bright dawn of salvation to rise on us and shine from heaven on all those who live in the dark shadow of death, to guide our steps into the path of peace."

6TH MUSICAL INTERLUDE: *(Another brief instrumental bridge is suggested here in place of a carol.)*

SECTION VI (An angel visits Joseph)

SUGGESTED MIME: An actor portraying Joseph is asleep. A bright light shines in his face. He awakens. An angel appears before him. He bows in awe as the angel gestures to the young Mary who is seen sitting at the opposite side of the stage. Joseph, at first, refuses but then at the angel's beckoning, he crosses over to her and embraces her. She smiles up at him.

MARY: *(Narrates)* **In the meantime, Joseph had found out that I was to deliver, a very scandalous happening since we were not yet married, and he wanted to secretly break the engagement and send me away until after the baby was born. But the angel of the Lord appeared to him and said** *(MT. 1:20-21)* **"Joseph, descendant of David, do not be afraid to take Mary to be your wife. For it is by the Holy Spirit that she has conceived. She will have a son, and you will name him Jesus — because he will save his people from their sins." So Joseph agreed to go ahead with our marriage as planned.**

1   *7TH MUSICAL INTERLUDE:*   *(Another brief musical bridge is*
2   *suggested here.)*
3
4   **SECTION VII (The innkeeper has no room)**
5
6   *SUGGESTED MIME:*   Joseph and Mary walk to an imaginary door.
7   They are bone-weary and weak. Joseph knocks. An innkeeper
8   opens the door and shakes his head. Joseph points to Mary. The
9   innkeeper gestures to stable at the side and below the inn.
10   **MARY:**   *(Narrates)* **Now as if things weren't confused enough,**
11   **the Roman emperor declared that a census be taken and**
12   **Joseph and I had to travel to Bethlehem. Bethlehem,**
13   **being the birthplace of King David, was a very crowded**
14   **village during the time of a census and Joseph was quite**
15   **concerned when the innkeeper refused us room in the**
16   **inn. He did offer us the use of his stable, an offer we**
17   **gratefully accepted.**
18   **Actually, it was a sheltered, private place for which**
19   **I was thankful because the baby arrived during our stay.**
20   **I wrapped him in swaddling clothes and laid him in the**
21   **manger. At first, all was peaceful and quiet. But then we**
22   **began to have unusual visitors.**
23   *SUGGESTED MIME:*   *(This mime proceeds as the narrator continues*
24   *talking.)* Shepherds travel to manger. They kneel to worship
25   child in the arms of Mary. Both shepherds and Mary and Baby
26   Jesus stay in view.
27   **MARY:**   *(Continues narration)* **The first to arrive were the**
28   **shepherds of the Bethlehem flocks. They explained that**
29   **while they were in the fields spending the night with**
30   **their flocks, an angel of the Lord appeared to them and**
31   **said** *(Luke 2:10-12)* **"Don't be afraid! I am here with good**
32   **news for you, which will bring great joy for all the people.**
33   **This very day in David's town your Savior was born —**
34   **Christ the Lord! And this is what will prove it to you.**
35   **You will find a baby wrapped in cloths and lying in a**

1   manger." And then an angel chorus sang a hymn of praise.

2   *8TH CAROL:* *(Entire congregation sings:)* "Away in a Manger"
3   [anonymous].

4   *SUGGESTED MIME:* Wise men enter the staging area and join
5   the shepherds worshipping the baby Jesus in Mary's arms.

6   **MARY:** *(Continues narration)* **But an even more amazing set of**
7   **visitors arrived some time later. Some astronomers from**
8   **the east came and brought expensive gifts. And the story**
9   **of why they came and how they found us was a fascinating**
10   **one, too. They had noticed an unusual star in the sky**
11   **and, according to their beliefs, this star signified the**
12   **birth of a king, so they followed it in order to worship**
13   **the new king.**

14   **The star seemed to them to stop over Jerusalem so**
15   **they went to King Herod and asked** *(MT. 2:2)* **"Where is**
16   **the baby born to be the king of the Jews? We saw his star**
17   **when it came up in the east, and we have come to worship**
18   **him." Herod called his priests and scribes together and**
19   **asked them** *(MT. 2:4)* **"Where will the Messiah be born?"**
20   **The priests quoted Micah for him.** *(MT. 2:5-6)* **"In the town**
21   **of Bethlehem in Judea, for this is what the prophet wrote:**
22   **'Bethlehem in the land of Judah, you are by no means**
23   **the least of the leading cities of Judah; for from you will**
24   **come a leader who will guide my people Israel.' "**

25   **So the wise men left Jerusalem and came to Bethlehem**
26   **where they found us. The gifts they brought were gold**
27   **and frankincense and myrrh. Such odd gifts for my little**
28   **son, but very proper, in their opinion, for the king they**
29   **thought they had found. Goodness, but it gives me an**
30   **odd feeling to remember all of this again — the angels,**
31   **the shepherds, the wise men, the prophecies that were**
32   **fulfilled.**

33   **Elizabeth's son is a prophet. He is prophesying the**
34   **coming of a savior. The name "Jesus" means savior. I**
35   **wonder if he's talking about my son? I don't exactly know**

how Jesus would save us or from what. Somehow I don't think it will be from the Romans. I don't know. I don't understand and I'm afraid. Perhaps I feel fear merely because I don't understand. So many things could happen — not all of them pleasant. The thought scares me. I don't want things to change. I wish I could always be as happy as I was the day he was born. *(The lights dim as the narrator, MARY, lights a candle and walks slowly down the length of the aisle and leaves the church sanctuary.)*

SUGGESTED MIME: Mary, the shepherds and the wise men remain up front in spotlight.

9TH CAROL: *(Entire congregation sings:)* "What Child Is This, Who Laid to Rest" [traditional English melody].

READERS THEATRE
FOR CHRISTMAS

Now Christmas Has Come
by MELVIN R. WHITE

CAST

Now Christmas Has Come can be performed by a cast of six readers, each interpreting a number of roles, or it can be read by some 20 or 30 readers, singers and dancers. The size of the cast depends on the director and how simple or how elaborate he or she wishes the performance to be. It is arranged so that units may be dropped for a shorter program, or music added to lengthen it.

PRODUCTION NOTES

This compiled script for Christmas includes three main items: "A Twentieth-Century Christmas Carol," "A Christmas Interview," by George P. McCallum; and a scene from the book *Mrs. Wiggs of the Cabbage Patch;* along with materials by Washington Irving, Robert Herrick, Christina Rosetti, William Shakespeare, Eugene Field, Francis P. Church and Martin Luther. It combines biblical passages, choral reading, traditional Christmas carols and dance (if desired) with poetry, prose and drama.

STAGING DIRECTIONS

Chairs for each reader may be placed on the performing area, either on the sides, at the back, or both. These may be moved about the stage as needed in the various scenes, either by members of the cast, or by a stage crew of one or two members. Transitions between scenes are accomplished by cast members either returning to their seats to freeze, or by turning their backs to the audience (noted in the script as BTA). If substantial changes are made in the script, it may be necessary to change and/or provide additional narration to the Master of Ceremonies and other narrators.

As is customary in Readers Theatre, performers move into the scene as they are needed, and retreat to their seats when not included in the unit being performed. If desired, the narrators may be provided with lecterns to rest their scripts — and with stools.

1	*(As "Now Christmas Has Come" opens, the cast comes Onstage*
2	*and is seated, the exception being the MASTER OF CEREMONIES,*
3	*who crosses Down Center to talk with the audience.)*
4	**MASTER OF CEREMONIES: Now Christmas is come,**
5	**Let us beat up the drum,**
6	**And call all our neighbors together,**
7	**And when they appear,**
8	**Let us make them such cheer,**
9	**As will keep out the wind and the weather.**
10	
11	**This is a song Washington Irving quoted in his essay,**
12	**"Christmas Eve," which he wrote after he visited in**
13	**England in 1815. Irving reveled in all the antique customs**
14	**he found in England which he had never seen in America.**
15	**Some of these English traditions are well-known to us**
16	**today, like the hanging of mistletoe, the serving of mince**
17	**pie and the singing of carols, as we have incorporated**
18	**them in our own traditions of Christmas. But to Irving**
19	**they were a delight, since in his day, Christmas was**
20	**scarcely noticed in America. Of the feast, he wrote:**
21	**WASHINGTON IRVING: Supper was announced shortly**
22	**after our arrival. Besides the accustomed lights, two**
23	**great wax tapers called Christmas candles, wreathed**
24	**with greens, were placed among the family silver**
25	**plate . . . I was happy to find my old friend, minced pie,**
26	**in the retinue of the feast; and finding him to be perfectly**
27	**orthodox and that I need not be ashamed of my**
28	**predilection, I greeted him with all the warmth**
29	**wherewith we usually greet an old and very genteel**
30	**acquaintance.** *(If period dance is desired, it may be introduced*
31	*with this excerpt from Irving.)*
32	**The dance, like most dances after supper, was a merry**
33	**one; some of the older folks joined in it, a rigadoon, a lively**
34	**dance with much jumping.** *(Insert here a period dance with*
35	*musical accompaniment, with the rest of the cast as audience.)*

1   MASTER OF CEREMONIES: Today, the old custom of dancing
2   at Christmas is not usually a part of our observance of
3   the birth of Christ. And yet, traditionally, 'tis a season to
4   be jolly!
5   SOLO OR CHORAL READING: Sing hey! Sing hey!
6   For Christmas Day;
7   Twine mistletoe and holly,
8   For friendship glows
9   In winter snows,
10   And so let's all be jolly.
11   ONE: The story of the first Christmas has been told and retold,
12   written and rewritten, true. But there is only one, and
13   no writer can improve on it: *(ONE steps aside, Down Right*
14   *or Down Left.)*
15   TWO: *(Rises to take a Down Center position.)* **And there were in**
16   the same country shepherds, abiding in the field, keeping
17   watch over their flock by night. And, lo, the angel of the
18   Lord came upon them, and the glory of the Lord shone
19   around them; and they were sore afraid.
20   And the angel said unto them:
21   ANGEL: *(Or TWO continues.)* Fear not; for, behold, I bring you
22   good tidings of great joy, which shall be to all people.
23   For unto you is born this day in the city of David, a Savior,
24   which is Christ the Lord. *(TWO and ANGEL return to seats.)*
25   ONE: *(Return to Down Center.)* True, that is the original story.
26   But so many stories about Christmas, about its traditions,
27   about the custom of giving gifts at Yuletide, and about
28   Santa Claus have become such a part of our celebration
29   of the birth of Christ, we hardly separate them from the
30   original story anymore. One of these is a letter which
31   appeared in the now defunct *New York Sun*, written by
32   a little girl whose friends had told her there was no Santa
33   Claus.
34   8 YEAR-OLD-GIRL: *(Reads letter.)* Dear Editor: I am eight
35   years old. Some of my little friends say there is no Santa

1	Claus. Papa says, "If you see it in *The Sun*, it's so." Please
2	tell me the truth. Is there a Santa Claus?
3	— Virginia O'Hanlon,
4	115 West 95th Street
5	ONE: In 1897, Francis P. Church wrote this beautiful response,
6	an answer to little Virginia that has become a famous
7	and well-loved classic?
8	CHURCH: Dear Virginia: Your little friends are wrong. They
9	have been affected by the skepticism of a skeptical age.
10	They do not believe except what they see. They think
11	that nothing can be which is not comprehensible by their
12	little minds. All minds, Virginia, whether they be men's
13	or children's, are little.
14	In this great universe of ours, man is a mere insect,
15	an ant, in his intellect, as compared with the boundless
16	world about him, as measured by the intelligence capable
17	of grasping the whole of truth and knowledge.
18	Yes, Virginia, there is a Santa Claus. He exists as
19	certainly as love and generosity and devotion exist, and
20	you know that they abound and give to your life its
21	highest beauty and joy. Alas! How dreary would be the
22	world if there were no Santa Claus! It would be as dreary
23	as if there were no Virginias.
24	There would be no childlike faith then, no poetry,
25	no romance to make tolerable this existence. We should
26	have no enjoyment, except in sense and sight. The eternal
27	light with which childhood fills the world would be
28	extinguished.
29	Not believe in Santa Claus! The most real things in
30	the world are those that neither children nor men can
31	see. Did you ever see fairies dancing on the lawn? Of
32	course not, but that's no proof that they are not there.
33	Nobody can conceive or imagine all the wonders there
34	are unseen and unseeable in the world.
35	Only faith, fancy, poetry, love, romance, can push

aside that curtain and view and picture the supernal beauty and glory beyond. Is it all real? Ah, Virginia, in all this world, there is nothing else real and abiding.

"No Santa Claus! Thank God he lives, and he lives forever. A thousand years from now, Virginia, nay ten times ten thousand years from now, he will continue to make glad the heart of childhood."

MASTER OF CEREMONIES: In earlier days in America, the Christmas pudding, so typical of England, was a part of the special Christmas dinner — and it is still found in many homes on that special day.

VOICE: "Into the basin, put the plums,

CHORUS: Stirabout, stirabout, stirabout!

VOICE: Next, the good white flour comes,

CHORUS: Stirabout, stirabout, stirabout!

VOICE: Sugar and peel and eggs and spice,

CHORUS: Stirabout, stirabout, stirabout!

VOICE: Mix them and fix them and cook them twice.

CHORUS: Stirabout, stirabout, stirabout!"

MASTER OF CEREMONIES: Yes, Christmas is a time for feasting, of that there is no doubt. From Robert Herrick and his "Ceremonies for Christmas," we hear:

VOICE 2:   "Drink now the strong beer,
Cut the white loaf here,
The while the meat is a-shredding;
For the rare mince pie
And the plums stand by
To fill the paste that's a-kneading."

MASTER OF CEREMONIES: And Christmas is a time for decorating:

VOICE 3:   "But give me holly, bold and jolly,
Honest, prickly, shining holly;
Pluck me holly leaf and berry
For the day when I make merry."

(Christina Georgina Rossetti)

1   MASTER OF CEREMONIES: Yet, while we feast and dance
2   and decorate and celebrate, we do remember, as William
3   Shakespeare reminded us:
4   VOICE 4: "Some say, that ever 'gainst that season comes
5   Wherein our Savior's birth is celebrated,
6   The bird of dawning singeth all night long;
7   So hallow'd and so gracious is the time."
8   MASTER OF CEREMONIES: "Why do bells for Christmas ring?
9   Why do little children sing?"
10   RESPONSE: "Once a lovely, shining star,
11   Seen by shepherds from afar,
12   Gently moved until its light
13   Made a manger's cradle bright."
14   2ND RESPONSE: "There a darling baby lay,
15   Pillowed soft upon the hay;
16   And its mother sang and smiled,
17   'This is Christ, the holy child!' "
18   MASTER OF CEREMONIES: "Therefore bells for Christmas
19   ring,
20   Therefore little children sing."
21   *("Song" by Eugene Field.)*
22   *("Cradle Hymn" by Martin Luther may be sung by a group of*
23   *little children at this point; it may be read by a cast member as*
24   *a spoken solo, or may be sung or spoken by the cast.)*
25   "Away in a manger,
26   No crib for a bed,
27   The little Lord Jesus
28   Lay down his sweet head;
29   The stars in the heavens
30   Looked down where he lay,
31   The little Lord Jesus
32   Asleep in the hay.
33
34   The cattle are lowing,
35   The poor baby wakes,

1   **But little Lord Jesus,**

2   **No crying he makes.**

3   **I love thee, Lord Jesus,**

4   **Look down from the sky,**

5   **And stay by my cradle**

6   **Till morning is nigh."**

7   *("Cradle Hymn," by Martin Luther)*

8 **MASTER OF CEREMONIES:** Fear not; for behold, I bring

9   you good tidings of great joy, which shall be to all people.

10   For unto you is born this day in the city of David, a

11   Saviour, which is Christ the Lord. And this shall be a

12   sign unto you; ye shall find the babe wrapped in

13   swaddling clothes lying in a manger.

14 **CAST:** Glory to God in the highest, and on earth, peace, good

15   will toward men.

16 *CHOIR:* (If a choir is available, here we suggest such carols as "Hark

17   *the Herald Angels Sing," "It Came Upon the Midnight Clear,"*

18   *"Silent Night" or "The First Noel.")*

19 **MASTER OF CEREMONIES:** Beyond a doubt, best-known,

20   most loved, most read, and most often produced as a play,

21   is Charles Dickens' story, "A Christmas Carol," with its

22   hopes for peace and goodwill. A favorite scene from

23   Dickens' masterpiece is Christmas Day at the home of

24   Bob Cratchit, Scrooge's clerk.

25

26 *CAST:* MRS. CRATCHIT, a pleasant motherly type, perhaps 35

27   years of age, a typical "homebody," outgoing and friendly; plain,

28   not well-educated. MARTHA CRATCHIT, a wholesome

29   ingenue, 15-18 years of age, but plain like her mother. PETER

30   CRATCHIT, the older of the two Cratchit boys. SECOND

31   CRATCHIT, the younger of the two Cratchit boys. TINY TIM,

32   a very small boy, ill and weak; may have a crutch. BOB

33   CRATCHIT, a middle-aged man of 35-40, rather thin and

34   beaten-looking, but pleasant in voice and manner.

35

1 *(The Cratchit scene may be played in a wide Down Center area.*
2 *If available, period costumes add tremendously to this excerpt,*
3 *but are not necessary, of course.)*
4 **MRS. CRATCHIT: What has ever got your precious father,**
5 **then? And your brother Tiny Tim? And Martha warn't as**
6 **late last Christmas Day by half an hour!**
7 **MARTHA:** *(Coming down into the scene, joining the two young*
8 *CRATCHITS and MRS. CRATCHIT)* **Here's Martha,**
9 **Mother!**
10 **TWO YOUNG CRATCHITS:** *(Ad-libbing such lines as:)* **Here's**
11 **Martha, Mother! Hurrah! There's such a goose, Martha!**
12 **MRS. CRATCHIT:** *(Kissing MARTHA several times)* **Why, bless**
13 **your heart alive, my dear; how late you are!**
14 **MARTHA: We'd a deal of work to finish up last night, and**
15 **had to clear away this morning, Mother.**
16 **MRS. CRATCHIT: Well, never mind, so long as you are come.**
17 **Sit ye down before the fire, my dear, and have a warm,**
18 **Lord bless ye!**
19 **PETER CRATCHIT: No, no! There's Father coming.**
20 **SECOND YOUNG CRATCHIT: Hide, Martha, hide!** *(MARTHA*
21 *hides behind MRS. CRATCHIT as BOB CRATCHIT and TINY*
22 *TIM enter the scene.)*
23 **BOB CRATCHIT:** *(After hugging his wife)* **Why, where's our**
24 **Martha?**
25 **MRS. CRATCHIT: Not coming.**
26 **BOB CRATCHIT: Not coming! Not coming on Christmas**
27 **Day?** *(Then, as MARTHA reveals herself, ad-lib greetings and*
28 *laughter by all as BOB CRATCHIT hugs and kisses his*
29 *daughter.)*
30 **MRS. CRATCHIT: And how did little Tim behave?**
31 **BOB CRATCHIT: As good as gold. Now, is our Christmas**
32 **dinner ready?**
33 **MRS. CRATCHIT: Yes, just waiting for you and Tim.**
34 **BOB CRATCHIT: Everyone, get chairs to the table.** *(Each*
35 *takes a chair to the imaginary table except TINY TIM; his father*

1   *gets one for him.)* **Here's a chair for you, Tim.** *(As they seat*
2   *themselves, ad-lib reactions to "Such a goose," "applesauce,*
3   *mashed potatoes," and "Mother made pudding too.")* **Now, a**
4   **toast!** *(General reaction of merriment)* **A Merry Christmas to**
5   **us all, my dears! God bless us!** *(Which the family echoes,*
6   *raising imaginary glasses high.)*
7   **TINY TIM:** *(The last of all)* **God bless us, every one!**
8   **BOB CRATCHIT:** **To Mr. Scrooge! I'll give you Mr. Scrooge,**
9   **the founder of the feast!**
10 **MRS. CRATCHIT:** **The founder of the feast, indeed! I wish I**
11 **had him here. I'd give him a piece of my mind to feed**
12 **upon, and I hope he'd have a good appetite for it.**
13 **BOB CRATCHIT:** **My dear, the children. Christmas Day!**
14 **MRS. CRATCHIT:** **It should be Christmas Day, I am sure, on**
15 **which one drinks the health of such an odious, stingy,**
16 **hard, unfeeling man as Mr. Scrooge. You know he is,**
17 **Robert! Nobody knows it better than you do, poor fellow!**
18 **BOB CRATCHIT:** *(Mildly)* **My dear, Christmas Day.**
19 **MRS. CRATCHIT:** **I'll drink his health for your sake and the**
20 **day's, not for his. Long life to him! A merry Christmas**
21 **and a happy New Year! He'll be very merry and very**
22 **happy, I have no doubt!** *(Those playing in the CRATCHIT*
23 *scene return their chairs as they end the scene.)*
24 **MASTER OF CEREMONIES:** **George Patrick McCallum,**
25 **author of many Christmas stories, wrote one he calls "A**
26 **Twentieth-Century Christmas Carol." In it we meet a**
27 **Scrooge of today — but his name is Ebenezer Scoon, a**
28 **man most people call, behind his back, "Scrooge."**
29 **ONE, NARRATOR:** **We call him Scrooge not because of his**
30 **name but because he is the stingiest, most miserly person**
31 **in all of New York City.**
32 **SCOON:** **I live on the top floor of an old brownstone building**
33 **in the east eighties, but I work on 72nd Street. It's a long**
34 **walk, especially when the weather is bad, but I always**
35 **walk to save the money. "A penny saved is a penny earned,"**

1   I always say.

2   ONE: Needless to say, the forty-five-year-old bachelor is very,
3   very rich. He owns an accounting firm, Scoon and Morley.
4   It's a fine business — even if his partner, Jack Morley, is
5   dead. Now he runs it alone — that is, except for his
6   overworked secretary, Bobbie Crandell, a pretty young
7   widow who has to support her mother and her teen-aged
8   son, Tim. *(MOTHER and BOBBIE cross into the scene.)*

9   MOTHER: Bobbie, your boss, that "scrooge," is a selfish
10   tightwad! He hasn't raised your salary in five years!

11   BOBBIE: Mother, I'm sure Mr. Scoon will raise my salary as
12   soon as he can.

13   MOTHER: When that great day comes, maybe we can move out
14   of this firetrap and find some decent place to live.

15   BOBBIE: *(Sighing)* Yes, it would be better for all of us.
16   Especially for Tim. This is an awful neighborhood. I
17   worry about Tim's friends. Well, I'm ready. I'd better get
18   to work as it's the twenty-fourth and tonight is Christmas
19   Eve. I want to get home as early as I can. *(Turns BTA; then*
20   *moves into scene with SCOON.)*

21   SCOON: You'll have to work late, Mrs. Crandell. I have to
22   have these reports the first thing on the twenty-sixth. If
23   they'd been done properly in the first place, we wouldn't
24   have to be rewriting them now. Oh, I know it was my
25   mistake — but I was rushing them because you won't be
26   here on the twenty-fifth to type them, so it's really your
27   fault.

28   BOBBIE: I've finished them, Mr. Scoon, so if you don't mind,
29   I'll leave now. It *is* Christmas Eve, and my family is
30   waiting for me. Merry Christmas, Mr. Scoon.

31   SCOON: Merry Christmas, indeed! An excuse to rob a man
32   of the little that remains after he's paid his bills, that's
33   all. *(NEPHEW enters.)*

34   NEPHEW: Merry Christmas, Uncle Ebenezer! Oh, Mrs.
35   Crandell, Merry Christmas to you, too! I wish you, your

1   mother, and your son the season's best.
2 BOBBIE: Thank you. Merry Christmas to you and to your
3   family too. *(She leaves.)*
4 SCOON: Oh, it's you, is it? What're you doing here? If it's a
5   loan you want, forget it. I can just barely pay my own
6   bills the way things are these days.
7 NEPHEW: *(Laughs)* No, no Uncle. I've come for one thing only:
8   to invite you out to Tarrytown to Christmas dinner
9   tomorrow.
10 SCOON: Dinner tomorrow? I'm busy tomorrow. Got a lot of
11   work to do.
12 NEPHEW: On Christmas Day?
13 SCOON: Just another day to me, Nephew. And if you had an
14   ounce of sense, you'd see it the same way. A commercial
15   trick, that's what Christmas is, and the sooner you realize
16   it the better off you'll be. I warrant you've gone into debt
17   until next Christmas just to buy gifts for all of those kids
18   of yours.
19 NEPHEW: And I'll warrant you're right. *(Laughing)* But don't
20   worry, I'll get 'em paid for, one way or another. But Uncle
21   Ebenezer, for goodness sake, forget your work this one
22   day of the year and join us for Christmas dinner.
23 SCOON: No. No, I can't. Thank you very much, but no. Good
24   night, Nephew.
25 NEPHEW: Well then, if you're sure. Good night, Uncle — and
26   Merry Christmas! *(Leaves)*
27 SCOON: Bah!
28 ONE: *(Narrating)* As I told you, this old miser was rich. One
29   reason for this was he never spent anything much, just
30   saved every penny. When his nephew left, Ebenezer
31   donned his muffler, turned out the lights, and started
32   home. He ignored the Salvation Army Santa Claus on the
33   corner, vigorously ringing his bell and calling out "Merry
34   Christmas." In fact, he managed to make believe he
35   neither saw nor heard the man as he hurried past to enter

1	the Automat to have his supper. The Automat, the
2	cheapest place around — and tonight, the Christmas
3	special was just two dollars and seventy-nine cents —
4	turkey, dressing, cranberry sauce, potatoes and gravy,
5	and even a bit of mince pie. As always, he searched
6	around until he found a newspaper someone had left,
7	and read every page of it, even his horoscope:
8	SCOON: *(Reading)* "Your dreams tonight will be of special
9	significance to you." Bah! Rubbish!
10	ONE: With the explosion of "rubbish," Scoon stuffed the
11	paper into his pocket and headed home, once again
12	ignoring the Salvation Army Santa Claus and his cheerful
13	"Merry Christmas." At home, his apartment was freezing
14	cold, but he did not turn up the thermostat, and when
15	he tried his old black and white TV set, all he could get
16	on it was Christmas, Christmas, Christmas.
17	SCOON: "Silent Night." Ugh! Rubbish! I'll just go to bed —
18	save turning up the furnace if I do. What a fuss! Over
19	nothing! A baby born two thousand years ago and once
20	every three hundred and sixty-five days, millions go in
21	debt because of it. Big deal! Can you imagine, Bobbie
22	Crandell asking me for an advance on her salary so she
23	could buy present for her mother and that kid of hers.
24	Presents they don't need. The nerve of her. *(Yawning)* And
25	my nephew ... and that Salvation Army Santa Claus.
26	He'll probably end up with pneumonia, standing there
27	in the cold, bothering everybody with his "Merry
28	Christmas." *(Sees JACK MORLEY at the foot of his bed as he*
29	*has dozes off to sleep.)* Jack? Jack Morley? No, no, it must
30	be that mince pie I had for supper. Jack's been dead for
31	five years. Oh, that mince pie! I knew I should not have
32	eaten it!
33	JACK MORLEY: *(In sepulchral tones)* Ebenezer, you'll have
34	three dreams. Pay attention to each of them, because,
35	old friend, there is still time for you. There is still time.

1   Don't allow yourself to make the mistake in life that I did.

2 SCOON: Jack! Jack! Oh, I must have fallen asleep. What a

3   dream . . . a dream . . . no, a nightmare. *(Sees ghost.)* But

4   who are you? What do you want?

5 CHRISTMAS PAST: I am the Spirit of Christmas Past. Your

6   past, Ebenezer Scoon. Come with me.

7 ONE: With the Spirit of Christmas Past, Ebenezer relived

8   scenes from his youth. What happy days they had been!

9   He had loved life — even loved Christmas — and now, all

10   he loved was money. He drifted into dreamless sleep for

11   a while, and then, suddenly, another figure stood before

12   him.

13 CHRISTMAS PRESENT: I am the Spirit of Christmas

14   Present. Come with me. *(The two go to the apartment of the*

15   *CRANDELLS, where the three are sitting down to their*

16   *Christmas dinner.)*

17 MOTHER: That's the smallest turkey I've ever seen in my life.

18 BOBBIE: *(Ignoring her mother's remarks)* Pour the wine, Tim.

19   And because it is Christmas, you may have a glass with

20   Mother and me.

21 TIM: Aw, Mom, you treat me like I was two years old.

22 BOBBIE: I treat you like you're seventeen, which you are.

23 MOTHER: When your grandfather was your age, young man,

24   he had a full-time job.

25 BOBBIE: Times have changed, Mother. Besides, Tim is going

26   to college when he finishes high school. Aren't you, Tim?

27 MOTHER: These potatoes are cold, Bobbie. Can't you even

28   serve a hot meal to us?

29 BOBBIE: I'm sorry, Mother. Shall I warm them up a bit?

30 MOTHER: No, they're all right. Pass the carrots. I wish we

31   had a salad.

32 BOBBIE: Tim, I asked you, aren't you going to college when

33   you graduate from high school?

34 TIM: Maybe. I don't know yet what I want to do.

35 BOBBIE: What do you mean, you don't know? Of course you're

1 　　　 going to college. Now let's drink a toast to our benefactor,
2 　　　 Mr. Scoon.
3 　 MOTHER:　Mr. Scrooge, you mean. The old skinflint.
4 　　　 Benefactor indeed!
5 　 BOBBIE:　Well, without him, we wouldn't be sitting here
6 　　　 eating turkey and drinking wine.
7 　 MOTHER:　No, we might be living in a decent apartment in a
8 　　　 respectable part of town where Timmy could meet the
9 　　　 right kind of young folks, instead of . .
10 　 TIM:　*(Interrupting)* Instead of what, Grandma? What's wrong
11 　　　 with my friends?
12 　 BOBBY:　*(Soothingly)* Never mind. Come now, both of you. Eat
13 　　　 your dinner before it gets even colder. This is Christmas;
14 　　　 let's not argue! *(As scene ends, the CRANDELLS turn BTA.*
15 　　　 *SPIRIT OF YET-TO-COME enters.)*
16 　 SPIRIT OF YET-TO-COME:　Come with me Ebenezer Scoon.
17 　　　 I am the Spirit of Yet-To-Come. Take my hand. We're
18 　　　 going on a little tour. And here we are, the cemetery.
19 　　　 Look, a new grave. Listen . . .
20 　 MAN:　Well, old "Scrooge" is gone.
21 　 SECOND MAN:　And soon forgotten. What do you suppose
22 　　　 will happen to all that money he saved and saved and
23 　　　 saved? He can't take it with him, can he?
24 　 MAN:　*(Laughing)* In his case, it's possible. Ebenezer "Scrooge"
25 　　　 probably figured a way. If there was anything he loved,
26 　　　 it was money.
27 　 SECOND MAN:　It was the only thing the old miser ever loved.
28 　　　 *(BTA to mark the end of the cemetery scene.)*
29 　 SCOON:　Spirit, they called me Scrooge. But that's *my* grave,
30 　　　 isn't it? Why did they call me that? Am I such a miserly
31 　　　 person? Spirit, tell me.
32 　 SPIRIT OF YET-TO-COME:　Come with me. Here is a police
33 　　　 court, which may be of interest to you. See, it's your
34 　　　 secretary, Bobbie Crandell.
35 　 JUDGE:　I sentence you, Timothy Crandell, and your two

1	companions to ten years in prison for assault and
2	robbery.
3	SCOON: *(Shouting)* No, no! It mustn't be allowed to happen.
4	Tim is a good boy. There's some mistake!
5	JUDGE: *(Pounding gavel)* Ten years.
6	SCOON: Spirit, what can I do? I have to help that boy.
7	SPIRIT: You should have thought of that before, Ebenezer
8	Scoon. It may already be too late.
9	SCOON: I never realized I was such a miser, that I thought
10	only of money, and that for such a reason, people called
11	me Scrooge. Why, what's money for if you can't use it to
12	help others?
13	SPIRIT: You see that now, Ebenezer?
14	SCOON: Please, Spirit, say it isn't too late. I have lots of
15	money. I want to use it for the good of my friends — for
16	the good of anyone I can help.
17	SPIRIT: I don't know, Ebenezer Scoon.
18	SCOON: And Christmas! I'll never again treat it as just
19	another day. I promise! I promise!
20	SPIRIT: It may be too late, Ebenezer Scoon; it may already
21	be too late! *(BTA)*
22	ONE: The sun was shining in his eyes when Ebenezer woke
23	up. He ran to the window. It had snowed during the night,
24	and everything in New York City was white and pure.
25	Now the sun was out, with all the promise of a beautiful
26	day. He threw open the window and called down to a boy
27	passing by.
28	SCOON: Boy, what day is this? Tell me, what day is it?
29	BOY: You crazy or something, Mister? Why, it's Christmas
30	Day!
31	SCOON: Christmas Day? Good, I haven't missed it. Merry
32	Christmas, boy! Merry Christmas! *(Comes back from*
33	*window.)* Now, I've got work to do. First, I'll get the biggest
34	turkey that's left in the market and get it to Bobbie
35	Crandell and her family. Then, I'll phone my nephew,

1	see if they'll still invite me to dinner with them. And that
2	Salvation Army Santa Claus! I'll give him enough money
3	to make up for the times I ignored his "Merry Christmas"
4	to me, that I'll do. And when Bobbie comes to work
5	tomorrow morning, what a surprise I'll give her! *(BTA for*
6	*shifts of scenes, then sit at desk waiting BOBBIE's entrance, late*
7	*to work on the twenty-sixth. Calling)* Mrs. Crandell. Come in
8	here, yes.
9	BOBBIE: Mr. Scoon, I'm sorry . . .
10	SCOON: *(Interrupting)* You're fifteen minutes late, Bobbie.
11	BOBBIE: Yes, I'm terribly sorry, Mr. Scoon, but . . .
12	SCOON: *(Smiles all over his face)* Well, what can we do about
13	it? Let me see. You might as well take the rest of the day
14	off, Mrs. Crandell — or should I call you Bobbie? — and
15	rush down to hit the Christmas sales. Here, take this
16	money *(Shoves a stack of bills into her surprised hands)* and
17	go spend, spend, spend. And while we are on the subject,
18	I want you and your family to move out of that old rattrap
19	on the west side and find something bigger and more
20	modern near the office. Oh, don't worry about the cost.
21	BOBBIE: But Mr. Scoon . . .
22	SCOON: We can talk about that later. And call me Ebenezer,
23	please.
24	BOBBIE: Are you drunk or crazy, Mr. Scoon? I can't believe . . .
25	SCOON: *(Laughing with delight)* Don't try to figure it out. Just
26	accept the fact that Ebenezer Scoon — that's not Scrooge,
27	by the way — Scoon has finally come to his senses. About
28	time, too, don't you think? *(He grabs BOBBIE and hugs her*
29	*as he helps her out the door.)*
30	ONE: The Christmas miracle continued. Before the year had
31	passed, Bobbie, her mother, and Tim had moved across
32	town to a better apartment in a better neighborhood —
33	but Bobbie no longer lived with her mother and son, as
34	in another apartment in the same building lived the
35	Scoons. Yes, Bobbie and Ebenezer became man and wife.

1　　　The sign on the business on 72nd Street read Scoon and
2　　　Scoon, as Ebenezer had made Bobbie both his wife and
3　　　business partner. And Tim? Tim had been accepted to
4　　　begin his studies at Yale University the following
5　　　September.
6　SCOON:　Oh, I know all of this is hard for you to believe. So
7　　　I'll add one thing more. If you want to do business with
8　　　me at the end of the year, if it is December, you can just
9　　　wait for January. I take Christmas very seriously now,
10　　　and I can't concern myself with anything as unimportant
11　　　as business during the season. I just say, "Call me next
12　　　month — and in the meantime, Merry Christmas! Merry
13　　　Christmas!"
14　MASTER OF CEREMONIES:　Now, ladies and gentlemen, we
15　　　have something very unusual for you. We have arranged
16　　　for you to meet three gentlemen who may be somewhat
17　　　familiar to you all: Gaspar, Balthazar and Melchior,
18　　　better known as the Three Wise Men. *(Three stately figures*
19　　　*garbed in colorful period robes and wearing jeweled turbans*
20　　　*enter.)* Your majesties, we are honored to have you with
21　　　us. May we ask you a few questions about that first
22　　　Christmas two thousand years ago? *(They nod and ad-lib.)*
23　　　Down through the ages, we have understood that the
24　　　three of you followed a star to Bethlehem and there, in
25　　　a stable behind the inn, found the Christ child, whose
26　　　birthday we celebrate every year at this time. Is that
27　　　true?
28　BALTHAZAR:　Yes, it is quite true, but there is more to it than
29　　　that.
30　MELCHIOR:　Indeed, there is much more. For one thing . . .
31　GASPAR:　Melchior, let Balthazar tell it. His English is
32　　　superior to either yours or mine. Besides, he's a better
33　　　public speaker.
34　MELCHIOR:　Now really, Gaspar . . .
35　MASTER OF CEREMONIES:　Look, why don't all of you tell

| 1 | it? After all, the three of you were there and each has his |
| 2 | own impressions, I'm sure. |

1   it? After all, the three of you were there and each has his
2   own impressions, I'm sure.
3   BALTHAZAR: Right. Perhaps I should begin, and Gaspar
4   and Melchior can add their comments as the story moves
5   along.
6   MASTER OF CEREMONIES: Excellent!
7   BALTHAZAR: Well, as I believe you already know, we three
8   were at that time counselors to the king of our country,
9   and among other things, had to study the stars. Astronomy
10   was big then.
11   MASTER OF CEREMONIES: Still is.
12   BALTHAZAR: Really? Well, one evening I noticed a new star
13   in the east which seemed brighter than the others. I
14   thought perhaps my eyes were deceiving me, so I hurried
15   to consult with Gaspar and get his opinion. Melchior
16   happened to be with him, and when I pointed out the
17   star to them, both agreed it was much brighter than the
18   rest. That same night, I had a dream in which I was told
19   to take my two friends and follow the star. According to
20   the dream, it would guide us to where a great new king
21   was about to be born.
22   MELCHIOR: *(Eagerly)* A king who was the Son of God and who
23   would bring peace to the world.
24   GASPAR: That's right. And we should say that the star was
25   moving.
26   MASTER OF CEREMONIES: So what did you do?
27   BALTHAZAR: We mounted our camels, and that evening
28   when the star appeared brighter than ever, we began to
29   follow it.
30   MASTER OF CEREMONIES: For how long?
31   BALTHAZAR: Oh, for many months. At night, you see, as that
32   was when we could see the star.
33   GASPAR: At last, we came to Jersualem, where we called on
34   the king.
35   MELCHIOR: His name was Gerald or Harold or something

1   like that. I forget; it's been such a long time.

2   GASPAR: It was Herod. You always did get mixed up on

3   names, Melchior.

4   MELCHIOR: I do remember that I took an instant dislike to

5   him. Terrible man!

6   GASPAR: But he showed great interest in our story, and told

7   us to come back after we'd seen the new king — said he

8   wanted to worship him too.

9   MASTER OF CEREMONIES: Did you?

10   MELCHIOR: No, because in another dream, Balthazar was

11   told to return home another way, and not to report back

12   to Herod.

13   GASPAR: Melchior, you're getting ahead of the story.

14   MELCHIOR: Oh, so I am. Sorry.

15   BALTHAZAR: To go back: We finally arrived in the little town

16   of Bethlehem, just a few miles down the road from

17   Jerusalem. The star came to a halt there, right over a

18   cave where animals were kept — a kind of stable.

19   GASPAR: Cows, sheep, a couple of mules too, as I recall. We

20   were sure there was some mistake. Whoever heard of a

21   king being born in a stable?

22   BALTHAZAR: But there the star was, so we went in. There

23   was only one small lamp in the cave, but strangely

24   enough, the whole place was filled with light.

25   MASTER OF CEREMONIES: Please describe what you saw,

26   Balthazar.

27   BALTHAZAR: It was a very simple scene, really. In the

28   middle of the cave, seated on some straw, were a young

29   man and woman — Joseph and Mary, their names were —

30   and in Mary's arms lay a newborn baby boy.

31   GASPAR: The most beautiful child any of us had ever seen.

32   And there was a soft glow all around him — it seemed to

33   come right from him.

34   MELCHIOR: That's what lit up the cave.

35   BALTHAZAR: Right away, we realized this was the new

1 king. How we knew, I don't know. We just knew. We knelt
2 down and worshipped him.
3 MELCHIOR: And presented our gifts, of course. Mine was
4 myrrh — that's a kind of resin used to make perfume,
5 and it is quite pleasant to smell.
6 GASPAR: My gift was frankincense — a kind of incense, as
7 the name implies.
8 BALTHAZAR: I brought gold, something the family could
9 surely use. They did appear to be quite poor.
10 MELCHIOR: As far as we know, ours were the only gifts the
11 child received — although there were some shepherds
12 there too.
13 MASTER OF CEREMONIES: Your majesties, do you realize
14 that in remembrance of what you did that night, down
15 through the ages, people all over the world have
16 exchanged gifts on the Christ child's birthday? You three
17 really started something.
18 MELCHIOR: Well, what do you know? We had no idea.
19 MASTER OF CEREMONIES: Was there anyone else there
20 that night?
21 BALTHAZAR: As Melchior said, some shepherds were present
22 too. Angels in the sky told them to go to Bethlehem to
23 see the baby, that he was their new king.
24 GASPAR: Actually, they used the word *Messiah*, which we
25 interpreted to be "king."
26 MASTER OF CEREMONIES: Is there anything else you can
27 tell us, your majesties?
28 BALTHAZAR: No, that's our story. Oh, we did stay a while
29 with Mary and Joseph. Oh, did I tell you his name was
30 Jesus? — the baby, I mean.
31 MELCHIOR: A lovely boy. Such eyes! I'd love to know what
32 happened to him. Did he actually become a king? Did he
33 bring peace to the world?
34 MASTER OF CEREMONIES: Yes, he did become a king —
35 that is, to people who believed him to be God's Son. But

1	as he himself said, "My kingdom is not of this world." He
2	did bring peace too — an inner peace that helps believers
3	face the trials and tribulations of this world.
4	MELCHIOR: That is good to hear. Thank you for allowing us
5	to tell you our story.
6	MASTER OF CEREMONIES: Thank you for being with us.
7	But before you leave, we'd like you to hear a song that
8	has been written about you. "We Three Kings of Orient
9	Are." *(The three ad-lib that this would please them. CHORUS*
10	*plus three male soloists on "We Three Kings of Orient Are.")*
11	TRIO: We three kings of Orient are,
12	Bearing gifts, we traverse afar.
13	Field and fountain, moor and mountain,
14	Following yonder star.
15	CHORUS: Oh, star of wonder, star of night,
16	Star with royal beauty bright,
17	Westward leading, still proceeding,
18	Guide us to the perfect light.
19	BALTHAZAR: Born a babe on Bethlehem's plain,
20	Gold we bring to crown him again,
21	King forever, ceasing never,
22	Over us all to reign.
23	CHORUS: *(As before)*
24	GASPAR: Frankincense to offer have I;
25	Incense owns a Deity nigh,
26	Pray'r and praising all men raising,
27	Worship God on high.
28	CHORUS: *(As before)*
29	MELCHIOR: Myrrh is mine; its bitter perfume
30	Breathes a life of gath'ring gloom;
31	Sorrowing, sighing, bleeding, dying,
32	Sealed in the stone-cold tomb.
33	CHORUS: *(As before)*
34	ALL: Glorious now behold him rise,
35	King and God and Sacrifice;

1   Heav'n sings "Hallelujah!"

2   "Hallelujah!" earth replies.

3   **CHORUS:** *(As before)*

4   **NARRATOR:** When Alice Caldwell Hegan wrote *Mrs. Wiggs*

5   *of the Cabbage Patch* in 1901, she dedicated the book:

6   **MRS. HEGAN:** This little story is lovingly dedicated to my

7   mother, who for years has been the Good Angel of "The

8   Cabbage Patch."

9   **NARRATOR:** Her mother was Louise Marshall, who founded

10   The Cabbage Patch Settlement House in Louisville,

11   Kentucky, to help relieve the suffering of that city's poor.

12   When she was only sixteen, she persuaded her father to

13   buy a lot that later became the site of the settlement

14   house, named after the cabbage patches that dotted a

15   poor neighborhood of Louisville at the turn of the

16   century. Mrs. Marshall, by the way, died in 1981 at the

17   age of niney-two. *(Transition)* But, to our Christmas story

18   from *Mrs. Wiggs of the Cabbage Patch.* *(MRS. WIGGS*

19   *crosses Down Center.)*

20   **MRS. WIGGS:** My, but it's nice an' cold this mornin'! The

21   thermometer's done fell up to zero!"

22   **STORYTELLER:** *(May be read by the NARRATOR.)* Mrs. Wiggs

23   made the statement as cheerfully as if her elbows were

24   not sticking out through the boy's coat she wore. But,

25   then, Mrs. Wiggs was a philosopher, and the sum and

26   substance of her philosophy lay in keeping the dust off

27   her rose-colored spectacles. For example, when their

28   little country home burned, her comment was:

29   **MRS. WIGGS:** Thank God it was the pig instid of the baby

30   that was burned!

31   **STORYTELLER:** The Wiggses lived in the Cabbage Patch. It

32   was not a real cabbage patch, but a queer neighborhood

33   where ramshackle cottages played hopstotch over the

34   railroad tracks. The Wiggses' house was the most

35   imposing in the neighborhood. This was probably due to

1	the fact that it had two front doors and a tin roof, the
2	only tin roof in the Cabbage Patch. Jim and Billy had
3	made it of old cans, which they had picked up on the
4	commons.

MRS. WIGGS: Jim's my oldest, fifteen. And now that Mr. Wiggs
is dead, Jim's the head of the family. He's serious, is Jim,
not like his brother Billy. *(Laughs a bit.)* Billy's
responsibilities rest on him as lightly as the freckles on
his nose!

STORYTELLER: The cold wave that was ushered in that
December morning was the beginning of a long series of
days that vied with each other as to which could induce
the mercury to drop the lowest. On Christmas Eve, Mrs.
Wiggs and Jim sat over the stove after the little ones had
gone to bed and discussed that their meager supply of
food and coal was gone.

MRS. WIGGS: Seems like we'll have to ask for help, Jim. I
can't ask for more credit at Mr. Bagby's grocery. Seems
like I don't have the courage left to pull again a debt.
What do you think? I guess — it looks like mebbe we'll
have to apply to the organization.

JIM: *(His eyes flash.)* Not yet, Ma. It 'ud be with us like it was
with the Hornbys: they didn't have nothin' to eat, and
they went to the organization an' the man asked 'em if
they had a bed or a table, an' when they said yes, he said,
"Well, why don't you sell 'em?" No, Ma! As long as we can
pick up some coal on the tracks, I'll git the vittles some
way. *(Attack of coughing)*

MRS. WIGGS: But how, Jim?

JIM: I think I can get a night job next week. One of the market-
men comes in from the country every night to git a early
start next mornin', and he ast me if I'd sleep in his wagon
from three to six an' keep his vegetables from bein' stolen.
That 'ud gimme time to git home for breakfast, an' be
down to the factory by seven.

1 MRS. WIGGS: *(Cries out anxiously.)* **But Jimmy, you can't**
2 **stand it, night and day too. No, I'll go watch the wagon;**
3 **I'll** . . . *(Sound of knocking on door.)*
4 STORYTELLER: **A knock on the door interrupted her. She**
5 **hastily dried her eyes and smoothed her hair. Jim went**
6 **to the door.** *(JIM opens imaginary door, Stage Left.)*
7 LOUISE: *(Cheery voice)* **I've a Christmas basket for you!**
8 JIM: *(Dully)* **Is this Christmas?**
9 LOUISE: *(Laughs as she deposits an imaginary basket inside the*
10 *door.)* **It's from the church; a bunch of us are distributing**
11 **baskets.**
12 MRS. WIGGS: *(Coming to door)* **Well, how did you ever happen**
13 **to come here?**
14 LOUISE: **There's one for each of the mission-school families;**
15 **just a little Christmas greeting, you know.**
16 MRS. WIGGS: **Well, that certainly is kind an' thoughtful-like.**
17 **Won't you — uh — come right in and git warm. The stove's**
18 **died down some, but you could git thawed out.**
19 LOUISE: **No, thank you, I can't come in.** *(Glances around a bit.)*
20 **Have you plenty of coal?**
21 MRS. WIGGS: *(Catching a negative nod from JIM, smiles*
22 *reassuringly.)* **Oh, yes'm, thank you.**
23 LOUISE: *(A bit doubtfully)* **Well, if you ever want — to come to**
24 **see me, ask for Miss Louise Olcott at Terrace Park. Good**
25 **night, and a happy Christmas.** *(She leaves; JIM closes the*
26 *door and picks up the basket, takes it Down Center. MRS. WIGGS*
27 *follows him.)*
28 STORYTELLER: **She was gone, and the doorway looked very**
29 **black and lonesome in consequence. But there was a big**
30 **basket to prove she was not merely an apparition. Sitting**
31 **on the floor, they unpacked it.** *(MRS. WIGGS and JIM sit*
32 *on the floor, one on each side of the imaginary basket, and unload*
33 *it.)* **There were vegetables, oatmeal, fruit, and even tea**
34 **and coffee. But the big surprise was at the very bottom!**
35 JIM: *(Laughing outright)* **A turkey! Ma, a big turkey!**

1	MRS. WIGGS: *(Delightedly, perhaps holding up and even pinching*
2	*the fat fowl)* It's the first turkey that's been in this house
3	for many a day! I 'spect the little ones'll be skeered of it,
4	it's so big. My, but we'll have a good Christmas dinner
5	tomorrow! I'll git Miss Hazy an' Chris to come over an'
6	spend the day and I'll carry a plate over to Mrs. Schultz,
7	an' take a little of this here tea to ole Mrs. Lawson. *(JIM*
8	*has been doing a sum on a piece of paper.)*
9	JIM: Ma, I guess we can't have the turkey this year. I kin sell
10	it for a dollar seventy-five, and that 'ud buy us hog meat
11	for a good while.
12	MRS. WIGGS: *(Her face falling)* Of course, we'll sell it. You've
13	got the longest head for a boy! We'll sell it in the mornin',
14	and buy sausage for dinner, an' I'll cook some of these
15	here nice vegetables an' put a orange an' some candy at
16	each plate, an' the children'll never know nothin' 'about
17	it.
18	JIM: That's right, Ma.
19	MRS. WIGGS: Besides, if you ain't never et turkey meat, you
20	don't know how good it is. Yes, you sell it, Jim — but I
21	think I wouldn't 'a' minded so much ef they hadn't 'a' sent
22	the cranberries too!
23	STORYTELLER: So Mrs. Wiggs and her brood had a fine
24	Christmas dinner, with most of her neighbors enjoying
25	a shared "little snack," as she put it, along with her
26	cheerful:
27	MRS. WIGGS: Merry Christmas!
28	*(Six readers and the MASTER OF CEREMONIES line up*
29	*Downstage for the conclusion of the program.)*
30	MASTER OF CEREMONIES: Here we come a-caroling
31	Among the leaves so green;
32	Here we come a-wand'ring
33	So fair to be seen.
34	VOICE 1: Love and joy come to you
35	And a joyful Christmas too;

1 VOICE 2: And God bless you and send
2   You a Happy New Year!
3 ALL: And God send you a Happy New Year!
4 MASTER OF CEREMONIES: We are not daily beggars
5   That beg from door to door;
6   But we are neighbor folks
7   That you have seen before.
8 VOICE 3: Love and joy come to you
9   And a joyful Christmas too;
10 VOICE 4: And God bless you and send
11   You a Happy New Year —
12 ALL: And God send you a Happy New Year!
13 MASTER OF CEREMONIES: God bless the master of the
14   house
15   Likewise the mistress too:
16   And all the little children
17   That 'round the table go.
18 VOICE 5: Love and joy come to you
19   And a joyful Christmas too;
20 VOICE 6: And God bless you and send
21   You a Happy New Year —
22 ALL: And God send you a Happy New Year.
23 *("Here We Come A-Caroling")*
24 ALL: *(Singing)* We wish you a Merry Christmas,
25   We wish you a Merry Christmas,
26   We with you a Merry Christmas,
27   And a Happy New Year!
28
29 *(The End)*
30
31
32
33
34
35

Joseph, Mary, Bethlehem, A Manger, Angels, and All That
by JOHN BUTTREY

CAST

FIVE VOICES

1   VOICE 1:   It's almost Christmas. What is Christmas?
2   VOICE 2:   It's Santa Claus and gifts piled upon gifts piled
3   upon gifts,
4   ALL: And it's a spirit of sharing.
5   VOICE 3:   It's artificial, dehumanizing, bottled-up cheer,
6   ALL: And it's joyful singing.
7   VOICE 4:   It's this meeting — that party; shopping —
8   shopping; busy — busy — busy,
9   ALL: And it's a quiet night with time for thinking.
10   VOICE 5:   It's gaudy lights, distracting, sometimes
11   blasphemous, advertising,
12   ALL: And it's a mother, a father, and a tiny baby born in
13   Bethlehem.
14   VOICE 1:   It's a lot of things:
15   VOICE 2:   Some good,
16   VOICE 3:   Some bad.
17   VOICE 4:   Some things that make me happy,
18   VOICE 5:   And some that make me very sad — or even mad!
19   VOICE 1:   Tonight let's go back to the beginnings: to Joseph,
20   Mary, Bethlehem, a manger, angels — and all that.
21   VOICE 2:   That's nice. But I'm more interested in the present
22   — or the future.
23   VOICES 3, 4, 5:   We are too! The past has passed!
24   VOICE 1:   But think about that: the present is constantly
25   moving into the past.
26   VOICE 2:   Even future moments will one day move into the
27   past.
28   VOICE 1:   Not only that, but, oddly enough, the reverse is also
29   also true: the past moves into the present, and into the
30   future.
31   VOICE 2:   In memories,
32   VOICE 3:   In books and stories,
33   VOICE 4:   In both the good and bad consequences of past
34   actions.
35   VOICE 5:   In songs and celebrations.

1	VOICE 3:	In wedding anniversaries and birthdays.
2	VOICE 4:	Past and present and future are intertwined.
3	VOICE 5:	Combined.
4	ALL:	And so it is with the birth of a tiny baby born in
5		Bethlehem.
6	VOICE 1:	Yes, it happened in the past.
7	VOICE 2:	But many of the details are very familiar to us
8		today:
9	VOICE 3:	Political leaders,
10	VOICE 4:	A census,
11	VOICE 5:	Home towns,
12	VOICE 1:	Marriage,
13	VOICE 2:	Expectant parents.
14	VOICE 3:	A long journey,
15	VOICE 4:	No vacancy signs,
16	VOICE 5:	Childbirth,
17	VOICE 1:	A first-born son . . .
18	VOICE 2:	Carefully wrapped up in clean clothes.
19	VOICE 3:	A proud father and mother.
20	VOICE 4:	Visitors coming to see the baby . . .
21	VOICE 5:	Bringing gifts, and departing to tell others what
22		they saw.
23	ALL:	And even shepherds and a flock of sheep, and a manger,
24		aren't all that strange.
25	VOICE 1:	The emotions in the story are part of the history
26		of man in every age:
27	VOICE 2:	The pain and joy of childbirth,
28	VOICE 3:	The shepherds' fear of the unknown.
29	VOICE 4:	A mother's pondering and wondering about her
30		child's future.
31	VOICE 5:	Hopes for peace.
32	ALL:	Hopes for peace! We'll have to come back to that.
33	VOICE 1:	Yes, it happened in the past.
34	VOICE 2:	But it's made up of some of the basic stuff of life.
35	VOICE 3:	Common,

1   VOICE 4:   Natural,

2   VOICE 5:   Universal stuff.

3   VOICE 1:   There are extraordinary details.

4   VOICE 2:   Luke's story includes ancient, strange, uncommon

5   ways of describing special events:

6   VOICE 3:. Talking angels,

7   VOICE 4:   A singing heavenly host,

8   VOICE 5:   A Savior who is Christ the Lord.

9   VOICE 1:   We can take those details straight, if we want to,

10   VOICE 2:   Emphasizing the mystery and uniqueness of Jesus'

11   birth.

12   VOICE 3:   Or we can deal with them more playfully,

13   VOICE 4:   As poetry and symbol.

14   VOICE 5:   In either case, those strange details are meant to

15   say:

16   ALL: God was present.

17   VOICE 1:   In Jesus' birth in a dirty stable in Bethlehem,

18   VOICE 2:   In his growing up as a carpenter among the

19   common folk in Nazareth,

20   VOICE 3:   In his preaching, and teaching, and healing, with

21   a small group of ex-fishermen and such.

22   ALL: God was present —

23   VOICES 3, 4:   In Jesus' loving and caring for tax collectors

24   and the sick and lonely,

25   VOICES 3, 4, 5:   In his courage and determination to do God's

26   will when he went to the big city, Jerusalem.

27   VOICES 2, 3, 4, 5:   In his faithfulness, even unto death on a

28   cross between two common crooks.

29   ALL: And God was present in that mysterious event we

30   celebrate at Easter time.

31   VOICE 1:   If we really believe that ...

32   VOICE 2:   If we really believe that God was present in the

33   life of Mary and Joseph's boy, Jesus ...

34   VOICE 3:   If we really believe that God was active in a man

35   noted for love and compassion, courage and faithfulness ...

1	VOICE 4:	If we really believe that God was alive among those
2		common folk in Bethlehem and Nazareth and Jerusalem ...
3	VOICE 5:	Then we can really believe that God is active now,
4	VOICE 1:	Among the common folk in *(Your city or village)*,
5	VOICE 2:	Or in Minneapolis and St. Paul, or wherever it is
6		that you live.
7	VOICE 3:	Or in Russia and Red China,
8	VOICE 4:	Or in Europe and South Africa and Afganistan and
9		Lebanon, Colombia, Central America.
10	VOICE 5:	Or in Bethlehem of today, in which tiny babies are
11		still born, in the midst of great tension and the fear of war.
12	VOICE 1:	If we really believe that God was present in Jesus,
13		then we have a way to deal with those who fear — or
14		hope — that God is dead. We won't be looking for voices
15		from above, or some out-of-this-world ecstasy, or for some
16		proof with a label which says, "Look everybody, there's
17		God!"
18	VOICE 2:	Instead we'll look for signs of the presence of God
19		in the actions and attitudes of people.
20	VOICE 3:	In people who, if even in some small way, remind us
21		us of Jesus,
22	VOICE 4:	In human relationships which include even small
23		amounts of love and forgiveness,
24	VOICE 5:	In medical discoveries which give health and hope
25		to the sick,
26	VOICE 1:	In private and public efforts to feed the hungry,
27	VOICE 2:	In movements seeking to bring fair treatment and
28		equal opportunity to men of all races,
29	VOICE 3:	In attitudes which offer acceptance to the non-
30		conformist, the outcast,
31	VOICE 4:	In efforts which seek to protect and preserve the
32		natural world,
33	VOICE 5:	In the work of those seeking peace.
34	ALL:	Peace! That's what we want. That's what God wants.
35		That's what we so desperately need. That's what God

1   wants so much for us to find.

2   VOICE 1:   The prophet Isaiah spoke of a new day, in which . . .

3   ALL: They shall beat their swords into plowshares, and their

4   spears into pruning hooks, nation shall not lift up sword

5   against nation. Neither shall they learn war, anymore.

6   VOICE 2:   And those maybe poetic angels sang,

7   ALL: "Glory to God in the highest, and on earth, peace among

8   men."

9   VOICE 3:   They were celebrating the birth of the Prince of Peace!

10   ALL: We are celebrating the birth of the Prince of Peace!

11   VOICE 4:   Jesus taught about peace. He said . . .

12   ALL: "Blessed are the peacemakers, for they shall be called

13   Sons of God."

14   VOICE 5:   And Jesus lived a life of peace, a ministry of

15   reconciliation, of peace among men.

16   ALL: We are called to be instruments of his peace, God's

17   peace, promoting reconciliation between . . .

18   VOICE 1:   Husbands and wives,

19   VOICE 2:   Parents and children,

20   VOICE 3:   Rich and poor,

21   VOICE 4:   Black and white and red,

22   VOICE 5:   Friends and enemies,

23   VOICE 1:   Communists and capitalists,

24   VOICE 2:   Reactionaries and revolutionaries,

25   VOICE 3:   Young and old.

26   ALL: Peace is hard to find. It's harder to keep, even when we

27   find it.

28   VOICE 1:   Sometimes we dilute the meaning of the word

29   "peace." We say "peace" and we may think of . . .

30   VOICE 2:   A picture of pine trees standing amid smooth

31   snowdrifts unmarked by footprints or snowmobile tracks.

32   VOICE 3:   Or a mountain lake mirroring tall peaks, and blue

33   sky, and soft fluffy clouds.

34   VOICE 4:   Or a colorful sunset or a rainbow.

35   VOICE 5:   Or a little white church building in the country.

1   ALL: All these scenes are good, part of God's handiwork.
2   They look fine on Christmas cards, or anywhere else. But
3   they present peace without people. And the Christmas
4   message is for peace among men.
5   VOICE 1:   Peace between blacks and whites in U.S. cities;
6   VOICE 2:   Peace between Arabs and Israelis in Bethlehem
7   and Jerusalem and Damascus.
8   VOICE 3:   Peace between North and South Ireland . . .
9   VOICE 4:   Between Americans and Russians.
10   VOICE 5:   Peace between father and son, husband and wife,
11   sister and brother in our own homes.
12   ALL: The Peace of Christmas is for people!
13   VOICE 1:   That's the best kind of peace,
14   VOICE 2:   And the hardest to find.
15   VOICE 3:   It doesn't just come to us — that's obvious.
16   VOICE 4:   We have to work for peace,
17   VOICE 5:   Pray to God for it,
18   VOICE 1:   Demonstrate our hopes for it,
19   VOICE 2:   Write to congressmen for it,
20   VOICE 3:   Be patient for it,
21   VOICE 4:   Sometimes compromise for it,
22   VOICE 5:   Sometimes stick to our peaceful guns for it.
23   ALL: Peace. Peace among men. Peace among all men. That's
24   a big part of what Christmas is all about.
25   VOICE 1:   Christmas is, to be sure, a lot of things.
26   VOICES 2, 3:   But the best of it goes back to a mother, a father,
27   and a tiny baby born in Bethlehem.
28   VOICES 4, 5:   That beginning is part of the past that has moved
29   powerfully into the present.
30   VOICES 2, 4:   It's made up of the universal stuff of life.
31   VOICES 3, 5:   Human and divine all at the same time.
32   VOICES 1, 2:   But first of all, human events in which God was
33   present.
34   ALL: Human events in which God *is* present,
35   VOICE 1:   Today.

1   VOICE 2:   Right here.

2   VOICE 3:   Now.

3   VOICE 4:   This year!

4   ALL: Wherever there is . . .

5   VOICE 5:   Loving,

6   VOICE 4:   Forgiving,

7   VOICES 4, 5:   Acceptance of outcasts,

8   VOICES 3, 4, 5:   Healing of sick bodies,

9   VOICES 2, 3, 4, 5:   Peacemaking.

10   ALL: That's where God is. That's where the Spirit of Jesus is

11   being born once again. That's where the real meaning of

12   Christmas is. Amen.

Those Fools — The Wise Men
by MARION FAIRMAN

CAST

TWO WOMEN READERS

MELCHIOR
The eldest of the three wise men. He is in charge of the expedition. He never doubts, but he does not understand completely the meaning of the star.

BALTHASAR
A middle-aged man given the responsibility for supplies, etc. He is an "enthusiast," but he seldom thinks through the consequences. He thinks he understands more than he does. He tends to follow what others suggest.

CASPAR
A young man, volatile in temperament. He knows heights and depths. Of the three, he alone understands the fullest implications of their following the star.

NOTE: MELCHIOR, BALTHASAR, and CASPAR may wear choir robes, if desired, or they may wear cold weather gear: sweaters, trousers, etc. They should not be dressed in bathrobes, nor should they talk like "Bible" characters.

PRODUCTION NOTES

This play may be used at any time during the Christmas season. An optional candle-lighting service for the congregation is included for a Christmas Eve service. The play may be included in a regular worship service beginning at the point of Scripture and sermon. If the offering is ordinarily received after the sermon in your church, you might wish to have it, for this special occasion, before the play.

The play is imagined as a time in the lives of the wise men when they had been traveling four months on their two-year journey to Bethlehem, a time when the first flush of adventure is over, a time when the end is nowhere in sight, a time when "wise" men come to grips with the realities of their quest for "light." The play then, though it uses the traditional names of the wise men, is not really an historical play, but a contemporary one. Thus, the wise men need not be dressed in robes, nor should they talk as though they knew they were in the Bible! They should sound and look like real men, exhibiting anger and humor, weaknesses and strengths.

In the action of the play, the men look forward to birth, not only the birth of the God-child, but the "birth" of believers. Caspar sees further still. He knows no man can be "born" without the death of self; he sees that God himself must finally die to bring about this new birth of man. More than the others, he understands both pain and joy await those who follow the star. Let the conflicts in each of the men be strong and real, reflecting the emotions felt, if not articulated, by those who will be watching the play.

The meaning of the play moves back and forth among variations of the words "wise" and "foolish", meanings reinforced in the litany. If you do not feel your audience will understand the final words of the litany, "fools for Christ," you might wish to print in your programs the Scripture references, 1 Corinthians 3:18 and 19, and 1 Corinthians 4:10.

Marion Fairman

1

SETTING: This play is designed to be used in the church service
2 during the Christmas season. A place is provided for a candle-
3 lighting service, if desired. No props are needed. The candle for
4 the litany may be placed at a convenient spot near the playing
5 area. Two reading stands are placed, one to the right and one
6 to the left of the congregation. Two women readers take their
7 places at the reading stands. These parts, though read, should
8 be dramatized.
9
10 **PROLOGUE**
11 *Old Testament Readings*
12
13 **WOMAN 1:   God made two huge lights —**
14 **The sun and the moon**
15 **To shine down upon the earth —**
16 **The larger one, the sun,**
17 **To preside over the day,**
18 **And the smaller one, the moon,**
19 **To preside through the night.**
20 **He also made the stars.**
21 **And God set them in the sky to light the earth**
22 **And to preside over the day and night,**
23 **And to divide the light from the darkness.**
24 **And God was pleased.** *(Genesis 1:16-18)*
25 **WOMAN 2:   Where were you when I laid the foundations of**
26 **the earth?**
27 **Tell me, if you know so much?**
28 **Do you know how its dimensions were determined?**
29 **And who did the surveying?**
30 **What supports its foundations?**
31 **And who laid its cornerstone**
32 **As the morning stars sang together**
33 **And all the angels shouted for joy?** *(Job 38:4-7)*
34 **WOMAN 1:   Oh, Bethlehem, you are but a small Judean village,**
35 **Yet you will be the birthplace of my King**

1   Who is alive from everlasting ages past! *(Micah 5:2)*
2   Praise the Lord, Oh Heavens. Praise him, sun and moon,
3   And all you twinkling stars! *(Psalm 148:3)*
4   WOMAN 2:   The Lord sent this message to King Ahaz:
5   "Ask me for a sign, Ahaz.
6   Ask anything you like, in heaven or on earth."
7   But the king refused.
8   "No," he said, "I'll not bother the Lord
9   With anything like that!"
10   Then Isaiah said, "Oh, House of David,
11   You aren't satisfied to exhaust my patience,
12   You exhaust the Lord's as well!
13   All right then,
14   The Lord himself will choose the sign —
15   A child will be born to a virgin,
16   And she shall call him Immanuel." *(Isaiah 7:10-14)*
17   WOMAN 1:   It was our grief he bore,
18   Our sorrows that weighed him down.
19   We thought his troubles were a punishment from God,
20   For his own sins!
21   But he was wounded and bruised for our sins.
22   He was chastised that we might have peace;
23   He was lashed —
24   And we were healed! *(Isaiah 53:4)*
25   God laid on him the guilt and sins of every one of us!
26   But when his soul has been made an offering for sin,
27   Then shall we have a multitude of children,
28   Many heirs.
29   He shall live again! *(Isaiah 53:10)*
30   WOMAN 2:   I see in the future of Israel,
31   Far down the distant trail
32   That there shall come a star from Jacob! *(Numbers 24:17)*
33   *ANTHEM:*   Suggested: "Behold that Star," Thomas W. Tulley,
34   arranged by Frank Cunkle, Shawnee Press.
35   *(The two READERS may exit during the anthem or remain at*

1	*their stands.)*
2	
3	***New Testament Readings***
4	
5	**WOMAN 1:** **If you read these words aloud to the church,**
6	**You will receive a special blessing from the Lord.**
7	**Those who listen to it being read —**
8	**And do what it says —**
9	**Will also be blessed.** *(Revelations 1:3)*
10	**WOMAN 2:** **There is one glory of the sun,**
11	**And another glory of the moon,**
12	**And another glory of the stars;**
13	**For star differs from star in glory.** *(1st Corinthians 15:41)*
14	**WOMAN 1:** **And Jesus said,**
15	**"No one can come to me**
16	**Unless the Father who sent me draws him to me.**
17	**Those the Father speaks to,**
18	**Who learn the truth from him**
19	**Will be attracted to me.**
20	**I tell you,**
21	**No one can come to me**
22	**Unless the Father attract him to me."** *(John 6:44,45,65)*
23	**WOMAN 2:** **I, Jesus, have sent my angel to you**
24	**To tell the churches all these things.**
25	**I am both David's Root and his Descendant.**
26	**I am the bright Morning Star.** *(Revelations 22:16)*
27	**WOMAN 1:** **You will do well to pay close attention.**
28	**When you consider the wonderful truth,**
29	**Then the light will dawn in your souls —**
30	**And Christ the Morning Star**
31	**Will shine in your hearts.** *(2nd Peter 1:19)*
32	**WOMAN 2:** **To everyone who overcomes —**
33	**Who to the very end keeps on —**
34	**I will give to him the Morning Star!**
35	**He that hath an ear,**

1   **Let him hear!** *(Revelations 2:26, 28, 29)*

2   *(READERS exit. End of Prologue.)*

3

4   **THE PLAY**

5

6   *(BALTHASAR and CASPAR enter Stage Right or Left.*

7   *BALTHASAR walks Center Stage. CASPAR walks Down Left*

8   *where he stands, hands on hips, looking up and around in*

9   *disgust.)*

10 **CASPAR:**   **Clouds! Look at them! Clouds every night since we**

11   **started out four months ago! I can't see any stars at all,**

12   **let alone the dog star, the Mesori.**

13 **BALTHASAR:** *(Complaining tone)* **Well, this is some route**

14   **Melchior picked.** *(He slaps his arms around his shoulders.)*

15   **I'm cold!**

16 **CASPAR:**   *(Indifferently)* **It's cold all right. No fire, no wood**

17   **here in the desert.**

18 **BALTHASAR:** *(Petulantly)* **And I'm hungry. Melchior cut our**

19   **rations pretty close.**

20 **CASPAR:**   **What choice did he have, Balthasar? Who knows**

21   **how far we have to go, or how long it will take?**

22 **BALTHASAR:** *(Looking around him carefully, then speaking*

23   *confidentially)* **It's not too late to go back to Persia.** *(He*

24   *walks Downstage Right, speaking dreamily.)* **Ah, Persia! Warm**

25   **sunshine, cool breezes from the ocean, the summer palace**

26   **on the mountain, cool sherbet slipping down our**

27   **throats —** *(MELCHIOR enters Stage Right. He stands at edge*

28   *of stage for a moment.)*

29 **CASPAR:**   **And the girls.** *(Swings toward BALTHASAR.)* **Don't**

30   **forget the Persian girls!** *(He laughs when he sees MELCHIOR,*

31   *not at all embarrassed.)* **Oh, hello, Melchior; we didn't hear**

32   **you.**

33 **MELCHIOR:** *(He walks Center Stage and speaks dryly.)* **Obviously**

34   **not.** *(He looks at CASPAR for a moment and then over at*

35   *BALTHASAR who is upset at being overheard.)* **Suppose we**

1 forget about Persia and the girls. We've got enough
2 trouble. What are the men doing tonight, Caspar?
3 CASPAR: Well, Melchior — they're cussing us out and
4   getting dead drunk. *(He turns Downstage Left and he mutters.)*
5   And I don't blame them.
6 BALTHASAR: *(Turning toward MELCHIOR, his manner obsequious)*
7   I'm glad you came out, Melchior. Two of the camels wandered
8   away this evening, and I didn't know what to do. The men
9   were too drunk to go after them.
10 MELCHIOR: *(Angry)* You're supposed to check those tethers
11   yourself, Balthasar. You know we can't afford to lose camels
12   and supplies. *(Turning toward CASPAR)* Can't you stop those
13   men from drinking?
14 CASPAR: *(Without turning, he shrugs.)* If you want to tangle with
15   those camel drivers, go ahead. Not me!
16 MELCHIOR: *(His voice stern)* When did they get the liquor?
17 CASPAR: This morning. You were in your tent studying the
18   Scriptures when those Bedouins went through. And those
19   Bedouins aren't exactly what you'd call friendly. For liquor,
20   our men traded everything they could —
21 MELCHIOR: *(Swings toward BALTHASAR, interrupting CASPAR.*
22   *He speaks sharply.)* The gifts, Balthasar? What about the gifts?
23 BALTHASAR: *(Soothingly)* Now, now, Melchior, you worry too
24   much. They're safe. Everything's in my tent. Anyway, the
25   men don't know what we're carrying.
26 CASPAR: Good thing they don't know why. They think we're
27   crazy anyway — following a star they haven't even seen.
28 BALTHASAR: *(Indignantly)* They call us fools, Melchior.
29 CASPAR: Maybe they're right!
30 MELCHIOR: Neither of you thought so when we started. Why
31   didn't you stay in Persia, Balthasar? Why start out through
32   the dark into the desert?
33 BALTHASAR: *(Turning Downstage Right and speaking defensively)*
34   It seemed exciting then — romantic —
35 CASPAR: *(Incredulous)* Romantic? *(He swings toward the others.)* We

1	sweat every day — freeze every night! *(Angry)* **And ever**
2	**since we left Persia — clouds! Melchior, we can't even see**
3	**the fool star!**
4	**MELCHIOR:** *(He folds his arms across his chest and speaks icily.)*
5	**The star is there!** *(He turns Upstage Center, his back to*
6	*CASPAR and BALTHASAR.)*
7	**CASPAR:** *(An outburst)* **Then why am I so lonely?** *(CASPAR*
8	*takes a step toward MELCHIOR, his fists clenched. But*
9	*BALTHASAR turns, stops him with a motion of his hand.)*
10	**BALTHASAR: We're all tired and cold and hungry, Melchior.**
11	**When will our journey end?**
12	**MELCHIOR:** *(Turning slowly forward)* **Maybe this journey**
13	**never ends. Maybe we just go on, not able to see — yet**
14	**believing the star is there.**
15	**CASPAR:** *(Staring at him, then he swings abruptly Downstage Left.)*
16	**Then we are fools!**
17	**BALTHASAR:** *(Pleading tone)* **Oh, come on, Caspar. Where do**
18	**you think we are going, Melchior?**
19	**MELCHIOR:** *(Shrugging)* **Well, it's no journey to a land we**
20	**know —**
21	**CASPAR:** *(Throwing out his arms in exasperation)* **Any fool knows**
22	**that — even me!**
23	**BALTHASAR:** *(Angry)* **Caspar, shut up! Where, Melchior?**
24	**MELCHIOR: We're going west, toward Judea.** *(He smiles at*
25	*BALTHASAR.)* **Wherever we're going, it's a good place,**
26	**Balthasar.**
27	**BALTHASAR: You've been studying the Scriptures. What do**
28	**you think we'll find?**
29	**MELCHIOR:** *(Shaking his head)* **I don't know. Something**
30	**different — like that Morning Star, the Mesori — something**
31	**that's never been before.**
32	**CASPAR:** *(Folding his arms across his chest)* **And what would that**
33	**be, pray tell?**
34	**MELCHIOR: Somebody new — a birth —**
35	**CASPAR:** *(Sarcastically)* **Ah, a birth! That's new?**

1   BALTHASAR: *(As though explaining something to a dull child)*
2   **Caspar, a new star to signal a new birth.** *(To MELCHIOR)*
3   **Whose birth, Melchior? Whose?**
4   MELCHIOR: *(Laughing a little)* **Yours maybe? Caspar's? Mine?**
5   BALTHASAR: *(Taken aback, he turns away Downstage Right.)*
6   **Mine?**
7   CASPAR: **I wouldn't know about you two, but I've been born.**
8   **My mother told me.**
9   BALTHASAR: *(Swinging toward CASPAR)* **Oh, shut up, you**
10   **fool.** *(Slowly, patiently)* **Melchior must mean that if**
11   **somebody has been born who is like nothing ever born**
12   **before — then — then we'll be new too — born — born**
13   **again.**
14   CASPAR: *(Turning toward BALTHASAR and bowing in an*
15   *exaggerated way)* **Oh, wise Balthasar, you may not believe**
16   **this, but I understand the way Melchior talks. But, oh**
17   **wise Balthasar, don't stop with birth. What if you are**
18   **asked to die?**
19   BALTHASAR: *(Astounded)* **To die? Me?** *(He turns Downstage*
20   *Right.)*
21   MELCHIOR: *(Laughing, he walks to CASPAR.)* **You're no fool,**
22   **Caspar. You're right! For that kind of birth, something**
23   **has to die —**
24   BALTHASAR: *(Turning toward them, his hand extended.)* **Well,**
25   **what?**
26   MELCHIOR: *(He walks Downstage Left, turns, claps CASPAR on*
27   *the shoulder and pushes him Center Stage.)* **Tell him, Caspar.**
28   CASPAR: *(Reluctantly)* **Something in you — and in me — and**
29   **in Melchior —**
30   BALTHASAR: *(Bewildered)* **What are you talking about death**
31   **for on the way to a birth?** *(Turns Downstage Right.)* **I**
32   **brought frankincense for a priest!**
33   MELCHIOR: **And I gold — gold for a king — according to my**
34   **studies, the king of the Jews.**
35   CASPAR: *(Looking intently at each of them)* **But remember, I**

1 brought myrrh. And myrrh is the gift for one who is to
2 die. *(Slowly)* Perhaps, one day, as the price for our new
3 birth, even God must die. *(MELCHIOR and BALTHASAR*
4 *both turn, startled, look at CASPAR.)*
5 MELCHIOR: God!?
6 BALTHASAR: God — die?
7 CASPAR: *(Vehemently)* Yes, yes — God die! Wise men look for
8 truth, right? So seek the whole truth. If this God-child is
9 to grow up knowing pain and suffering only to die — think
10 Melchior. *(He crosses to MELCHIOR on the name.)* Why
11 should it be any different for us? *(Crosses to BALTHASAR.)*
12 Do you want to go on, Balthasar?
13 BALTHASAR: *(Moves to Center Stage, speaking to MELCHIOR.)*
14 Maybe we are fools to go on, Melchior — if that's what
15 lies ahead —
16 MELCHIOR: Or, since we've been following a light never
17 seen before — *(Turns Down Left)* would we be fools to go
18 back?
19 CASPAR: *(On Down Right corner)* Well, let's not give our camel
20 drivers a vote. They'd go back in a minute. *(Drops his satiric*
21 *tone, sighs.)* And I? I see too much through too much
22 darkness, too many clouds. *(He drops his head in his hands.)*
23 MELCHIOR: *(Looking up slowly)* Caspar! Balthasar! A morning
24 wind is stirring. The clouds are moving! We will see the
25 star again!
26 CASPAR: *(He raises his head slowly from his hands.)* My star — my
27 Morning Star!
28 BALTHASAR: *(Turns to both men, holding out his hands, his voice*
29 *trembling.)* Well, do we turn back to Persia while we can?
30 MELCHIOR: *(Shaking his head)* When once you've seen the
31 star, Balthasar, no wise man turns back from following.
32 BALTHASAR: Well, if you're sure. *(He starts to cross Upstage*
33 *Right — or Left — and pauses, looking back at the two men.)*
34 Then, uh, I suppose we better get ready to move. *(He walks*
35 *Upstage Right — or Left — turns to look at them again.)* I'll see —

1	**I'll see if I can waken some of the men.** *(He looks again at*
2	*CASPAR and MELCHIOR.)* **You *are* sure?** *(Both men nod*
3	*without looking at him. BALTHASAR exits Stage Right or Left.)*
4	**MELCHIOR:** *(Calling after him)* **Waken all the men, Balthasar!**
5	*(To CASPAR)* **Maybe they will see the star for themselves.**
6	**CASPAR:** *(Turns toward him and walks Center Stage, laughing a*
7	*little.)* **And be fools like us, Melchior?**
8	**MELCHIOR:** *(Walking to CASPAR, he puts both hands on his*
9	*shoulders and speaks slowly.)* **If they are wise, Caspar; if**
10	**they are wise!** *(After a moment, CASPAR nods in agreement.*
11	*MELCHIOR and CASPAR exit Stage Right or Left, MELCHIOR's*
12	*hand on CASPAR's shoulder.)*
13	
14	**THE LITANY**
15	*(Words of litany to appear in program)*
16	
17	*(After the exit of MELCHIOR and CASPAR, the table holding*
18	*the Christmas candle is moved Center Stage. A PAGE hands*
19	*the MINISTER the candlelighter. The MINISTER lights the*
20	*candle as he stands behind the table. Then he gives the PAGE*
21	*the candlelighter. The PAGE moves to one side or exits.)*
22	**MINISTER:** **I have lighted this Advent (Christmas) candle**
23	**To be the star that wise men follow.**
24	**CONGREGATION:** **We see this to be so.**
25	**MINISTER:** **To follow the Morning Star**
26	**Means to leave behind the places of comfort.**
27	**CONGREGATION:** **We understand this to be so.**
28	**MINISTER:** **To travel toward light**
29	**Means to journey through the dark night of the soul.**
30	**CONGREGATION:** **We believe this to be so.**
31	**MINISTER:** **To persist when the light is hidden**
32	**Means to be lonely and cold.**
33	**CONGREGATION:** **We know this to be so.**
34	**MINISTER:** **To follow the star**
35	**Means you will know both joy and pain.**

1 CONGREGATION: Still, we will follow the star.
2 MINISTER: Men will call you fools,
3   Like those fools, the wise men.
4 CONGREGATION: Like those wise men,
5   We will follow the Morning Star;
6   We will be fools —
7   For Christ!
8
9 *(A candlelighting service may follow here if desired.)*
10
11 *(From outside auditorium, where wise men exited, three unseen*
12 *men will sing the verses of hymn, "We Three Kings of Orient*
13 *Are." On each one, they should move further away to give the*
14 *effect of "journeying." The congregation will sing the chorus,*
15 *either from the hymnbook or from words printed on their*
16 *programs. Prayer and benediction may follow the last chorus.)*
17
18
19
20
21
22
23
24
25
26
27
28
29
30
31
32
33
34
35

Joseph of Nazareth
by MARTHA SLITER SHEERAN

CAST

NARRATOR
SIMEON
NATHANIEL
JOSHUA

NARRATOR: And so it came to pass that Joseph of Nazareth died and was taken to his fathers. In the court of heaven there was great rejoicing among the angels that another of Adam's sons had entered eternal life. But in the city of Nazareth the women wept and the menfolk bowed their heads in grief when the body of Joseph was laid in the tomb. Only Mary, the spouse, and Jesus, the son, stood quietly by and kept their sadness in their hearts. Then, as the procession of friends and neighbors wound its way from the place of burial back to the city streets, the sighs of mourning gave way to words of praise.

SIMEON: A just man was Joseph. Nazareth will miss his quiet wisdom.

NATHANIEL: A fair and honest worker. Where will we find his equal in the craft of carpentry?

JOSHUA: A kind and thoughtful husband . . .

SIMEON: An example to each man who calls himself a father. In truth, that was Joseph.

NARRATOR: Now in the city of Nazareth on that day a stranger observed all that was taking place. He was a man of Joseph's age, an Egyptian, who had only recently taken up residence in Galilee. The stranger watched the procession of mourners as it passed his house on the farthest street of the town. He listened to the words of praise that were spoken of the carpenter and he began to wonder just what kind of person this Joseph had really been and what were his accomplishments. The Egyptian's wonder led him from his house further into the city, up and down the steep and narrow streets, each with its particular trade. He crossed the street of the goldsmiths, past the street of the copper workers, onto the street of the carpenters. There, in front of the flat-roofed house which stood next to the dwelling of Joseph, the stranger came upon a group whom he recognized as part of the mourning procession. He approached them timidly at first, as became a stranger in the city, and then, gathering courage, asked the questions that had been puzzling him: "Who and what was this man Joseph whom you have just laid to rest? Why have I heard him spoken of in praise such as I have never heard before either here or in my homeland?" The men and women gathered there before the house were astounded by these questions. They started to turn away. But some, seeing the stranger was in good faith, began to paint for him a word-portrait of the man called "father" by Jesus.

SIMEON: Since boyhood, I, Simeon, have known the man named Joseph. As children we played together in these very streets. As young boys we talked together of the day when we would set up the shops of our trades. It was together that we first saw the marvelous city of Jerusalem. We were twelve years old at that time and we made the trip with our parents to celebrate the feast of the Passover in the shadow of the great temple. I remember how excited I was all during the journey and how I exclaimed with delight at my first sight of the wonders of Jerusalem.

NATHANIEL: The city of Jerusalem, with its ramparts and citadels, is truly a glorious sight. I, Nathaniel, remember the first time I looked down on it from the Mount of Olives. The gold and marble temple and the palaces and villas seemed brighter than the sun.

SIMEON: So it appeared to me as I gazed down on the Holy City. But Joseph, standing firmly on the overlooking hill, seemed to see far beyond the city to a place where my eye could not even follow. It was then that I realized how different Joseph and I had become. I was still a boy, easily filled with the enthusiasms of a boy. But Joseph already was a man in his ways and in his understanding. In that moment I could see in him a quietness and strength that had been unnoticed before. He was observant without being talkative; he was reflective without seeming rude. I think I knew then that Joseph was different from all the other Galilean youths I knew. And so he remained through all these years.

JOSHUA: The stranger looks puzzled, Simeon. Speak further, to explain your meaning. For myself, I think you touched the vital point only a moment ago when you described Joseph as standing firmly on the ground but looking to a place beyond. In more than a physical sense that was true of Joseph and it is an achievement which few men seem able to accomplish. Usually, those whose roots are earth-bound cannot see whatever is beyond their personal reach. Joseph, holy man that he was, never failed to give the things of earth their proper place.

SIMEON: You are right, Joshua, you are right. For years now I have tried to find the phrases to describe that peculiar quality in Joseph that set him apart from his friends. Now suddenly you have given me the words. Truly, Joseph had his eyes and heart fixed on the heavens and the things that belong thereto. But his feet were firmly planted on this Galilean soil. When Joseph prayed, he prayed with all his heart. And in that same manner, as any father should, he taught the boy Jesus to kneel beside him and pray. When Joseph worked, it was with all the strength of his muscles and the dexterity of his fingers. Again in that manner, also as any father should, he taught the boy Jesus to stand beside his bench and use the hammer and saw. And somehow, because Joseph's work was done wholeheartedly and offered as a supplement to his prayers, the two were blended until the work itself became a prayer. Stranger from Egypt, I bow today in memory of a man who could achieve such a perfect balance in his daily life — perpetual harmony with the things of God — and complete accord with the common-place tasks of everyday living. I bow to Joseph, the man

1 who showed me, as he showed his boy Jesus, the way to
2 work and pray.
3 NARRATOR: The stranger heard the words of Joseph's
4 boyhood friend and pondered them a moment. Then he
5 turned to others in the group and spoke to them.
6 "Friends, I see you nod in agreement with the man who
7 has just spoken to me of Joseph. But I would know more.
8 Speak on about this man you so admired." And they
9 looked one to another until an older man stepped forward
10 and spoke earnestly to the stranger.
11 JOSHUA: Stranger unto Galilee, listen while I tell you some
12 wondrous things about this Joseph whom we just so
13 lately mourn. My name is Joshua and I have lived here
14 in Nazareth many more years than Joseph, for I am far
15 older than he. My house is near the well in the center of
16 the city, close by the family home of Mary, Joseph's
17 widow. I knew Mary from the day of her birth and I recall
18 vividly her years in the temple during which she and
19 Joseph were first betrothed. I remember well the
20 happiness that filled all Nazareth at the time of their
21 betrothal. Mary was the purest and loveliest of maidens
22 and Joseph was a vigorous man in those far-off days. He
23 was silent, as becomes a man of strength — but capable
24 of just and honest speech when there was a need of words.
25 And the love he bore for Mary was deep and tender — and
26 protective. It was this love which has guarded Mary like
27 a shield through their many years of poverty and times
28 of traveling. The family of Joseph has traveled about,
29 even as you, stranger, must have traveled. But their
30 journeys were those of hardship and necessity rather
31 than of pleasure. They began not long after the wedding
32 ceremony of Joseph and Mary when Caesar Augustus
33 decreed that a census of the whole world should be taken.
34 NATHANIEL: Stranger, had you been here in Nazareth of
35 Galilee at that time you would have been astounded at

1	the fury in this peaceful city, for the edict decreed that
2	each man should register in his own city of his lineage.
3	JOSHUA: That meant that many of us men of Nazareth must
4	journey abroad, some of us to great distances. As
5	Nathaniel says, there was great anger among the people
6	at the unreasonable order from the tyrant Caesar. We
7	men grumbled and muttered angry threats against the
8	government as we prepared for our journey. Joseph
9	alone spoke no ill of Caesar and tried to calm the rest of
10	us. It was apparent that Joseph's concern was for Mary,
11	his wife, who was soon to bring forth a child. He realized
12	how difficult the journey across the Galilean hills would
13	be for her and he thoughtfully provided every small
14	comfort that his poor funds would permit. Would that I
15	and all husbands would unfailingly offer such
16	thoughtfulness.
17	NATHANIEL: The gentleness of Joseph will not be forgotten
18	among men. Perhaps it will even serve as an example.
19	JOSHUA: May it ever be so. But my story has scarcely begun.
20	Together Mary and Joseph made the journey into Judea
21	because Joseph was of the house and family of David. It
22	was there in Bethlehem, David's city, that Mary delivered
23	her first-born son. And, stranger, these are the wondrous
24	things I promised to tell you of this man Joseph and his
25	family here of Nazareth. In the town of Bethlehem, where
26	they registered for the census, there was no room for
27	them at the inn. So the child Jesus was born in a manger
28	in a cave which served as shelter for the beasts. But on
29	that night of the birth, it is said that a heavenly star
30	rested over the spot where the child was born. An angelic
31	choir resounded in the heavens. And shepherds coming
32	from afar knelt at the feet of Joseph and Mary and the
33	child and glorified God. Later, so we have heard, three
34	kings from the East who also saw the star, came with
35	gifts of great price. Then, when King Herod sent his soldiers

1   into Bethlehem to kill all male children under two years
2   of age, still another strange thing happened to the family
3   of Joseph. In a dream, so it has been hinted, Joseph was
4   warned by an angel to take the child and his mother and
5   to flee into your land of Egypt until it was safe for them
6   to return. When Herod died, in some mysterious way
7   Joseph received the word and brought his family back
8   to Nazareth.

9 SIMEON: Man from Egypt, when you consider these unusual
10   happenings which Joshua has told you, remember that
11   neither Mary nor Joseph recounted these occurrences
12   to those of us their friends. The stories trickled into
13   Nazareth by travelers who heard them elsewhere in
14   Palestine. Neither did Mary nor Joseph deny these tales,
15   but kept their own counsel and would not speak of them.

16 JOSHUA: But many of us believe that there is truth in these
17   accounts and that there is something exceptionally holy
18   about Joseph and Mary and even more so about their
19   son, Jesus. For there is yet one other happening which
20   some of us witnessed. I myself was present on the
21   occasion and saw the strangeness which I could not
22   explain. It was in the year when Jesus was twelve and
23   many families here from Nazareth, as was the custom,
24   journeyed to Jerusalem for the feast of the Passover. We
25   remained there eight days in the densely crowded city,
26   packed with pilgrims. When the Galilean caravan left the
27   city, Joseph and Mary became separated and each
28   thought their son was with the other. It was not until the
29   caravan set camp for the night that his absence was noted
30   and when day broke, several of us accompanied the
31   parents back to the city to find the boy.

32 SIMEON: I remember it well. For three days the search went
33   on — three days of worry for the anguished parents. And
34   then they found him in the temple.

35 NATHANIEL: I myself saw him there. He was standing

1   among the doctors, debating on matters of the Scriptures.
2   And his wisdom and knowledge were such as I had never
3   heard before. Indeed, it astounded the doctors in the
4   temple and confounded his rejoicing parents.
5 JOSHUA: We knew then that this was an exceptionally holy
6   family of Nazareth — that the house of Joseph bore a
7   special sign of sanctity. You asked, stranger, why we
8   mourn this man Joseph who has passed from our midst.
9   We ask in turn, why would we not mourn one who has
10   been selected for holy happenings which we only vaguely
11   know of and which we are too simple to understand? If
12   there is no heavenly meaning to these happenings — as
13   surely there must be from all we have heard and seen —
14   would we still not mourn a man who was ever a loyal
15   and loving husband — a father who risked his life to save
16   that of his infant son? No finer man has yet come out of
17   Nazareth. And I ask you, stranger, have you seen his
18   equal any place in the world beyond?
19 NARRATOR: The stranger listened thoughtfully to the
20   unexpected revelations of the old man of Nazareth. "No
21   man," he agreed, "either in Nazareth nor in the world
22   apart can merit greater honor than that due men like
23   Joseph for their regard for their families. But tell me
24   more of this just man whose perfect fatherhood you
25   stress. I have seen him through your words as a man of
26   God and the head of a family to whom mysterious
27   happenings of an almost supernatural nature seem to
28   have occurred. Tell me now of Joseph as a man among
29   men, for it is outside the family circle, as well as within
30   its folds, that a father shows his son the proper way to
31   live. You, Nathaniel, tell me of Joseph's life at work here
32   in the street of the carpenters."
33 NATHANIEL: Joseph, the carpenter, was the man I knew
34   best, for I, too, am a carpenter by trade and have been
35   for many years. I mourn for Joseph as a father, for though

1	we were of the same age, I learned from him the lessons
2	that a father might have taught. We lived in troubled
3	times, Joseph and I, even as young men when we first
4	set up our houses and our shops side by side. Despots
5	have ruled us from Rome and tyrants have reigned in
6	Palestine. As you have heard from Bethlehem to Judea,
7	Joseph was forced to flee with his family into your own
8	land of Egypt because of a cruel king. We have been taxed
9	almost to the point of starvation to keep up the armies
10	of Rome and we have watched our children go hungry
11	because the wages for our labor have been far below
12	what our labor is worth. All this has caused hatred and
13	unrest here in Galilee as in all the Hebrew lands.
14	SIMEON: True, Nathaniel. For years I have heard men curse
15	the governments that rule us and make useless threats
16	against the despots.
17	NATHANIEL: But not Joseph. From him I heard words of
18	peace and love alone. From Joseph I have taken new
19	courage that the Messiah will come soon to deliver his
20	people and that a new order will be established by his
21	coming. From Joseph I learned other things, too — about
22	the dignity that lies within each man and the homage
23	due to women. How to pray for those who worship pagan
24	gods and those who treat all conquered men as slaves.
25	Most important for my own peace of mind, I learned from
26	him not to despise the humble trade of carpentry, poorly
27	paid though it is. Through the wisdom of Joseph I know
28	that carpentry, as all other work, has its place in God's
29	plan of the universe, to provide shelter and comfort for
30	me. Carpentry, I understand now, is good and necessary,
31	just as tilling the soil to feed God's creatures, or weaving
32	linens to clothe them, or preaching in the temple to save
33	their souls are good and necessary works. Joseph, more
34	by his silent and prayerful example than by his few
35	spoken words, has taught me that there is dignity in any

1   work man does — if it is attuned to the will of God and
2   performed to the best of man's ability.
3 JOSHUA: Stranger, you appear as though you believe what
4   Nathaniel tells you of Joseph, as well as what Simeon
5   and I have said. Surely it answers your questions
6   concerning our praise of this holy man.
7 NATHANIEL: But wait, Joshua, there is more I must say. I
8   would speak to the stranger of the many journeys
9   undertaken by Joseph without a word of complaint.
10   Already we have told you of those journeys — now think
11   on them. Imagine, if you can, the quiet, gentle Joseph,
12   forced into the worrisome trip with Mary to Bethlehem,
13   across the hills and valleys that led to the city of David.
14   Imagine the dread with which he undertook the
15   unexpected flight to Egypt with his wife and young child,
16   into a land of different customs and strange tongues. On
17   his return to this quiet place of Nazareth, we might have
18   heard words of bitterness from Joseph's lips, for the
19   hardships of the displaced family were many. Instead, I
20   for one, learned further lessons in love from Joseph. All
21   men, he assured me, are basically the same, whether they
22   live in Galilee or Judea, or far off in Egypt where pagan
23   gods are worshipped.
24 SIMEON: Joseph also pointed out to us that the God of Israel
25   created every man and that each man everywhere asks
26   little more than to do his work and earn sufficient wages
27   to take care of his family.
28 NATHANIEL: Joseph taught me, too, that men must ever be
29   kind to those in need, regardless of their color or their
30   tongue or occupation. And this lesson, stranger, came
31   from one whose wife bore her son in a stable because
32   they would give them no room in the inn. Whose family
33   was sent into exile because of the cruelty of a tyrant king.
34   And whose comforts in life have ever been small because
35   the rich kept down the wages of the poor. Across the

1 years, stranger, I have learned these lessons from my
2 friend the carpenter, Joseph. And I shall teach them to
3 my sons and my sons' sons as though I have learned them
4 from Joseph as a father.
5 SIMEON: He was called husband by Mary and father by
6 Jesus . . . a man of the poor . . . a model for those who
7 work with their hands. This, stranger, was Joseph of
8 Nazareth — a just man and a father to imitate.
9 NARRATOR: And so it was that the stranger returned to his
10 house on the farthest street of Nazareth. And though
11 nothing that Joseph ever said had been directly quoted
12 to him, he praised his gods and the God of Israel for the
13 lessons learned from this humble carpenter of Nazareth —
14 this man whom he recognized as the perfect model of
15 fatherhood. And all this happened on the day that Joseph
16 of Nazareth was laid in the tomb.
17
18
19
20
21
22
23
24
25
26
27
28
29
30
31
32
33
34
35

The Customs of Christmastide
by MARTHA-JEAN ROCKEY

CAST

NINE SPEAKERS

OTHERS AS NOTED THROUGHOUT SCRIPT
Non-speaking parts

PRODUCTION NOTES

This program was created as a Christmas program to be presented in the sanctuary of a church, but it could be adapted to any location.

If used in a sanctuary with a front altar, the greenery may be draped over the altar, and a poinsettia placed at one side and a miniature Christmas tree at the other, with the living nativity scene created in the middle in front of the altar.

This has been written to involve nine speakers, although any number may be used, with musical interludes. As written the audience is invited to participate by singing one verse each of a number of familiar carols, for which the words should not need to be printed.

Musical numbers are also suggested for choirs of adults, youth, and children, but feel free to alter this as wished, and also feel free to add any other special numbers that seem suitable.

This was performed using children from preschool through sixth grade, with some assistance by older youths to direct the younger ones. Also, older youths (seventh-twelfth grades) were used for the youth choirs, although again, this is flexible.

For performance, each speaker stood wherever he was and read his part from there, but a front podium could be used.

For rehearsals each choral group worked separately to learn the songs. Then the children (and youths who were helping the children) with props were rehearsed three times with an adult reading the cue lines to signal action. The entire work was never rehearsed with all speakers and music, yet the final performance went very smoothly.

1	SPEAKER 1:	Tonight we mark the celebration of Christmas
2		— and we shall do that by examining the origins of many
3		of the customs we perform at Christmas time. Let us all
4		join in singing one verse of "O, Come All Ye Faithful."
5		Literally Christmas means Christ Mass or the Mass
6		of Christ. The month of December has been a month of
7		celebration for centuries, originally centering on the
8		winter solstice. For Jews, December has brought
9		Hanukah, the Festival of the Lights, celebrating their
10		victory over their Syrian oppressors.
11		Although there is controversy over the actual date
12		of the birth of Christ, December 25 is commonly accepted,
13		and it fits in well with a heritage of other winter
14		celebrations.
15		Where do our customs come from? They come from
16		a very diverse heritage, a mix of pagan and Christian
17		customs from many parts of the world. Yet all we do, we
18		do today as part of our traditional Christian celebration.
19		Join in singing one verse of "Deck the Halls."
20	SPEAKER 2:	Christians traditionally celebrate by using
21		greenery to decorate their homes, particularly holly and
22		holly wreaths. *(A few CHILDREN begin to bring in holly*
23		*branches to place at front of church.)* Holly, an evergreen
24		plant, was revered by early Anglo-Saxons and Norsemen
25		who used it in their homes to ensure the return of other
26		vegetation with the spring.
27		A Christian legend states that holly first grew where
28		the feet of Christ touched the earth. Another legend has
29		it that the crown of thorns which Christ wore was of
30		holly, whose berries, originally white, turned red on his
31		forehead.
32	*CHOIR:*	Sings "The Holly and the Ivy."
33	SPEAKER 2:	*(Continued)* The poinsettia is also a traditional
34		Christmas plant, coming to the United States from
35		Mexico. Its significance is explained in a lovely legend

1   which tells of a young peasant boy or girl — the stories
2   vary — who prays for a gift for the Christ child, and is
3   rewarded when weeds change into the poinsettia.
4   **SPEAKER 3:**   Most of us also have a Christmas tree as part of
5   our holiday decorations.
6   *YOUTH CHOIR:*   Sings "O Christmas Tree."
7   **SPEAKER 3:** *(Continued)* **Traditionally Boniface, an early**
8   **missionary to Germany, is thought to have placed a fir**
9   **tree in place of an oak sacred to the Norsemen, and many**
10   **call that the first Christmas tree. Others point to early**
11   **mystery plays in which a paradise tree decorated with**
12   **fruit and nuts, had a prominent place.** *(CHILDREN bring*
13   *in a small tree, place it at one side of the front, and begin to*
14   *decorate it.)*
15   **Still others credit Martin Luther for the origin of**
16   **the tree, who, after noticing a lovely woodland tree,**
17   **supposedly put one up in his home. The earliest trees**
18   **used in America were those used by Hessian soldiers**
19   **during the American Revolution by men who were lonely**
20   **for home.**
21   **By 1856, the tree was so popular at Christmas that**
22   **President Pierce had one put up in the White House, and**
23   **in 1923 President and Mrs. Coolidge lit the first national**
24   **Christmas tree on the White House grounds. Let us all**
25   **sing one verse of "Hark, the Herald Angels Sing."**
26   **SPEAKER 4:**   What decorates the tree? Lights of one sort or
27   another, and many ornaments — often those relating to
28   the Christmas story itself, such as figures of angels. Join
29   in singing "Angels from the Realms of Glory."
30   A vital Christmas custom in many homes is the
31   placing of the crèche in a prominent spot. This, of course,
32   dates directly from the Christmas story. Let's all sing one
33   verse of "O Little Town of Bethlehem." *(A manger or cradle*
34   *with two chairs is placed at front.)*
35   Often times a crèche itself is first set up, and perhaps

1 other buildings to represent the town of Bethlehem.
2 SPEAKER 5: Luke 2:1-5. Thus, the key figures in the scene
3 become Mary and Joseph. *(Two representing MARY and*
4 *JOSEPH take places behind the altar and stand by cradle.)*
5 *SPECIAL:* A duet may be sung here: "Joseph, Dear, Oh Joseph,
6 Mine."
7 SPEAKER 5: *(Continued)* Luke 2:6-7. And now we may add the
8 Christ child to the scene. *(Child representing ANGEL gives*
9 *MARY doll to place in cradle. Then ANGEL stands behind*
10 *cradle.)* Join in singing one verse of "Silent Night."
11 Luke 2:8-14. Sing one verse of "Angels We Have
12 Heard on High.
13 *CHOIR:* Sings "Rise Up, Shepherd."
14 SPEAKER 5: *(Continued)* Luke 2:15-20.
15 *CHILDREN:* Sing "Away in a Manger." *(Children representing*
16 *SHEPHERDS take places around manger — kneeling or sitting.)*
17 Perhaps the children can sing "O Come, Little Children."
18 SPEAKER 5: *(Continued)* And with this passage of Luke the
19 scene is nearly complete.
20 SPEAKER 6: Then, as Christmas approaches, we turn from
21 decorating to celebrating. One familiar custom is the
22 sending of Christmas cards. *(At one side, near Christmas*
23 *tree, CHILDREN bring cards and exchange them . . . settle down*
24 *to look at them.)* The earliest known holiday card was
25 printed in Germany in the 1400s, but the one that started
26 our trend was printed in 1843 in London for Sir Henry
27 Cole. It read "Merry Christmas and Happy New Year."
28 In 1874 the first cards were printed in America and the
29 custom spread so that five billion are exchanged each
30 year. Let's all sing one verse of "We Wish You a Merry
31 Christmas."
32 SPEAKER 7: Another traditional way of spreading Christmas
33 spirit is through caroling. The earliest carols were ring
34 dances accompanied by singing, but eventually the word
35 came to mean the song itself. Troubadors and wandering

1   minstrels first toured villages of Italy, but the custom
2   spread throughout France, Germany and England.
3   The wandering carolers were often rewarded with
4   food and drink.
5 **CHOIR:**   Sing "Hey, Ho, Nobody Home," if available. Maybe sung
6   as a round.
7 **SPEAKER 7:** *(Continued)* **During the Puritan reign in**
8   **seventeenth century England the traditional caroling**
9   **died out only be to revived again in the nineteenth**
10   **century.**
11 *YOUTHS:*   "Here We Come A-Caroling." *(YOUTHS sing and walk,*
12   *and end up front staying until song is finished.)*
13 **SPEAKER 8:**   **On Christmas Eve many children hang their**
14   **Christmas stockings and wait for Santa to fill them with**
15   **goodies. This custom comes from the story of Saint**
16   **Nicholas, now more commonly called Santa Claus.**
17   **Saint Nicholas lived in Asia Minor in the fourth**
18   **century and, as the legend goes, he wanted to provide**
19   **dowry money for three daughters of a poor merchant. So**
20   **he poured the coins down the chimney into their**
21   **stockings which were hung to dry. Stockings as we know**
22   **them were not worn until the eleventh century, so much**
23   **of this story is just a legend.**
24   **The Dutch who settled in New York brought with**
25   **them this saint whom they called Sinterklaas.**
26   **Then in 1822, a New York professor, Clement Clark**
27   **Moore, transformed the tall, kindly saint into the fat,**
28   **jolly Santa Claus we know today, with his poem, "A Visit**
29   **from Saint Nicholaus."** *(CHILDREN place stockings at altar*
30   *and lie down.)*
31   **It is this Santa of whom children dream of on**
32   **Christmas Eve as they wait for Christmas morning to**
33   **arrive. Join in singing one verse of "Joy to the World."**
34 **SPEAKER 9:**   **On Christmas morning many Christians**
35   **exchange gifts — although this is a custom observed at**

1   many different times throughout the season. Many feel
2   this custom dates from the story of the three wise men.
3   *MEN OF CHOIR:*   Sing "March of the Three Kings."
4   **SPEAKER 5:**   Matthew 2:1-14.
5   **SPEAKER 9:**   According to tradition the kings were Melchior,
6   **King of Arabia, who brought gold, the symbol of a king's**
7   **position; Balthasar, King of Ethiopia, who brought**
8   **frankincense, symbol of a high priest's position; and**
9   **Gaspar, King of Tarsus, who brought myrrh, symbol of**
10   **medicine and representative of Christ's future role as**
11   **Great Physician.** *(KING figures march down aisle and end up*
12   *at manger, where they deposit gifts and then take places around*
13   *scene, completing the nativity scene.)*
14   **Although the kings are not thought to have arrived**
15   **until the twelfth day of Christmas, January 6, they make**
16   **the final figures normally included in the manger scene.**
17   **Sing one verse of "We Three Kings."**
18   **The gifts they brought are represented each year**
19   **by the gifts we exchange.**
20   **Thus, even though the sources of our traditions are**
21   **varied, together they have come to make up what we**
22   **think of as a truly American Christmas.**
23   **Please join in singing the rest of "Joy to the World,"**
24   **beginning with verse two.**
25
26
27
28
29
30
31
32
33
34
35

ADAPTATIONS FROM CLASSICS AND LEGENDS

Gabriel Grubb's Christmas Dance
adapted from THE PICKWICK PAPERS
by CHARLES DICKENS
dramatized by DOUGLAS ROOME

CAST

NARRATOR

BOY

VOICES
(Offstage)

GABRIEL

DEATH

YOUNG WOMAN
(Walk-on)

CURATE
(Walk-on)

PRODUCTION NOTES

This play is adapted from a short story in *The Pickwick Papers* by Charles Dickens. It can be performed on a bare stage or with scenery as suggested. A few simple lighting effects, as indicated in the script, are all that's required for an effective presentation.

1

SCENE 1

2

3 ***SETTING:*** Projected onto the forestage are several patches of light

4   in which can be seen the shadows of people standing and

5   dancing. There is also the sound of music mixed with that of

6   people talking and laughing.

7

8 ***AT RISE:*** NARRATOR enters from right and comes to the edge of

9   the stage. May be a man or a woman wearing street clothes.

10

11 **NARRATOR:** A long, long while ago — so long that the story

12   **must be a true one because our great-grandfathers**

13   **implicitly believed it — there officiated as sexton and**

14   **gravedigger in a churchyard near here, one Gabriel**

15   **Grubb, an ill-conditioned, cross-grained, surly fellow**

16   **who consorted with nobody but himself — and who eyed**

17   **each merry face, as it passed by, with a deep scowl of**

18   **malice and ill humor.**

19   **A little before twilight, this Christmas Eve, Gabriel**

20   **shouldered his spade, lighted his lantern, and betook**

21   **himself toward the old churchyard,** *(GABRIEL enters from*

22   *left. He wears dark clothing and is carrying a spade and lantern)*

23   **for he had a grave to finish by next morning, and feeling**

24   **very low, he thought it might raise his spirits if he went**

25   **on with his work at once.**

26   **As he went his way up the ancient street, he saw**

27   **the cheerful light of the blazing fires gleam through the**

28   **old windows and heard the loud laugh and the cheerful**

29   **shouts of those who were assembled within. All this was**

30   **gall and wormwood to the heart of Gabriel Grubb. And**

31   **when children were heard at their Christmas games,**

32   **Gabriel smiled grimly and clutched the handle of his**

33   **spade with a firmer grasp as he thought of measles,**

34   **scarlet fever, whooping cough, and a good many other**

35   **sources of consolation besides.** *(GABRIEL exits right. The*

1   *sound and lighting effects cease.)*
2   In this happy frame of mind, *(GABRIEL enters from*
3   *right)* Gabriel turned into the dark lane which led to the
4   churchyard. Now, Gabriel had been looking forward to
5   reaching the dark lane because it was, generally
6   speaking, a nice gloomy, mournful place into which the
7   townspeople did not much care to go except in broad
8   daylight and when the sun was shining. *(Off left and*
9   *approaching, BOY singing a carol)* Consequently, he was not
10   a little indignant to hear a young urchin *(BOY enters)*
11   roaring out a jolly song in this very sanctuary which was
12   called Coffin Lane.
13   BOY: Merry Christmas to you, Mr. Grubb!
14   GABRIEL: I'll merry you, you howling cur! *(Sets on BOY, trying*
15   *his best to hit him with lantern and spade. BOY just does elude*
16   *him, and exits running.)*
17   NARRATOR: And as the boy hurried away singing quite a
18   different sort of tune, Gabriel Grubb chuckled very
19   heartily to himself and entered the churchyard.
20   *(GABRIEL exits left, NARRATOR right.)*
21
22   SCENE 2
23
24   *SETTING:*   Churchyard. At Right Center and Left Center are screens
25   on which are painted the stones, statues, and tombs of a
26   cemetery. Area lighting. GABRIEL has just entered from left.
27   He puts down the lantern and spade in front of screen at Left
28   Center.
29
30   GABRIEL: *(Singing as he takes off his coat)*
31   Brave lodgings for one, brave lodgings for one,
32   A few feet of cold earth, when life is done;
33   A stone at the head, a stone at the feet,
34   A rich, juicy meal for the worms to eat;
35   Rank grass overhead, damp clay around,

1   **Brave lodgings for one, here, in holy ground!**

2   *(Laughs)* **Ho! Ho! Ho! A coffin at Christmas!**

3   **A Christmas box! Ho! Ho! Ho!**

4   **DEATH:** *(Behind screen at Left Center)* **Ho! Ho! Ho!**

5   **GABRIEL:** *(Starts and looks around)* **. . . It was the echoes.**

6   **DEATH:** *(Enters from behind screen. Long robe with hood of ash*

7   *white, gloves of the same color, and a half mask depicting a skull.*

8   *From cord around waist hangs an hourglass.)* **It was *not*.**

9   **GABRIEL:** *(Jumps)* **Whooo . . .!?**

10   **DEATH:** **It was not the echoes.**

11   **GABRIEL:** **Yes . . . yes, sir!**

12   **DEATH:** **What are you doing here on Christmas Eve?**

13   **GABRIEL:** **I came to dig a grave, sir.**

14   **DEATH:** **What man wanders among graves and churchyards**

15   **on such a night as this?**

16   **VOICES:** *(From Offstage)* **Gabriel Grubb! Gabriel Grubb!**

17   *(GABRIEL looks around wildly.)*

18   **DEATH:** **I said, what man?**

19   **VOICES:** **Gabriel Grubb! Gabriel Grubb!**

20   **DEATH:** **Have you no answer?**

21   **GABRIEL:** *(Stammering, not looking at DEATH)* **It's — it's —**

22   **very curious, sir. Very curious, and very pretty, but I**

23   **have my work to do, sir, if you please.**

24   **DEATH:** **What work?**

25   **GABRIEL:** **The grave, sir; making the grave.**

26   **DEATH:** **Oh, the grave, eh? And who makes graves at a time**

27   **when all other men are merry and take pleasure in it?**

28   **VOICES:** **Gabriel Grubb! Gabriel Grubb!**

29   **DEATH:** **Do you know me?**

30   **GABRIEL:** **No, sir.**

31   **DEATH:** **Come, Gabriel! You have been following after me**

32   **these forty years, man and boy.**

33   **GABRIEL:** **It cannot be, sir. You must be a reveler or semblance,**

34   **sir. Death never makes sport, sir. Death only does what**

35   **he's bid — neither more nor less.**

1 DEATH: *(Offers his hand.)* **Take my hand, then. If I am not**
2 **Death, what is there to fear?**
3 GABRIEL: **Why do you sport?**
4 DEATH: **Then you do know me?**
5 GABRIEL: **Is it writ? Has my time come?**
6 DEATH: **Perhaps.**
7 GABRIEL: *(Afraid, but also sullen)* **That can't be! Either you've**
8 **come to part me, body from soul, or you haven't! There's**
9 **no "perhaps" to it!**
10 DEATH: **And if it pleases God to have me do otherwise?**
11 GABRIEL: **He can't! He can't let you loose to make sport and**
12 **bargain! That'd be the end of all justice!**
13 DEATH: **Except this night, Gabriel Grubb. This night even**
14 **Death may turn away from the darkness and face the**
15 **light. This night I have the power to refuse the writ and**
16 **overthrow myself. God would have even Death honor the**
17 **birth of his son.**
18 GABRIEL: *(Stares, grim)* **If it's so, and my name be writ, take**
19 **me — I'll not bargain with you or do tricks like a fool!**
20 *(YOUNG WOMAN enters from right carrying an infant wrapped*
21 *in a blanket. She is sad and poorly dressed. She disappears*
22 *behind the screen at Right Center.)*
23 DEATH: **That is who I have come for — that infant.**
24 GABRIEL: *(Vastly relieved, has given YOUNG WOMAN the*
25 *briefest of glances.)* **I knew it couldn't be me. I'm in the**
26 **prime of health.**
27 DEATH: **The mother is a widow and a stranger here. She is**
28 **very young and very timid. Having been ill treated before,**
29 **she is afraid to ask for help.**
30 GABRIEL: **She isn't the only one ever to know ill treatment.**
31 DEATH: **The child is hungry and burns with fever. The**
32 **mother believes it will die soon, that is why she has come**
33 **to this place of death.**
34 GABRIEL: *(Shrugs)* **Do what's writ.**
35 DEATH: **You will not help?**

1 GABRIEL: What are they to me? I have my own skin to look
2   after. Besides, without a child, the woman'll find it easier
3   to get work.
4 DEATH: This is true.
5 GABRIEL: And the child is better off. It'll fly straight to God
6   without sin or blemish. If it stays here, it'll only know
7   want and sorrow. You're doing the child a favor.
8 DEATH: You will not help?
9 GABRIEL: Do your bidding! Do what's writ!
10 DEATH: You wish Death to touch the child?
11 GABRIEL: *(Stamps his foot.)* It's not my concern! You pass and
12   free the soul, and I come after and bury what remains.
13   That's how the world is arranged!
14 DEATH: Tell me to touch the child, Gabriel Grubb!
15 GABRIEL: I tell you it isn't for me to say!
16 DEATH: Did you take a close look at the mother's face?
17 GABRIEL: Why?
18 DEATH: Go and look at her face.
19 GABRIEL: *(Hesitates, then takes lantern and crosses to screen at*
20   *Right Center. Holding the lantern high, he peers behind the*
21   *screen. He starts violently. Terrified.)* Can't be! Can't be!
22 DEATH: What did you see?
23 GABRIEL: I remember! She told me the story! But it can't be!
24   All that's fifty years ago!
25 DEATH: God is also Time, Gabriel Grubb.
26 GABRIEL: But — but the curate found us! He took us in.
27   There was food. There was medicine for my fever. You
28   can't mean you want to take my life? You can't do that!
29   A man's life is more than something writ in chalk on a
30   slate! You can't make it as if I never was!
31 DEATH: *(Pointedly)* And who was it that prompted the curate
32   to go walking in the churchyard? *(GABRIEL stares at*
33   *DEATH open-mouthed. Harshly.)* And why shouldn't I
34   regret! Who would miss you? Who would mourn you? Who
35   would feel the loss of a man who digs graves on Christmas

1   Eve? Who would believe that life was dear to such a man?

2 GABRIEL: You said you could overthrow yourself! In Christ's

3   name!

4 DEATH: And so, by God's leave, I may — if I wish. But I

5   neither can nor will do it alone.

6 GABRIEL: I'll find someone to help! *(Starts off.)*

7 DEATH: No!

8 GABRIEL: *(Frantic)* But how else can I help the child if it's me?

9 DEATH: Become as a child.

10 GABRIEL: How?!

11 DEATH: Have you no remembrance of your childhood . . . of

12   your mother?

13 GABRIEL: Yes . . . some. Some. *(Wrings his hands.)* But it was

14   so long ago . . . and my mother is long dead, poor soul . . .

15 DEATH: But were you not delicately nurtured and tenderly

16   brought up? Wasn't your mother, once her hope had been

17   restored, ever cheerful under privations and superior to

18   suffering? Didn't she bear within her heart an

19   inexhaustible well-spring of affection and devotion?

20   *(Harshly, taking a step closer to GABRIEL)* Or was it she who

21   taught you to snarl at mirth and cheerfulness? Was it she

22   who taught you to strike children out of envious malice

23   because they could be merry and you could not?

24 GABRIEL: *(Has been making protesting gestures.)* No! No! She

25   was ever cheerful! There was no unkindness in her!

26 DEATH: And she kept Christmas well?

27 GABRIEL: Yes, yes!

28 DEATH: Then I ask you again, Gabriel Grubb: Would you

29   have Death touch the child?

30 GABRIEL: No! I will become a child! Only show me how.

31 DEATH: *(Begins to clap and to keep time with his foot.)* Dance,

32   Gabriel — dance your way back in life.

33 GABRIEL: *(Desperate, helpless)* I don't know how!

34 DEATH: Begin. You will remember — just as you remembered

35   your mother. The dance will come back to you if only you

1   will go toward it.

2   GABRIEL: *(Begins an awkward, almost ludicrous, hopping dance*

3   *step.)* **This is your sport! You're just making a fool of me.**

4   DEATH: **No, Gabriel Grubb, I am *un*making a fool.**

5   GABRIEL: **God help me!**

6   DEATH: **He is trying to.**

7   GABRIEL: *(Dancing with slightly more ease and grace)* **Is this**

8   **enough?** *(DEATH takes a step away, then another.)* **Is this the**

9   **way? Is this better?** *(CURATE enters Up Left, hands behind*

10   *his back, deep in thought. GABRIEL has moved to Down Left.*

11   *DEATH is now by the left edge of the screen at Left Center. When*

12   *CURATE reaches Up Center, he looks up and toward screen at*

13   *Right Center. With a concerned expression, he crosses and*

14   *disappears behind screen. A moment later CURATE reappears*

15   *supporting YOUNG WOMAN on his arm. DEATH ceases to*

16   *mark the tempo and disappears behind screen at Left Center.*

17   *GABRIEL exits left, dancing. CURATE and YOUNG WOMAN*

18   *exit Up Left.)*

19

20   **SCENE 3**

21

22   *SETTING:*   Same at Scene 1.

23

24   *(GABRIEL enters from left. His step is livelier, and he shows*

25   *signs of enjoying the dance.)*

26   GABRIEL: **I'm getting my second wind now ... Not so bad**

27   **once you get going ... Odd the way it seems to come back**

28   **to you.** *(He moves, by turns, to Center. The light and sound*

29   *effects return.)*

30   VOICES: *(Ad-lib)* **Who's that? Can't be! Old Grubb's**

31   **possessed! It's a fit for sure! St. Anthony's fire, if you ask**

32   **me!**

33   GABRIEL: **Merry Christmas! Bless you all!**

34   VOICES: *(Ad-lib)* **Can't be! Is! Miracle! Miracle and a half!**

35   **God be praised! Who'd have believed?**

```
1    GABRIEL:   Merry Christmas!
2    VOICES:    And a Merry Christmas to you, Gabriel Grubb.
3
4
5
6
7
8
9
10
11
12
13
14
15
16
17
18
19
20
21
22
23
24
25
26
27
28
29
30
31
32
33
34
35
```

The First Christmas Crèche
by BETTY KELLY and ARTHUR ZAPEL

CAST

NARRATOR
The pastor or any good reader.
He is apart from the action.

FATHER FRANCIS
A man about 30 dressed in a monk's robe.
He was not bearded, but this is optional. A gentle person.

BERNARDO
Should be a contrasting type to Francis.
He can also be dressed in a monk's robe if two are available.
Not required. He could be just a villager and follower of Francis.

MARIA
A woman about 35.
Age optional. Her son is still in his teens. A good actress.
Emotional.

MAYOR
A portly fellow, perhaps, about 50.
Age is optional.

ANGELA
A young girl about 15.
She's impressionable. All the world is a wonder to her.

CHILDREN
Can be six brief speaking parts.

OTHER PARTS
These remaining roles are all nonspeaking parts.
They can be chosen from men and women as described
in the script.

PRODUCTION NOTES

This program is meant to be staged as conveniently as possible. No ostentatious sets or costumes are required. This is a simple story of a small village called Assisi in Italy during the Middle Ages — very likely 1212 during St. Francis' early ministry at this place.

This story is for all Christians. St. Francis is revered by Christians of all faiths and denominations. Francis was canonzied before the reformation, so technically we must suppose he's a saint for everyone in Christendom.

This apocryphal story can be adapted to fit your situation. We suggest the dramatic action take place in the church altar area and the NARRATOR can speak from a side pulpit. Simple lighting can help direct attention from each scene to the NARRATOR and back to the players. The scenes will change as the NARRATOR speaks.

The action and props are indicated in the script. The director can work out the best way to use the play action for your church.

1	NARRATOR: There is a legend that St. Francis built the first
2	Christian crèche or manger scene. It happened in Assisi,
3	Italy. Some say it was built in the town square — others
4	say in a hillside cave on the outskirts of the village.
5	Actually, no one knows because this was long ago in
6	medieval times. I would guess about the year 1212. And
7	how do you suppose St. Francis came to make the first
8	Christmas crèche? Did he just decide one day that this
9	would be a good thing to do or was he inspired by some
10	real-life event in his time. Of course, we shall never know
11	because history has no true record of this. But today, let
12	us imagine what might have happened in Assisi to cause
13	St. Francis to make the first manger crèche many
14	centuries ago . . . *(Fade up lights on altar area where we see*
15	*BERNARDO and MARIA in disagreement.)*
16	BERNARDO: My good lady, Maria, I have told you, he is not
17	to be disturbed.
18	MARIA: But I must see him. Please.
19	BERNARDO: Father Francis is in the cathedral garden. He
20	prays for you and me among the white doves of the
21	mountains. They have flown here this morning from
22	Corsica. They come here only once a year. He waits all
23	year for this day.
24	MARIA: But Signor Bernardo, can't you see that I need him
25	now? *(She weeps.)* Please, I beg you! You do not
26	understand.
27	BERNARDO: It is you who do not understand. Don't you
28	know that Father Francis . . .?
29	FRANCIS: *(Walking into scene)* What is it, Bernardo? I heard
30	someone weeping. If it is this good woman let her come
31	to me.
32	BERNARDO: But Francis, the doves. You have waited so
33	long.
34	FRANCIS: And I can wait longer. *(To MARIA)* Please come
35	with me and tell me your need.

1 MARIA: Bless you, Father Francis. My name is Maria
2 Sanchetti. My son and I are new to Assisi. We come here
3 for work but we find none. My good husband, may God
4 bless his soul, he died three weeks ago. It was a long
5 illness and my son and I have no money left. Our friends
6 they help us. But how much can they do? They have their
7 own families to look after. Others in our little village try
8 to help us but they have too little for themselves. So we
9 leave. We do not want to take from others. My son, Pepi,
10 he has tried to care for me but he is not able to find work
11 in Assisi.
12 FRANCIS: You and your son may stay here, Maria. I will find
13 you work.
14 MARIA: No, Father, that is impossible. My son Pepi, he is in
15 jail.
16 FRANCIS: What has he done that they should put him in
17 jail?
18 MARIA: He saw how weak and thin I had become and so he
19 went to the wheat fields of the man named Salvatore and
20 he stole grain for bread. He was caught on the roadway
21 and beaten by Salvatore's workers.
22 FRANCIS: And the cabineri, how did they come to put him in
23 jail?
24 MARIA: Signor Salvatore insisted that the cabineri jail him
25 as an example to others who would steal. But Father
26 Francis, my son is not a criminal! He is a good boy — a
27 loving son. Please, Father, help my Pepi.
28 FRANCIS: I will speak to the mayor, Maria. With our Lord's
29 help Pepi will be free again. Our people of Assisi are
30 sometimes harsh and even cruel but they do have it in
31 their hearts to forgive. Maria, you stay here and rest. *(To*
32 *BERNARDO)* Bernardo, please give this woman warm
33 broth, meat and bread. It will restore her strength. I will
34 go to the village. *(Fade lights on scene. Spotlight on*
35 *NARRATOR.)*

1   NARRATOR: But it was not an easy task that Father Francis
2   had taken on for himself. The village of Assisi at that
3   time was an unhappy place. The people were being
4   heavily taxed, many were without work, and there was
5   violence between groups — each fighting for its own
6   special interests. Even though it was nearly Christmas
7   the troubled mayor was not in a friendly mood. *(Fade up*
8   *lights on new scene.)*
9   MAYOR: What do you expect me to do, Father Francis? This
10   boy was caught stealing. You know the law as well as I.
11   If I were to release him then all the village's anger would
12   fall on me. No. No. It is a bad time, Father.
13   FRANCIS: But it should be a good time, Signor Mayor, for
14   soon it will be the day of our Savior's birth. This should
15   be a time of forgiveness, of goodwill to men.
16   MAYOR: Of course, but that is not the way it is, Padre. I am
17   sorry but I must refuse your request.
18   FRANCIS: You are a kind man, Signor Mayor. May I ask your
19   cooperation in another matter I have long been
20   considering?
21   MAYOR: Speak and I will listen. But no promises.
22   FRANCIS: Perhaps this is the time for us to remind our people
23   of Assisi that Jesus was born to teach us how to love —
24   how to forgive. I believe we can . . . *(Lights fade along with*
25   *his words. Spotlight on NARRATOR.)*
26   NARRATOR: Father Francis explained in detail his inspiration
27   of how the village might celebrate the birth of Jesus. The
28   mayor was, in truth, a good Christian man. He listened
29   carefully. He liked what Father Francis suggested, and
30   as a result, an important decision was made that
31   afternoon — far more important than either of them
32   could possibly have guessed. It was agreed that there
33   would, in two weeks, on the day before Christmas, be a
34   special village pageant. It would be a re-enactment of the
35   Nativity in the village square. All villagers young and old

1 would be invited to participate. *(Lights up on new scene.)*
2 ANGELA: *(Excited)* **We will have a manger right here in our**
3 **village, Father Francis?!**
4 FRANCIS: **Yes, my child.**
5 ANGELA: **With Mary and Joseph?**
6 FRANCIS: **Yes, and the baby Jesus, too.**
7 ANGELA: **And what about the shepherds and the wise men?**
8 **Will we have them?**
9 FRANCIS: **Everything, my child. Spread the word and I will**
10 **do the same. This will be a beautiful Christmas Eve in**
11 **Assisi.** *(Fade lights. Spotlight on NARRATOR.)*
12 NARRATOR: **And indeed it was. It didn't happen as easily**
13 **as you might think — but it did happen. The word was**
14 **passed along to all of the citizens of Assisi and the mayor**
15 **wrote a proclamation. There was talk and grumblings**
16 **about this silly new idea. In fact, some said it was**
17 **blasphemous — that Father Francis had overstepped his**
18 **authority. You know how some people are about change.**
19 **Yes, sadly, nothing happened for over a week and it**
20 **appeared that the event would never come to be. It seems**
21 **that everyone was afraid to be the first to volunteer. But**
22 **then the least likely person of all stepped forward.** *(MAN*
23 *walks down center church aisle carrying a wooden manger. He*
24 *places it at center of altar.)* **It was the man who ran the**
25 **armory. The man whose small foundry was dedicated to**
26 **producing battle-axes, swords, truncheons and**
27 **armor — instruments of war and violence. One evening**
28 **this man, Giovanni Rappalo, brought a wooden manger**
29 **he had made.** *(SECOND MAN comes down aisle. He carries*
30 *a wooden stool.)*
31 **Later that evening, one of his workers brought a**
32 **crude wooden stool which they placed beside the manger.**
33 **It was here that Mary was to sit to watch after her infant**
34 **Jesus.** *(Now several costumed TOWNSPEOPLE come down*
35 *aisle and gather around the manger.)* **The word passed quickly**

1	among the townspeople and soon they all gathered at the
2	village square to see the manger, the chair, and the hand-
3	carved baby Jesus some unknown person had put in the
4	manger. *(SHOPKEEPER gives blanket.)* **A shopkeeper then**
5	**donated a Persian wool embroidered blanket to cover**
6	**the Holy Child. Very quickly everyone was caught up in**
7	**the spirit of the event.** *(FATHER FRANCIS walks among*
8	*the group assigning parts.)* **It was easy then for Father**
9	**Francis to persuade the villagers to each portray one of**
10	**the many roles of the nativity.** *(YOUNG WOMAN is given*
11	*the "baby Jesus" by FATHER FRANCIS.)* **A young woman,**
12	**whom the gossips called a prostitute, was chosen by**
13	**Father Francis to be Mary. They were shocked at his**
14	**choice but they were soon quieted when they saw the**
15	**transformation in the young woman's face as she lifted**
16	**the figure of the baby Jesus from the manger. She seemed**
17	**instantly to change into another person.** *(FRANCIS directs*
18	*others where to stand.)* **The role of Joseph was assigned to**
19	**an agente di polizia — a policeman. Then four village**
20	**politicos volunteered to be shepherds.**
21	**The wise men were a dressmaker, a butcher and a**
22	**rich landowner. Yes, Salvatore, from whose farm Pepi**
23	**had stolen the grain. Soon it was Christmas Eve and**
24	**Francis was finding a place for everyone in the manger**
25	**scene. All was nearly ready when Father Francis stopped**
26	**and said:** *(Spotlight on FRANCIS.)*
27	FRANCIS: **I have a surprise for you all. You may have thought**
28	**I had forgotten the animals. You know they, too, were**
29	**very much a part of our Lord's Nativity. There is a legend**
30	**that they talked the night that Jesus was born. I believe**
31	**it is true. Let us welcome them to our holy crèche.** *(The*
32	*VILLAGE CHILDREN come down the center aisle of the church.*
33	*Each carries a painted cardboard cutout of an animal. When*
34	*they reach the altar where the Nativity scene is situated, they*
35	*place their animals in position surrounding the manger. They*

remain standing next to their animal cutout as the carol "The
Friendly Beasts" is sung by a soloist or by each of the children.

FIRST CHILD: Jesus, our brother, strong and good,
        Was humbly born in a stable crude,
        And the friendly beasts around him stood.
        Jesus, our brother, strong and good.

SECOND CHILD: I, said the donkey, shaggy and brown,
        I carried his mother up hill and down,
        I carried her safely to Bethlehem town.
        I, said the donkey, all shaggy and brown.

THIRD CHILD: I, said the cow, all white and red,
        I gave him my manger for his bed.
        I gave him my hay to pillow his head.
        I, said the cow, all white and red.

FOURTH CHILD: I, said the sheep, with the curly horn.
        I gave him my coat on Christmas morn.
        I gave him my wool to keep him warm.
        I, said the sheep, with the curly horn.

FIFTH CHILD: I, said the dove, from the rafters high,
        I cooed him to sleep that he should not cry,
        We cooed him to sleep, my mate and I.
        I, said the dove, from the rafters high.

SIXTH CHILD: Every beast by some good spell,
        In the stable dark was glad to tell
        Of the gifts he gave Immanuel,
        Of the gifts he gave Immanuel.

(Everyone holds their position in a tableau-like scene.)

NARRATOR: That night in Assisi many people were
        changed. The spirit of Christ had entered into them
        through the rebirth of the baby Jesus at the crèche in
        their village square. The jealousy and suspicion between
        rival factions disappeared and they began talking with
        each other about the problems they shared. The young
        lady that was Mary, mother of the Lord for one night,
        found forgiveness and a new start. And even Salvatore,

the rich landowner in whose wheat fields young Pepi was caught stealing, found forgiveness in his heart. He asked the town officials to release the boy saying that he would not press charges. He was moved to remember the passage from Matthew 6:14 in the Bible: "If ye forgive men their trespasses, your heavenly Father will also forgive you." Father Francis had called upon his Father in heaven to show him the way and he was inspired to create the first manger scene which we all today call a crèche.

I hope this story helps us all remember the forgiveness and humility it represents. Father Francis remembered all his life and came to be called Saint Francis of Assisi. Let us all now sing the carol "Joy to the World." *(Players can join in the singing.)*

The Second Shepherd's Play

Adapted from the Wakefield plays
by THOMAS HATTON

CAST

COLL, GYB, DAW
Shepherds

MAK
A sheep thief

GYLL
Mak's wife

ANGEL

READERS
Can be two women narrators

JOSEPH, MARY
Young children, non-speaking, to form a tableau

NOTE: No scenery is necessary for this play as it is intended to be performed in church sanctuaries. Props include staffs for the shepherds, a cardboard sheep, and cradles for Gyll's infant and the Christ Child.

FOREWORD

One of the earliest forms of English drama was the medieval cycle plays. In the fourteenth and fifteenth centuries, the various guilds — trade union organizations — in many English towns produced a series of short dramatizations of Bible stories for various church holidays. These playlets were acted out on ox-drawn wagons which paraded through the city's streets, stopping at various appointed places called "stations" so that the plays could be performed. In this way, the entire pageant of biblical history was presented to a general public which was still predominantly illiterate and thus could not read the Bible themselves.

Most of these cycle plays are merely recreations of the biblical texts — all the action and dialog are taken straight from the account in the Bible. A few plays, however, are more elaborate, and probably the best of these are six plays written by an anonymous master writer for the cycle produced at Wakefield. The Wakefield Master freely added characters, dialog and even plot to the Bible stories he chose to dramatize. The most popular of his plays is the second of two dramatizations he made of the Christmas story of the shepherds on the hillside outside of Bethlehem on Christmas Eve. This famous little play is still acted today in its medieval version, but in this form it appeals mainly to a scholarly audience.

In this modernization we have tried to adapt "The Second Shepherd's Play" for use as a Christmas program given either by older children or adults in the average church. We hope we have kept the spirit of the Wakefield Master's original work while making it more accessible to a modern audience. We have also added two non-speaking parts and parts for readers so that younger children may have a chance to take part in the program.

1   SCENE ONE
2
3   *SETTING:*   A hillside outside Bethlehem.
4
5   **READER:** *(Onstage or Offstage over a microphone)* **In the**
6   **beginning was the Word and the Word was with God, and**
7   **the Word was God.** And the Word became flesh and dwelt
8   among us. The true light that enlightens every man was
9   coming into the world. He was in the world, and the world
10   was made through him, yet the world knew him not. And
11   in that region there were shepherds out in the field,
12   keeping watch over their sheep by night. *(If READER is*
13   *Onstage, he now exits.)*
14 **COLL:**   *(Entering left)* **Lord, the weather's cold! My fingers and**
15   **toes are numb, and my face is so chapped, I've got no**
16   **feeling there either. And besides that, I'm hungry. I**
17   **haven't had a decent meal in weeks. Got no money.**
18   **Everybody's making money nowadays but the farmer.**
19   **Oh, sure, everybody thinks we're cleaning up what with**
20   **market prices sky high, but precious little of that gets**
21   **back to us — except the prices. A good ewe costs twice**
22   **what she did ten years ago. Sometimes I feel like just**
23   **giving up.**
24 **GYB:**   *(Entering left without noticing COLL)* **Cold, cold, cold! I've**
25   **never been so cold in my life! I've never seen it this bad**
26   **this early. It's even worse than last winter. I don't see**
27   **how I can stand it; I don't! And precious little thanks I**
28   **get for freezing my fingers off out here. Do you think my**
29   **wife cares about that? I tell you, a man makes a lot of**
30   **mistakes in life, but the biggest one is when he gets**
31   **married. I've been married three years now and I haven't**
32   **had a day of peace. That woman is something else. Gyb**
33   **do this! Gyb do that! And her mother! I'd rather face a**
34   **pack of wolves any day than that old mountain lion!**
35 **COLL:**   **Gyb, is that you?**

1	GYB:	What's left of me.
2	COLL:	Have you seen anything of Daw?
3	GYB:	Not a hair.
4	COLL:	I thought he was supposed to relieve us.
5	GYB:	He was, but you didn't expect him to be on time, did
6		you? That fool kid is always late.
7	COLL:	I don't know what's got into these young folks
8		nowadays. No sense of responsibility.
9	GYB:	Nothing's the way it used to be. The whole world's going
10		to pot.
11	COLL:	You can say that again.
12	DAW:	*(Entering left)* What am I doing here? What am I doing
13		here? Daw, you're a smart boy. How in the world did you
14		let yourself be dragged out here on a night like this? I've
15		never seen it so cold. It didn't used to be like this. I can
16		remember Decembers when my mother's roses were
17		blooming. Once when I was little we spent the whole
18		night tending the sheep, and we never even wore jackets.
19		But winter before last it turned cold, and last winter was
20		worse. And this winter! I can't believe it! Well, I'll tell you
21		one thing. As soon as I get a little money together, I'm
22		splitting. There's got to be a better life than sheep
23		tending. Let my old man freeze out here. I'm going to the
24		big town — maybe even Jerusalem!
25	COLL:	Do my ears deceive me, or is that Daw?
26	GYB:	Couldn't be Daw. He's only an hour late.
27	COLL:	Sounds like him. Hey, Daw!
28	DAW:	Evenin', Mr. Gyb, Mr. Coll. I've come to relieve you.
29	COLL:	I'll just bet you did.
30	GYB:	It's about time. We're freezing.
31	DAW:	Well, I ain't none too warm myself.
32	COLL:	Now, no smart talk, boy! We're in no mood for it!
33	DAW:	Yes, sir. Anyway, I'm here. I suppose you two'll be
34		heading for your warm beds. It's always us young folks
35		who get the graveyard shift!

1   GYB: No fresh talk now, Daw! Just you know that we've done
2   our share. *(MAK enters left, singing and talking to himself to*
3   *the rhythm of a blues tune.)*
4   MAK: Rather drink muddy water, sleep in a hollow log.
5   Rather drink muddy water, sleep in a hollow log.
6   Than to be way out here,
7   Treated like a dirty dog!
8   COLL: Hold it! Somebody's coming.
9   GYB: I know that voice. That's Mak, the sheep shearer.
10 DAW: Isn't he the one they say steals sheep?
11 COLL: The same. And I know for a fact that he's stolen more
12   head of sheep than we've got in our flock right now.
13   Everybody knows it, but nobody can ever catch him at it.
14 MAK: *(Still singing his blues tune)* Got the Bethlehem blues,
15   Just as blue as I can be.
16   Got the Bethlehem blues,
17   Just as blue as I can be.
18   I'm just a poor sheep shearer,
19   And it'll be the death of me.
20 COLL: Who goes there?
21 MAK: A poor man down on his luck.
22 GYB: Is that you, Mak?
23 MAK: You were expecting something better?
24 DAW: What are you doing out here this late at night? Looking
25   for another sheep to steal?
26 MAK: That's not very funny, son. You'd be out here, too, if
27   you lived in my house. I've got ten kids already and
28   another on the way. I'm so sick of those brats crying I
29   come out here every night just to get away from the noise.
30   You wouldn't have a warm blanket about you so I can
31   curl up and get some sleep?
32 GYB: You want to stay out here with us?
33 MAK: I'd be obliged. If you wouldn't mind.
34 COLL: Come here a minute, Gyb. I want to talk to you alone.
35   *(Pulls him to one side.)* You know what this old boy's really

1	out here for. The minute we leave he'll pull the wool over
2	the eyes of that dumb Daw and make off with a fat ewe.
3	You can bet on it.
4	GYB: Let's tell him to move on then.
5	COLL: What good would that do? As soon as we're gone, he'll
6	just come back.
7	GYB: What can we do?
8	COLL: I've got a plan, but it'll mean staying out here tonight.
9	GYB: Oh, my aching back! But it's better than losing a sheep
10	to that skunk, I guess.
11	COLL: You'd better believe it. Play along with me. *(To MAK)*
12	Me and Gyb's talked it over, Mak. I expect we could put
13	you up for the night. We were just going to lay down and
14	get some shuteye ourselves.
15	DAW: You were? But I thought you two . . .
16	COLL: Sure we were. But the truth is, we're short on
17	blankets. I'll tell you what we'll do though. We'll let you
18	sleep in the middle of the three of us — right between us.
19	MAK: Uh . . . between you?
20	COLL: Sure, that way our bodies'll keep you warm.
21	GYB: Unless, of course, you get up in the night and sleepwalk.
22	I hope you don't sleepwalk. If you make a move, you know,
23	you'll wake us all up.
24	DAW: Oh, I see . . .
25	MAK: Oh, I'm a sound sleeper — very sound.
26	COLL: Well then, let's get to it. I'm dead tired.
27	GYB: So am I. *(The four lie down with MAK in the middle. There*
28	*are several counts of silence. The SHEPHERDS start to snore*
29	*softly. MAK rises up.)*
30	MAK: What a bunch of numbskulls. Sleep in the middle so
31	you'll stay warm. Don't sleepwalk, you'll wake us up. The
32	devil himself couldn't wake those three. Well, time to get
33	to business. *(MAK picks up a cardboard sheep positioned Stage*
34	*Right and exits left. Lights down. Exit SHEPHERDS.)*
35	READER: And Jesus said, "Truly, truly I say unto you, he

1   that does not enter the sheepfold by the door but climbs
2   in another way, that man is a thief and a robber. The
3   thief comes to kill and destroy; I come that they may have
4   life more abundant. I am the good shepherd. The good
5   shepherd lays down his life for his sheep."
6
7   SCENE TWO
8
9   *SETTING:*   Fade up lights to reveal MAK's house. As the lights
10   come up, GYLL is seated by an empty cradle, knitting.
11
12 GYLL: Now where do you suppose that husband of mine is?
13   He's supposed to be out doing some business. I hope he
14   hasn't stopped in some tavern or done something stupid
15   and gotten caught. That's all I need with ten kids and
16   another on the way — a husband in jail. I've heard you
17   can even get hanged for sheep rustling.
18 MAK: *(Knocking Offstage)* Open the door! Open the door!
19 GYLL: Lord a mercy! Who is it? Are you the law?
20 MAK: You stupid old woman, don't you recognize my voice?
21   It's me, Mak.
22 GYLL: Are you sure?
23 MAK: Of course, I'm sure! Open this door!
24 GYLL: I'm coming, I'm coming! *(Rises and opens door.)*
25 MAK: *(Entering with sheep)* It's about time, woman. Look what
26   I've got.
27 GYLL: Not a bad specimen. Looks like a bell weather.
28 MAK: It is. I got it from those dumb shepherds, Coll, Gyb and
29   Daw. Those dummies thought that if they had me sleep
30   in the middle of them, they'd be safe. I just waited for
31   them to drop off and here I am with their best sheep.
32 GYLL: Wait a minute. They saw you there? They know you
33   were out in the fields?
34 MAK: Yeah, I ran into them. Couldn't help it.
35 GYLL: You idiot!

1 MAK: What's the matter?
2 GYLL: You know what kind of reputation you have. When
3   those shepherds wake up, where do you think they're
4   going to look when they miss a sheep?
5 MAK: I hadn't thought of that.
6 GYLL: You hadn't thought of that! You never think of
7   anything. Why do I always have to do all the thinking in
8   this family?
9 MAK: We'll have to hide this sheep somewhere.
10 GYLL: In a one room house? Where are we going to hide a
11   sheep in a one room house?
12 MAK: How about the shed?
13 GYLL: The kids are all sleeping in the shed. You wake all
14   them up and we'll really have trouble.
15 MAK: There must be some place. Hey, I've got it! Your cradle!
16 GYLL: What?
17 MAK: We'll put the sheep in the cradle and cover him up. When
18   the shepherds come, I'll tell them it's your new baby.
19 GYLL: You think they'll believe that?
20 MAK: Those guys are dumb enough to believe anything.
21   Trust me.
22 SHEPHERDS: *(Knocking Offstage)* Hey, Mak! Open up! We
23   want to talk with you!
24 MAK: It's the shepherds! Help me get the sheep in the cradle.
25   Hurry up!
26 GYLL: I hope this works. *(MAK and GYLL put the sheep in the*
27   *cradle and cover it with blankets. MAK goes to the door. The*
28   *SHEPHERDS are still knocking.)*
29 MAK: Who's making all this noise? What do you want? *(Enter*
30   *SHEPHERDS right.)*
31 COLL: We want to talk to you, Mak.
32 GYB: We woke up a little while ago and you were gone.
33 DAW: And one of our best sheep was gone, too.
34 COLL: Someone just might think the two of you left together.
35 MAK: Are you crazy? Listen, while I was sleeping with you

1		guys, I had a dream. I dreamed Gyll here had just had
2		another baby and was calling me. I rushed home, and
3		what do you think? I was right. We've just had a baby boy!
4	GYB:	I thought you just had a girl about four months ago.
5	MAK:	Uh, we did, we did. This one was premature.
6	COLL:	Gyll's having a baby wouldn't keep you from stealing
7		our sheep now, would it?
8	MAK:	How can you think such a thing?!
9	GYB:	We think we'll just come in and have a look around
10		your house. Just to make sure.
11	MAK:	Are you crazy? My wife just had a rough time of it. She
12		needs her rest.
13	DAW:	She can rest when we've gone. We're coming in. *(The*
14		*SHEPHERDS force their way into the room and begin looking*
15		*around.)*
16	GYLL:	This is an outrage! What do you think you're doing?
17		Upsetting a woman in my condition! After what I've been
18		through!
19	MAK:	For heaven's sake, don't wake up the baby. We've just
20		gotten him to sleep.
21	GYLL:	If you don't get out of here, we'll have the law on you.
22		You're trespassing, you know?
23	COLL:	I can't find anything. Can you, Gyb?
24	GYB:	Not a thing. Daw?
25	DAW:	Me neither. I could have sworn they had our sheep.
26	COLL:	Well, Mak, I guess we owe you an apology.
27	MAK:	You sure do. And a big one.
28	GYB:	We're awfully sorry, but you have to admit it looked
29		suspicious.
30	MAK:	Only to them that don't trust nobody.
31	DAW:	We're sure sorry, Mrs. Gyll. We didn't mean any harm.
32		Hope the baby's all right.
33	GYLL:	You've probably given him the colic, that's what
34		you've done.
35	DAW:	Let me have a peek at the little feller. *(Goes to cradle and*

1   *lifts blanket.)*

2   **MAK:** *(Shoving him aside)* **You leave that baby alone! We had a**
3   **devil of a time getting that kid to sleep. You wake him up,**
4   **and you'll be in big trouble.**

5   **DAW: OK, OK. Sorry. I didn't mean any harm.**

6   **COLL: Well, come on, fellows. We'd best be getting back to**
7   **our other sheep. We sure are sorry, Mak . . . ma'am.**

8   **GYLL: We don't want your stupid apologies. Just get out of**
9   **here.**

10   **SHEPHERDS: We're going. We're going.** *(They leave the house*
11   *and walk Downstage Center.)*

12   **COLL: Well, would you believe that?**

13   **GYB: I could've sworn he took that sheep. I feel like a darn**
14   **fool barging in and upsetting everything with the baby**
15   **and all.**

16   **DAW: So do I. But I'll tell you one thing, fellers, that baby'll**
17   **need all the help he can get. Did you see him?**

18   **GYB: Just a little when you pulled the blanket away.**

19   **DAW: Boy, what an ugly kid! I mean, I've seen ugly, but that**
20   **kid's something else! I've seen prettier looking sheep!**

21   **COLL: Poor little tyke! Say, you know what?**

22   **GYB: What?**

23   **COLL: We forgot to give the kid birthday presents. You know**
24   **it's the custom.**

25   **GYB: By golly, you're right. But what have we got to give a**
26   **little baby?**

27   **DAW: I've got this little ball.**

28   **COLL: Well, I've got this little sheep's bell. He might like that.**

29   **GYB: And I've got this old spoon. Let's go back and give him**
30   **our presents.** *(They return to the house.)*

31   **COLL: *(Knocking)* Mak! Mak! Open up!**

32   **MAK: Oh, no, not you again!** *(Opens door.)*

33   **GYB: Look, Mak, we're sorry about what just happened.**

34   **COLL: Yeah, and to make everything right, we want to give**
35   **your baby these presents. See this spoon, the ball and the bell.**

1   MAK: He doesn't need your presents.

2   GYLL: Go away! You're bothering me!

3   COLL: *(Forcing his way past MAK)* Now, now. This'll just take a

4   minute. Here, baby, here's a nice tinkly bell for you.

5   DAW: And here's a ball for the baby.

6   GYB: And this here spoon. Look baby. Look at the spoon.

7   *(Raises blanket on cradle.)*

8   **MAK and GYLL:**   *(Seizing blanket and pulling it down)* **Don't wake**

9   **him up! Leave the blanket on!** *(They struggle. The cradle is*

10   *overturned and out falls the sheep.)*

11   COLL: Well, well, well. What do we have here?

12   GYLL: Oh, my lord! Some fairy has turned my poor baby into

13   a sheep!

14   GYB: Do you expect us to buy that?

15   MAK: Would you believe the baby crawled out and a sheep

16   wandered in here by mistake?

17   DAW: No, I wouldn't.

18   MAK: I didn't think so. All right, I'll admit it. I took your dumb

19   sheep.

20   COLL: Do you know what you can get for sheep rustling,

21   Mak?

22   MAK: I know. Twenty, thirty years. Sometimes they even

23   hang you.

24   GYLL: Oh, please don't turn my husband in. He's a good man,

25   but he's got a dozen mouths to feed. We're desperate.

26   You've got so many sheep. We didn't think you'd miss just

27   one.

28   GYB: I say we get the sheriff out here first thing in the

29   morning.

30   MAK: I guess I've got it coming.

31   GYLL: But we're going to have another baby. Really we are.

32   Just think, eleven little ones with no daddy to take care

33   of them. What'll become of us?

34   COLL: Well, gee, I'd hate to take a daddy away from all those

35   kids.

1   DAW: But what about our sheep?

2   GYB: Well, we've gotten it back. No harm done there, I
3   suppose.

4   MAK: I swear I'll never take another. I swear it.

5   COLL: Aw, save your breath. We know how much your word's
6   worth.

7   GYB: Look, we'll let you go this time, but if we ever catch you
8   hanging around our flocks again . . .

9   MAK: Oh, I won't, I won't. You can bank on that!

10   COLL: Well, get a good night's sleep then. And try to take
11   good care of that kid when he's born, eh? Set him a good
12   example.

13   GYLL: We will, sir. And . . . thank you. We don't deserve it.

14   COLL: If we all got what we deserve, we'd all be black and
15   blue, I expect. Come on, fellows.

16   GYB and DAW: Good night.

17   MAK: Good night. And bless you all. *(Exit SHEPHERDS. Lights*
18   *down.)*

19   READER: And Jesus said, "What man among you, having a
20   hundred sheep, if he has lost one of them, does not leave
21   the ninety and nine in the wilderness and go after the
22   one which is lost? And when he has found it, he lays it
23   on his shoulders, rejoicing. And when he comes home,
24   he calls together his friends and his neighbors saying to
25   them, 'Rejoice with me, for I have found the sheep which
26   was lost.' "

27

28   SCENE THREE

29

30   *SETTING:*   Fade up lights to reveal the fields. Enter the SHEPHERDS
31   left.

32

33   GYB: I don't know, Coll. I still think maybe we let that old boy
34   get off too easy.

35   COLL: Aw, we got our sheep back. Mak's got a lot of problems.

1   Let's just be glad it worked out the way it did.
2   GYB: Yeah, I guess . . .
3   DAW: Say, fellows, it sure is getting light.
4   COLL: That's funny. It can't be dawn already.
5   DAW: Fellows, I'm scared. *(The SHEPHERDS fall to their knees.*
6   *An ANGEL appears right.)*
7   READER: And an angel of the Lord appeared unto them, and
8   the glory of the Lord shone around them, and they were
9   filled with fear. And the angel said to them:
10   ANGEL: Be not afraid, for behold I bring you good news of a
11   great joy which will come to all the people; for to you is
12   born this day in the city of David a Savior who is Christ
13   the Lord. And this will be a sign for you. You will find
14   the babe wrapped in swaddling clothes lying in a manger.
15   READER: And suddenly there was with the angel a multitude
16   of the heavenly host praising God and saying, "Glory to
17   God in the highest and on earth peace among men with
18   whom he is well pleased." *(Lights out. Exit all.)*
19   READER: When the angels went away from them into
20   heaven, the shepherds said one to another, "Let us go
21   over to Bethlehem and see this thing which the Lord has
22   made known to us." So they went with haste and found
23   Mary and Joseph and the babe lying in a manger.
24   *TABLEAU:*   Lights up. MARY and JOSEPH around the cradle,
25   ANGEL standing at rear. Enter SHEPHERDS. They approach
26   the cradle one by one, speaking as they kneel before it.
27   COLL: The angel said that he would rule the world and all
28   that's in it. I worship you, babe. Look, I am a poor man.
29   All I have to give you is this sheep's bell. Take it for your
30   own, and when you have all power, remember me.
31   GYB: I, too, am poor, son, who shall save both sea and land.
32   All I can give is this old spoon. Take it and remember me
33   when you rule the skies.
34   DAW: Now look on me, dear Lord. I have only this little ball to
35   give you. Take it as a sign of your majesty when you rise

1	above the earth.
2	READER: And so the Lord of Hosts was made known to these
3	simple shepherds, men not particularly different from
4	the rest of mankind. As they were able to find their own
5	sheep disguised as a child, so they were able to find the
6	Lamb of God in the same disguise. And in both cases it
7	was their charity that led them aright. Let us join them
8	this Christmas as they worship at the manger to which
9	eventually all Christians must come. *(All actors and*
10	*audience may now join together to sing the Christmas carol, "Oh,*
11	*Come All Ye Faithful," if desired.)*
12	
13	
14	
15	
16	
17	
18	
19	
20	
21	
22	
23	
24	
25	
26	
27	
28	
29	
30	
31	
32	
33	
34	
35	

The Very Best Kind of Christmas Tree
by HENRY VAN DYKE

Adapted for Readers Theatre
by ALETHEA GASSER

CAST

NARRATOR
Fay — Fairy — All

READER 1
Tree

READER 2
Trouble — Gale — Goat — Dream — Fay — Fairy
Reader — All

READER 3
Envy — Peddler — Joyful Beam — Fay — Fairy
Reader — All

READER 4
Fay — Young Wind — Troubled Sleep
Reader — All

1 NARRATOR: Have you ever looked across the fence and said,
2 "Gee, I wish we had a beautiful green lawn like Mr.
3 Jones"? While on a Sunday drive have you thought, "Gee,
4 I wish my family had a beautiful home in which to
5 entertain our friends"? How about Fred's new car? Do
6 you wish you had one too?
7 Why do we spend our lives wishing we had a better
8 lawn, a bigger house, a nicer car? Maybe it's because the
9 grass always looks greener on the other side of the fence.
10 We just never feel "up to par" with our neighbors. In
11 other words, we never seem happy and content with what
12 God has given us.
13 Fret not on "what might have been," but instead, give
14 thanks "for what you are," as you listen to the tale of "The
15 Very Best Kind of Christmas Tree," by Henry Van Dyke.
16 *(READER 1 is standing Up Centerstage with back to audience.)*
17 NARRATOR: *(Continued)* A little tree grew in the midst of the
18 wood.
19 Contented and happy, as little trees should.
20 READER 4: His body was straight,
21 READER 2: And his branches were green;
22 READER 4: And summer and winter
23 READER 2: The bountiful sheen
24 NARRATOR: Of his needles bedecked him, from top to root,
25 ALL: In a beautiful, all-the-year holiday suit. *(ALL stop.)*
26 READER 3: But a trouble *(READER 2 reacts)* came into his
27 head one day,
28 When he saw how the other trees *(NARRATOR and*
29 *READER 4 react)* were gay.
30 In the wonderful raiment that summer weaves,
31 Of a hundred different kinds of leaves;
32 READER 4: He looked at his needles so stiff and so small,
33 READER 2: And he thought that his dress was the cheapest
34 of all.
35 READER 4: Then envy *(READER 3 reacts)* beclouded the little

1   tree's mind,

2   And he said to himself,

3   READER 1: "It was not very kind

4   "To give such an ugly old dress to a tree!

5   "If the fays *(NARRATOR and READERS 1, 2, 3 react)* of the

6   forest would only ask me,

7   "I'd tell them the way I should like to be dressed,

8   "In a garment of gold, to outshine all the rest!"

9   READER 2: Trouble, trouble, trouble —

10   READER 3: Envy, envy, envy —

11   READER 1: "I'd tell them *(Cross to Down Right)* gold, *(Cross to*

12   *Down Left)* gold, *(Cross to Down Center)* gold for my

13   dress." *(ALL stop.)*

14   NARRATOR: Then he fell asleep, but his dreams *(READERS*

15   *2 and 3 react)* were bad;

16   When he woke in the morning, my! wasn't he glad?

17   READER 2: *(READER 1 reacts to following dialog.)* For every leaf

18   that his bough could hold

19   Was certainly made out of beaten gold.

20   NARRATOR 1: I tell you, my children, that tree was proud;

21   READER 2: He was something above the common crowd;

22   READER 4: And he tinkled his leaves, as if he would say

23   READER 2: To a peddler *(READER 3 reacts)* who walked in

24   the wood that day,

25   READER 1: "Just look at me! Don't you think I am fine?

26   "And wouldn't you like such a dress as mine?"

27   READER 3: "Ach, ja!"

28   NARRATOR: Said the man,

29   READER 3: "Und I shust pelieves

30   "Dot I fills mein pack mit dose peautiful leaves."

31   ALL: Just look at me, fine, fine, fine e - e - e - e - e

32   Like my dress m - m - m - m - m

33   Pack peautiful leaves, leaves, leaves, leaves es - es - es

34   - es - es

35   READER 4: So he picked them, every one, with care —

1   READER 3:   And left the little tree standing bare.
2   ALL: Oh, oh, oh, oh,
3   Standing, oh, oh, oh, oh
4   Bare, oh, oh, oh, oh,
5   Bare, oh, oh, oh, oh,
6   Bare, oh, oh, oh, oh. *(ALL stop.)*
7   READER 1:   "Oh, why did I wish for golden leaves?"
8   NARRATOR: The little tree said,
9   READER 1:   "I forgot that thieves
10   "Would be sure to rob me in passing by. *(FAIRIES react*
11   *to "passing by.")*
12   "If the fairies would give me another try,
13   FAIRIES: No, no, no, no,
14   READER 1:   "I'd wish for something that cost much less,
15   FAIRIES: Much less, much less, *(React among themselves.)*
16   READER 1:   "And be satisfied with glass for my dress!"
17   FAIRIES: *(Confer and agree to another chance.)* Another try,
18   another try, - m - m - m - m - m
19   m - m - m - m - satisfied - m - m - m - m - m
20   m - m - m - m - much less - m - m - m - m - m
21   m - m - m - m - glass - oh - oh - oh - oh - oh
22   "We shall see e - e - e - e - e!"
23   READER 2:   So he fell asleep; and, just as before,
24   The fairies answered his wish once more. *(FAIRIES react*
25   *on "once more.")*
26   READER 3:   When the night was gone, and the sun rose clear,
27   The tree was a *(READER 1 reacts to "crystal chandelier")*
28   crystal chandelier;
29   FAIRIES: Oh, oh h - h - h - h - h
30   How beautiful!
31   How delicate!
32   How exquisite!
33   READER 4:   And it seemed, as he stood in the morning light,
34   That his branches were covered with jewels bright.
35   READER 1:   "Ach!"

1   NARRATOR: Said the tree,
2   READER 1: "This is something great!"
3   READER 4: And he held himself up, very *(FAIRIES react to*
4   *"haughty and straight")* haughty and straight;
5   NARRATOR: But a rude young wind *(READER 4 reacts)*
6   through the forest dashed,
7   *(READER 4 reacts to "temper," "suddenly smashed," "shining*
8   *leaves," and "shivering sound.)*
9   In a "rough house" temper, and suddenly smashed
10   The shining leaves. With a shivering sound. *(ALL stop.)*
11   NARRATOR: They broke into pieces and fell to the ground.
12   *(READERS 2, 3, 4 fall to ground. ALL stop.)*
13   Like a silvery, shimmering shower of hail,
14   And the tree *(READER 1 reacts)* stood naked and bare to
15   the gale *(READER 2 reacts. ALL stop.)*
16   Then the tree was sad; and he cried,
17   READER 1: "Alas
18   "For my beautiful leaves of shining glass!
19   "Perhaps I have made a little mistake
20   "In choosing a dress so easy to break.
21   "If the fairies would only hear me again
22   "I'd ask them for something both pretty and plain.
23   *(FAIRIES do not hear.)*
24   "It wouldn't cost much to grant my request, *(Some*
25   *FAIRIES hear.)*
26   "In leaves of green lettuce I'd like to be dressed!" *(ALL*
27   *hear.)*
28   READER 2: By this time the fairies were laughing, I know;
29   But they gave him his wish in a second; and lo!
30   READER 3: With leaves of green lettuce, all tender and sweet,
31   The tree was rigged out, from his head to his feet. *(READERS*
32   *2 and 4 react.)*
33   READER 1: "I knew it! I was sure I could find
34   "The sort of a suit that would be to my mind.
35   "There's none of the trees has a prettier dress,

1   "And none as attractive as I am, I guess."

2   READER 4:   But a goat, *(READER 2 reacts)* who was strolling

3   along that way,

4   Overheard what the foolish tree did say.

5   So he came up close for a nearer view;

6   READER 3:   "My salad!"

7   READER 4:   He bleated,

8   READER 3:   "I think so too!

9   FAIRIES: My salad!

10 READER 3:   "You're the most attractive kind of a tree,

11 FAIRIES: My salad!

12 READER 3:   "And I want your leaves for my five o'clock tea."

13 FAIRIES: My salad! My five o'clock tea.

14 NARRATOR: So he ate them all without saying grace,

15 FAIRIES: My salad, my five o'clock tea. Without saying grace.

16 NARRATOR: And walked away with a grin on his face;

17 FAIRIES: My salad, my five o'clock tea, without saying grace.

18   *(ALL walk away, grinning.)*

19 NARRATOR: And the little tree stood in the twilight dim,

20   With never a leaf on a single limb. *(READER 1 standing*

21   *Down Left Center arms down. ALL Up Stage full back.)*

22 ALL: Never a leaf f - f - f - f on a single limb b - b - b - b *(ALL*

23   *stop.)*

24 READER 3:   Then he sighed and groaned; but his voice was

25   weak;

26   He was so ashamed that he couldn't speak.

27 READER 2:   He knew at last that he'd been a fool,

28   To think of breaking a forest rule,

29   And choosing a dress himself to please,

30   Because he envied the other trees. *(ALL stop.)*

31 READER 4:   But it couldn't be helped, it was now too late,

32   He must make up his mind to a leafless fate!

33 NARRATOR: So he let himself sink in a slumber deep,

34 READER 3:   But he moaned and he tossed in his troubled

35   sleep, *(READER 4 reacts.)*

1	READER 2:	Till the morning came, with its joyful beam,
2		*(READER 3 reacts.)*
3	READER 3:	And he woke to find it was all a dream. *(READER*
4		*2 reacts.)*
5	READER 4:	For there in his evergreen dress he stood,
6		A pointed fir in the midst of the wood!
7	READER 2:	Troubled sleep . . .
8	READER 3:	Joyful beam . . .
9	READER 4:	All a dream . . .
10	NARRATOR:	His boughs were sweet with the balsam smell,
11	FAIRIES:	Sweet, sweet, sweet . . . balsam smell.
12	NARRATOR:	His branches were fresh when the white snow
13		fell,
14	FAIRIES:	Fresh, fresh, fresh . . . white snow.
15	NARRATOR:	And nevermore fretful or jealous was he,
16	FAIRIES:	Nevermore, nevermore . . . jealous was he.
17	NARRATOR:	The very best kind of a Christmas tree. *(ALL*
18		*stop.)*
19	READER 1:	A little tree grew in the midst of the wood
20		Contended and happy, as little trees should.
21	NARRATOR:	His body was straight and his branches were
22		green;
23	READER 2:	And summer and winter the beautiful sheen
24	READER 3:	Of his needles bedecked him, from top to root,
25	READER 4:	In a beautiful, all-the-year holiday suit. *(End)*
26		
27		*("Oh, Christmas Tree" or any other appropriate song may be*
28		*added at the end.)*
29		
30		
31		
32		
33		
34		
35		

CHRISTMAS READINGS

A Visit from St. Nicholas
by CLEMENT CLARKE MOORE

PRODUCTION NOTES

The author wrote this poem as a Christmas gift for his family in 1822. A year later it was published by *The Sentinel*, a newspaper in Troy, New York. It has since been reprinted over and over in countless publications relating to Christmas.

1	'Twas the night before Christmas, when all through the
2	house
3	Not a creature was stirring, not even a mouse;
4	The stockings were hung by the chimney with care,
5	In hopes that St. Nicholas soon would be there;
6	The children were nestled all snug in their beds,
7	While visions of sugarplums danced in their heads;
8	And mamma in her kerchief and I in my cap
9	Had just settled our brains for a long winter's nap,
10	When out on the lawn there arose such a clatter,
11	I sprang from my bed to see what was the matter.
12	Away to the window I flew like a flash,
13	Tore open the shutters, and threw up the sash;
14	The moon, on the breast of the new-fallen snow,
15	Gave a luster of midday to objects below;
16	When what to my wondering eyes should appear
17	But a miniature sleigh and eight tiny reindeer,
18	With a little old driver, so lively and quick,
19	I knew in a moment, it must be St. Nick.
20	More rapid than eagles his coursers they came,
21	And he whistled and shouted and called them by name:
22	"Now Dasher! now Dancer! now Prancer! now Vixen!
23	On, Comet! on Cupid! on, Donner and Blitzen!
24	To the top of the porch! To the top of the wall!
25	Now, dash away, dash away, dash away, all!"
26	As dry leaves that before the wild hurricane fly,
27	When they meet with an obstacle, mount to the sky,
28	So up to the housetop the coursers they flew,
29	With the sleigh full of toys and St. Nicholas too.
30	And then, in a twinkling, I heard on the roof
31	The prancing and pawing of each little hoof.
32	As I drew in my head and was turning around,
33	Down the chimney St. Nicholas came with a bound.
34	He was dressed all in fur, from his head to his foot,
35	And his clothes were all tarnished with ashes and soot;

1	A bundle of toys he had flung on his back,
2	And he looked like a peddler just opening his pack.
3	His eyes: how they twinkled! his dimples: how merry!
4	His cheeks were like roses, his nose like a cherry;
5	His droll little mouth was drawn up like a bow,
6	And the beard on his chin was as white as the snow.
7	The stump of a pipe he held tight in his teeth,
8	And the smoke, it encircled his head like a wreath:
9	He had a broad face, and a little round belly,
10	That shook, when he laughed, like a bowl full of jelly;
11	He was chubby and plump, a right jolly old elf;
12	And I laughed, when I saw him, in spite of myself,
13	A wink of his eye and a twist of his head
14	Soon gave me to know I had nothing to dread.
15	He spoke not a word, but went straight to his work,
16	And filled all the stockings; then turned with a jerk,
17	And laying his finger aside of his nose,
18	And giving a nod, up the chimney he rose.
19	He sprang to his sleigh, to his team gave a whistle,
20	And away they all flew like the down of a thistle;
21	But I heard him exclaim, ere he drove out of sight,
22	"Happy Christmas to all, and to all a good night!"
23	
24	
25	
26	
27	
28	
29	
30	
31	
32	
33	
34	
35	

The Gift of the Magi

by O. HENRY

(Sydney William Porter)

One dollar and eighty-seven cents. That was all. And sixty cents of it was in pennies. Pennies saved one and two at a time by bulldozing the grocer and the vegetable man and the butcher until one's cheeks burned with the silent imputation of parsimony that such close dealing implied. Three times Della counted it. One dollar and eighty-seven cents. And the next day would be Christmas.

There was clearly nothing to do but flop down on the shabby little couch and howl. So Della did it. Which instigates the moral reflection that life is made up of sobs, sniffles, and smiles, with sniffles predominating.

While the mistress of the home is gradually subsiding from the first stage to the second, take a look at the home. A furnished flat at eight dollars per week. It did not exactly beggar description, but it certainly had that word on the lookout for the mendicancy squad.

In the vestibule below was a letter box into which no letter would go, and an electric button from which no mortal finger could coax a ring. Also appertaining thereunto was a card bearing the name "Mr. James Dillingham Young."

The "Dillingham" has been flung to the breeze during a former period of prosperity when its possessor was being paid thirty dollars per week. Now, when the income was shrunk to twenty dollars, the letters of "Dillingham" looked blurred, as though they were thinking seriously of contracting to a modest and unassuming D. But whenever Mr. James Dillingham Young came home and reached his flat above he was called "Jim" and greatly hugged by Mrs. James Dillingham Young, already introduced to you as Della. Which is all very good.

Della finished her cry and attended to her cheeks with a powder puff. She stood by the window and looked out dully at a gray cat walking a gray fence in a gray back yard. Tomorrow would be Christmas Day, and she had only one dollar and eighty-seven cents with which to buy Jim a present. She had been saving every penny she could for months, with this result. Twenty dollars a week doesn't go far. Expenses had been greater than she had calculated. They always are. Only one dollar eighty-seven cents to buy a present for Jim. Her Jim. Many a happy hour she had spent planning for something nice for him. Something fine and rare and sterling — something just a little bit near to being worthy of the honor of being owned by Jim.

There was a pier glass between the windows of the room. Perhaps you have seen a pier glass in an eight-dollar flat. A very thin and very agile person may, by observing his reflection in a rapid sequence of longitudinal strips, obtain a fairly accurate conception of his looks. Della, being slender, had mastered the art.

Suddenly she whirled from the window and stood before the glass. Her eyes were shining brilliantly, but her face had lost its color within twenty seconds. Rapidly she pulled down her hair and let it fall to its full length.

Now, there were two possessions of the James Dillingham Youngs in which they both took a mighty pride. One was Jim's gold watch that had been his father's and his grandfather's. The other was Della's hair. Had the Queen of Sheba lived in the flat across the airshaft, Della would have let her hair hang out the window some day to dry just to depreciate Her Majesty's jewels and gifts. Had King Solomon been the janitor, with all his treasure piled up in the basement, Jim would have pulled out his watch every time he passed, just to see him pluck at his beard from envy.

So now Della's beautiful hair fell about her, rippling and shining like a cascade of brown waters. She did it up again nervously and quickly. Once she faltered for a minute and stood still while a tear or two splashed on the worn red carpet.

On went her old brown jacket; on went her old brown hat. With a whirl of skirts and with the brilliant sparkle still in her eyes, she fluttered out the door and down the stairs to the street.

Where she stopped the sign read: "Mme. Sofronie. Hair Goods of All Kinds." One flight up Della ran and collected herself, panting. Madame, large, too white, chilly, hardly looked the "Sofronie."

"Will you buy my hair?" asked Della.

"I buy hair," said Madame. "Take yer hat off and let's have a sight at the looks of it."

Down rippled the brown cascade.

"Twenty dollars," said Madame, lifting the mass with a practiced hand.

"Give it to me quick," said Della.

Oh, and the next two hours tripped by on rosy wings. Forget the hashed metaphor. She was ransacking the stores for Jim's present.

She found it at last. It surely had been made for Jim and no one else. There was no other like it in any of the stores, and she had turned all of them inside out. It was a platinum watch chain, simple and chaste in design, properly proclaiming its value by substance alone and not by meretricious ornamentation — as all good things should do. It was even worthy of The Watch. As soon as she saw it she knew that it must be Jim's. It was like him. Quietness and value — the description applied to both. Twenty-one dollars they took from her for it, and she hurried home with the eighty-seven cents. With that chain on his watch Jim might be properly anxious about the time in any company. Grand as the watch was, he sometimes looked at it on the sly on account of the old leather strap that he used in place of a chain.

When Della reached home her intoxication gave way a little to prudence and reason. She got out her curling irons and lighted the gas and went to work repairing the ravages made by generosity added to love. Which is always a tremendous task, dear friends — a mammoth task.

Within forty minutes her head was covered with tiny close-lying curls that made her look wonderfully like a truant school boy. She looked at her reflection in the mirror long, carefully, and critically.

"If Jim doesn't kill me," she said to herself, "before he takes a second look at me, he'll say I look like a Coney Island chorus girl. But what could I do — oh! what could I do with one dollar and eighty-seven cents?"

At seven o'clock the coffee was made and the frying pan was on the back of the stove, hot and ready to cook the chops.

Jim was never late. Della doubled the watch chain in her hand and sat on the corner of the table near the door that he always entered. Then she heard his step on the stair away down on the first flight, and she turned white for just a moment. She had a habit of saying little silent prayers about the simplest everyday things, and now she whispered: "Please, God, make him think I am still pretty."

The door opened and Jim stepped in and closed it. He looked thin and very serious. Poor fellow, he was only twenty-two — and to be burdened with a family! He needed a new overcoat and he was without gloves.

Jim stepped inside the door, as immovable as a setter at the scent of quail. His eyes were fixed upon Della, and there was an expression in them that she could not read, and it terrified her. It was not anger, nor surprise, nor disapproval, nor horror, nor any of the sentiments she had been prepared for. He simply stared at her fixedly with that peculiar expression on his face.

Della wriggled off the table and went for him.

"Jim, darling," she cried, "don't look at me that way.

I had my hair cut off and sold it because I couldn't have lived through Christmas without giving you a present. It'll grow out again — you won't mind, will you? I just had to do it. My hair grows awfully fast. Say 'Merry Christmas!' Jim, and let's be happy. You don't know what a nice — what a beautiful, nice gift I've got for you."

"You've cut off your hair?" asked Jim, laboriously, as if he had not arrived at that patent fact yet even after the hardest mental labor.

"Cut if off and sold it," said Della. "Don't you like me just as well, anyhow? I'm me without my hair, ain't I?"

Jim looked about the room curiously.

"You said your hair is gone?" he said, with an air almost of idiocy.

"You needn't look for it," said Della. "It's sold, I tell you — sold and gone too. It's Christmas Eve, boy. Be good to me, for it went for you. Maybe the hairs of my head were numbered," she went on with a sudden serious sweetness, "but nobody could ever count my love for you. Shall I put the chops on, Jim?"

Out of his trance Jim seemed to quickly wake. He enfolded his Della. For ten seconds let us regard with discreet scrutiny some inconsequential object in the other direction. Eight dollars a week or a million a year — what is the difference? A mathematician or a wit would give you the wrong answer. The Magi brought valuable gifts, but that was not among them. This dark assertion will be illuminated later on.

Jim drew a package from his overcoat pocket and threw it upon the table.

"Don't make any mistake, Dell," he said, "about me. I don't think there's anything in the way of a haircut or a shave or a shampoo that could make me like my girl any less. But if you'll unwrap that package you may see why you had me going awhile at first."

White fingers and nimble tore at the string and paper. And then an ecstatic scream of joy; and then, alas! a quick feminine change to hysterical tears and wails, necessitating the immediate employment of all the comforting powers of the lord of the flat.

For there lay The Combs — the set of combs that Della had worshiped for long in a Broadway window. Beautiful combs, pure tortoise shell, with jeweled rims — just the shade to wear in the beautiful vanished hair. They were expensive combs, she knew, and her heart had simply craved and yearned over them without the least hope of possession. And now they were hers, but the tresses that should have adorned the coveted adornments were gone.

But she hugged them to her bosom, and at length she was able to look up with dim eyes and a smile and say: "My hair grows so fast, Jim!"

And then Della leaped up like a little singed cat and cried, "Oh, oh!"

Jim had not yet seen his beautiful present. She held it out to him eagerly upon her open palm. The dull precious metal seemed to flash with a reflection of her bright and ardent spirit.

"Isn't it a dandy, Jim? I hunted all over town to find it. You'll have to look at the time a hundred times a day now. Give me your watch. I want to see how it looks on it."

Instead of obeying, Jim tumbled down on the couch and put his hands under the back of his head and smiled.

"Dell," said he, "let's put our Christmas presents away and keep 'em awhile. They're too nice to use just at present. I sold the watch to get the money to buy your combs. And now suppose you put the chops on."

The Magi, as you know, were wise men — wonderfully wise men — who brought gifts to the Babe in the manger. They invented the art of giving Christmas presents. Being wise, their gifts were no doubt wise ones, possibly bearing the privilege of exchange in case of duplication. And here I have lamely related to you the uneventful chronicle of two foolish children in a flat who most unwisely sacrificed for each other the greatest treasures of their house. But in a last word to the wise of these days let it be said that of all who give gifts these two were the wisest. Of all who give and receive gifts, such as they are wisest. Everywhere they are wisest. They are the Magi.

Is There a Santa Claus?

An Editorial by
FRANCIS P. CHURCH

Reprinted from the
NEW YORK SUN
September 21, 1897

———

We take pleasure in answering at once and thus
prominently the communication below, expressing at the
same time our great gratification that its faithful author
is numbered among the friends of *The Sun:*

Dear Editor:
I am eight years old.
Some of my little friends say there is no Santa Claus.
Papa says "If you see it in 'The Sun' it's so."
Please tell me the truth, is there a Santa Claus?

Virginia O'Hanlon,
115 West 95th Street,
New York City

Virginia, your little friends are wrong. They have
been affected by the skepticism of a skeptical age. They
do not believe except what they see. They think that
nothing can be which is not comprehensible by their little
minds. All minds, Virginia, whether they be men's or
children's, are little. In this great universe of ours man
is a mere insect, an ant, in his intellect, as compared with
the boundless world about him, as measured by the
intelligence capable of grasping the whole of truth and
knowledge.

Yes, Virginia, there is a Santa Claus. He exists as
certainly as love and generosity and devotion exist, and
you know that they abound and give to your life its
highest beauty and joy. Alas! how dreary would be the
world if there were no Santa Claus! It would be as dreary
as if there were no Virginias. There would be no childlike
faith, then, no poetry, no romance to make tolerable this
existence. We should have no enjoyment, except in sense
and sight. The eternal light with which childhood fills
the world would be extinguished.

You might as well not believe in fairies! You might

get your papa to hire men to watch in all the chimneys on Christmas Eve to catch Santa Claus, but even if they did not see Santa Claus coming down, what would that prove? Nobody sees Santa Claus, but that is no sign that there is no Santa Claus. The most real things in the world are those that neither children nor men can see. Did you ever see fairies dancing on the lawn? Of course not, but that's no proof that they are not there. Nobody can conceive or imagine all the wonders there are unseen and unseeable in the world.

You tear apart the baby's rattle and see what makes the noise inside, but there is a veil covering the unseen world which not the strongest man, nor even the united strength of all the strongest men that ever lived, could tear apart. Only faith, fancy, poetry, love, romance, can push aside that curtain and view and picture the supernal beauty and glory beyond. Is it all real? Ah, Virginia, in all this world there is nothing else real and abiding.

No Santa Claus! Thank God he lives, and he lives forever. A thousand years from now, Virginia, nay, ten times ten thousand years from now, he will continue to make glad the heart of childhood.

Christmas at the White House
by PRESIDENT THEODORE ROOSEVELT
written to
Master James A. Garfield

JIMMIKINS:

...Yesterday morning at a quarter of seven all the children were up and dressed and began to hammer at the door of their mother's and my room, in which their six stockings, all bulging out with queer angles and rotundities, were hanging from the fireplace. So their mother and I got up, shut the window, lit the fire (taking down the stockings, of course), put on our wrappers and prepared to admit the children. But first there was a surprise for me, also for their good mother, for Archie had a little Christmas tree of his own, which he had rigged up with the help of one of the carpenters in a big closet; and we all had to look at the tree and each of us got a present off of it. There was also one present each for Jack, the dog; Tom Quartz, the kitten; and Algonquin, the pony, whom Archie would no more think of neglecting than I would neglect his brothers and sisters. Then all the children came into our bed and there they opened their stockings. Afterwards we got dressed and took breakfast, and then all went into the library, where each child had a table set for his bigger presents. Quentin had a perfectly delightful electric railroad, which had been rigged up for him by one of his friends, the White House electrician, who has been very good to all the children. Then Ted and I, with General Wood and Mr. Bob Ferguson, who was a lieutenant in my regiment, went for a three hours' ride; and all of us, including all the children, took lunch at the house with the children's aunt, Mrs. Captain Cowles — Archie and Quentin having their lunch at a little table with their cousin Sheffield. Late in the afternoon I played at single stick with General Wood and Mr. Ferguson. I am going to get your father to come on and try it soon. We have to try to hit as light as possible, but sometimes we hit hard, and today I have a bump over one eye and a swollen wrist. Then all our family and kinsfolk and Senator and Mrs. Lodge's family and kinsfolk had our Christmas dinner at the White House, and afterwards dancing in the East Room, closing up with the Virginia Reel.

Keeping Christmas
by HENRY VAN DYKE

He that regardeth the day, regardeth it unto the Lord.
— Romans, XIV: 6

PRODUCTION NOTES

Henry Jackson Van Dyke was one of the leading Christian writers of the Victorian period of literature. *Keeping Christmas* was originally written as a short Christmas sermon. It was first published in 1905 as part of a book entitled *The Spirit of Christmas*.

It is a good thing to observe Christmas Day. The mere marking of times and seasons, when men agree to stop work and make merry together, is a wise and wholesome custom. It helps one to feel the supremacy of the common life over the individual life. It reminds a man to set his own little watch, now and then, by the great clock of humanity which runs on sun time.

But there is a better thing than the observance of Christmas Day, and that is, keeping Christmas.

Are you willing to forget what you have done for other people, and to remember what other people have done for you; to ignore what the world owes you, and to think what you owe the world; to put your rights in the background and your duties in the middle distance, and your chances to do a little more than your duty in the foreground; to see that your fellow men are just as real as you are, and try to look behind their faces to their hearts, hungry for joy; to know that probably the only good reason for your existence is not what you are going to get out of life, but what you are going to give to life; to close your book of complaints against the management of the universe, and look around you for a place where you can sow a few seeds of happiness — are you willing to do these things even for a day? Then you can keep Christmas.

Are you willing to stoop down and consider the needs and the desires of little children; to remember the weakness and loneliness of people who are growing old; to stop asking how much your friends love you, and ask yourself whether you love them enough; to bear in mind the things that other people have to bear on their hearts; to try to understand what those who live in the same house with you really want, without waiting for them to tell you; to trim your lamp so that it will give more light and less smoke; and to carry it in front so that your shadow will fall behind you; to make a grave for your ugly thoughts, and a garden for your kindly feelings, with the gate open — are you willing to do these things even for a day? Then you can keep Christmas.

Are you willing to believe that love is the strongest thing in the world — stronger than hate, stronger than evil, stronger than death — and that the blessed life which began in Bethlehem nineteen hundred years ago is the image and brightness of the Eternal Love? Then you can keep Christmas.

And if you keep it for a day, why not always?

But you can never keep it alone.

The Little Match Girl
by HANS CHRISTIAN ANDERSEN

Reproduced here is the earliest American translation we could find of
this sentimental favorite of the 19th century. This reproduction is from
the electrotype edition of Goodrich's Fifth School Reader published in
Louisville, Kentucky by John P. Morton Co. in the year 1857. This
version of rhyming couplets may be used as a reading or simply as a
reference copy of the original American interpretation.

Little Maggie, little Maggie wanders up and down the street;
    The snow upon her yellow hair, the frost upon her feet;
With the little box of matches she could not sell all day,
    And the thin, thin, tattered mantle which the wind blows
        every way.
The rows of large, dark houses without look cold and drear;
    But within glad hearts are waiting for Christmas to appear.
By the bright and cheerful firelight smile the father and the
    mother,
    While the children talk of presents, in whispers to each
        other.
But no one talks to Maggie, and no one hears her speak;
    No breath of little whisperers comes warmly to her cheek.
No little arms are round her — alas! that there should be,
    With so much happiness on earth, so much of misery!
Little Maggie, little Maggie goes shivering on her way;
    There's no one looketh out at her, there's no one bids her
        stay;
Her home is cold and desolate — no smile, no food, no fire;
    But sisters clamorous for bread, and an impatient sire.
She sits down in a corner where two great houses meet,
    And she curleth up beneath her, for warmth, her little feet.
And she remembers the loved tales her mother used to tell,
    And the cradle-songs she sang, when the summer twilight
        fell;
Of good men, and of angels, and of the Holy Child
    Who was cradled in a manger when winter was so wild.
Colder it grows and colder; but she does not feel it now,

1 For the pressure at her heart, and the weight upon her
2   brow.
3 But she struck one little match on the wall so cold and bare,
4   That she might look around her, and see if He was there.
5 The single match was kindled; and by the light it threw,
6   It seemed to little Maggie that the wall was rent in two.
7 And she could see the room within, the room all warm and light,
8   With the fire-glow red and blazing, and the tapers burning
9   bright.
10 And kindred there were gathered round the table richly spread,
11   With heaps of goodly viands, red wine, and pleasant bread.
12 She could smell the fragrant odor; she could hear them talk
13   and play;
14   Then all was darkness once again — the match had burned
15   away.
16 She struck another hastily, and now she seemed to see,
17   Within the same warm chamber a glorious Christmas tree.
18 The branches all were laden down with things that children
19   prize;
20   Bright gifts for boy and maiden they showed before her
21   eyes.
22 And she almost seemed to touch them, and to join the welcome
23   shout;
24   Then darkness fell around her, for the little match was out.
25 Another, yet another she has tried — they will not light;
26   Then all her little store she took, and struck with all her
27   might.
28 And the whole place around her was lighted with the glare!
29   And lo! there hung a little Child before her in the air!
30 There was blood-drops on his forehead, and a spear-wound
31   in his side,
32   And cruel nail-prints in his feet and in his hands spread
33   wide.
34 And he looked upon her kindly, and she felt that he had known
35   Pain, hunger, cold, and sorrow, still greater than her own.

1   And he pointed to the laden board, and to the Christmas tre

2   　　　Then up to the blue sky, and said, "Will Maggie come

3   　　　　　me?"

4   And she folded both her thin-white hands, and turned f

5   　　that bright board,

6   　　　And from the golden gifts, and said, "With thee, with t

7   　　　　　O Lord!"

8   The chilly winter morning breaks in the cold gray skies,

9   　　　On the city wrapped in vapor, on the spot where Ma

10 　　　　　lies.

11 In her scant and tattered garment, with her back against

12 　　wall,

13 　　　She sitteth cold and rigid — she answers not their c

14 Then they lifted her up carefully; they shuddered as they sa

15 　　　"It was a bitter, bitter night — the child is frozen dead.

16 While angels sang their greeting to another saved from s

17 　　　Men said, "It was a bitter night — would no one let her in

18

19

20

21

22

23

24

25

26

27

28

29

30

31

32

33

34

35

– 294 –

Order Form

Meriwether Publishing Ltd.
P.O. Box 7710
Colorado Springs, CO 80933
Telephone: (719) 594-4422
Website: www.meriwetherpublishing.com

Please send me the following books:

_____ **Christmas on Stage #BK-B153** $16.95
       by Theodore O. Zapel
       An anthology of Christmas plays for performance

_____ **Joy to the World #BK-B161** $14.95
       by L.G. Enscoe and Annie Enscoe
       A variety collection of Christmas programs

_____ **Costuming the Christmas and Easter Play** $10.95
       #BK-B180
       by Alice M. Staeheli
       How to costume any religious play

_____ **Stagecraft for Christmas and Easter Plays** $ 9.95
       #BK-B170
       by James Hull Miller
       A simplified method of staging in the church

_____ **Elegantly Frugal Costumes #BK-B125** $14.95
       by Shirley Dearing
       A do-it-yourself costume maker's guide

_____ **Costuming Made Easy #BK-B229** $19.95
       by Barb Rogers
       How to make theatrical costumes from cast-off clothing

_____ **'Twas the Night Before #BK-B143** $14.95
       by Rachel Olson and Arthur L. Zapel
       A Christmas picture book for children

These and other fine Meriwether Publishing books are available at your local bookstore or direct from the publisher. Prices subject to change without notice. Check our website or call for current prices.

Name: _____

Organization name: _____

Address: _____

City: _____ State: _____

Zip: _____ Phone: _____

  ❑ **Check enclosed**

  ❑ **Visa / MasterCard / Discover #** _____

                                   Expiration
Signature: _____ *date:* _____
      (required for Visa/MasterCard/Discover orders)

Colorado residents: Please add 3% sales tax.
Shipping: Include $2.75 for the first book and 50¢ for each additional book ordered.

  ❑ *Please send me a copy of your complete catalog of books and plays.*